OUT FOR A DUCK

For
my mother,
with love

OUT FOR A DUCK

A Celebration of Cricketing Calamities

Ian Valentine

Illustrations by Oliver Preston

Quiller

Text Copyright © 2010 Ian Valentine
Illustrations Copyright © 2010 Oliver Preston

First published in the UK in 2010
by Quiller, an imprint of Quiller Publishing Ltd

British Library Cataloguing-in-Publication Data
A catalogue record for this book
is available from the British Library

ISBN 978 1 84689 087 1

The right of Ian Valentine to be identified as the author of this work has been asserted in accordance with the Copyright, Design and Patent Act 1988

The information in this book is true and complete to the best of our knowledge. All recommendations are made without any guarantee on the part of the Publisher, who also disclaims any liability incurred in connection with the use of this data or specific details.

Printed in China

Quiller

An imprint of Quiller Publishing Ltd
Wykey House, Wykey, Shrewsbury, SY4 1JA
Tel: 01939 261616 Fax: 01939 261606
E-mail: info@quillerbooks.com
Website: www.countrybooksdirect.com

Contents

Introduction

The idea for this book arrived in the upper tier of the Compton Stand at Lord's on a lazy summer's afternoon in 2009. The batsmen and bowlers had bought into the crowd's post-lunch stupor, neither side straining for runs or wickets. Such carefree moments, shared with a dear friend provide the perfect environment for discussing the finer points of our favourite sport. Any updates on work, family and mutual friends are dutifully traded during the morning session, leaving the rest of the day's play for earnest cricket chat fuelled by the occasional visit to the refreshment kiosks.

Just before tea, our conversation meandered towards the subject of batting as a trial of character. How many other sports give you just one chance to express yourself? Even that one fleeting opportunity can be snuffed out prematurely. The unplayable ball, brilliant catch, errant umpire or needless run out are all waiting to test your sense of humour. In a split second, your day has ended.

Batting is not a matter of life and death – no innings is that important – but the finality and inevitability of getting out does draw comparison, even at a superficial level. No batsman, not even the greatest to have taken guard, can escape the pain of being dismissed for a low score or a duck. A perfect season or career is not possible. Nobody is immortal at the crease.

How often do we hear this on commentary? 'He did well to nick that one. A lesser batsman would have missed it.' Cold comfort to the debutant who has just bagged a duck. Likewise: 'The umpire didn't see the inside edge and he's given him lbw. The finger is raised and the batsman isn't happy, but he has to go'. Spectators may be sympathetic, selectors less so.

And it's not only the batsmen who are a hostage to fortune. A leading bowler can find himself flogging a dead pitch that gives no assistance, as a moderate batsman smacks him round the park. Any edges fly into gaps, while the fielders drop sitters and dive over the ball. 'You'll bowl half as well tomorrow and take five wickets,' will not change the '0 for 120' in the scorebook. For every hundred, five-for, partnership or blinding catch, there is the anguish of a duck, Chinese cut, collapse or dolly drop. Of course, the best sportsmen quickly erase the memory and make the most of the next opportunity. But cricket can be damned unfair sometimes. Perhaps that is what makes this the best of team sports – certain individuals are destined to fail during a contest, often through no fault of their own. Those players in form or enjoying the rub of the green must win or save the match for those whose touch or luck has deserted them.

All of the cricketers mentioned in this book have played to at least first-class level, so any failure was a mere blip in a highly successful career. I wish I had even half their ability! But I do hope that their struggles will provide consolation for the rest of us who never reached such lofty heights. No blushes are spared on the cricket field, whether you are Bradman or Hammond, Sobers or Tendulkar. Sooner rather than later the cricketing gods will smack you to the ground and give you a kick in the guts while you're down there.

Amidst the sense of loss and futility, however, the occasional moment of glorious achievement makes it all feel worthwhile. Why else would we keep coming back for more punishment?

Acknowledgements

Many people have helped me to compile this book, so my thanks to all of you. In particular, I am grateful to Henry Blofeld for writing the foreword; Oliver Preston for his excellent illustrations: the committee of the Primary Club, especially Chris Larlham; Peter Baxter and Jonny Hammond-Chambers for their insights my editor Kirsty Ennever for her attention to detail; and Andrew Johnston for taking another punt on me.

For their encouragement during the long winter months of 2009–10, my thanks to: Richard Butler, David Pick, Jonathan Hamilton-Jones, Dominic Ash, Sara Trechman, Alastair and Clare Valentine.

And, as always, to my parents for their unstinting love and support: thank you both.

Writing this book would not have been possible without the wealth of information available in *Wisden Cricketer's Almanack* (John Wisden & Co Ltd) and the ESPN Cricinfo website, which has been a daily friend for the last ten years. Cricket fans are blessed to have such comprehensive resources.

Useful books included: *The Complete Who's Who of Test Cricketers* by Christopher Martin-Jenkins (Macmillan, 1987); *The Complete History of Cricket Tours at Home and Abroad* by Peter Wynne-Thomas (Hamlyn, 1989); *Test Match Special: 50 Not Out* edited by Peter Baxter (BBC Books, 2007); *The Best XI* by Geoffrey Boycott (Penguin, 2009); *Out of the Rough* by Peter Baxter, Jonathan Agnew and David Lloyd (Andre Deutsch, 1997); *Stiff Upper Lips and Baggy Green Caps* by Simon Briggs (Quercus, 2009).

Foreword by Henry Blofeld

Ian Valentine has done cricket a great and rather surprising service. The game has a larger and more comprehensive bibliography then any other sport and just about every facet of the game has been covered – and most of them many times over. With shrewd forethought Ian has ingeniously discovered an area of the game which has never before been put under the microscope. As a result of enormous and, I daresay, forbidding research he has not only filled the gap, but in doing so he has also produced a book which is as humorous as it is informative.

The great deeds of the game, both individually and collectively, have been written about *ad infinitum*. On the other hand the horror stories of teams and of individual players and the merciless and scurvy way the unfortunates of cricket have been treated by bad luck, have mostly been allowed to go harmlessly past the off stump. Embarrassing ducks, red-faced bowling figures of 0/200 and more, howlers in the field when catches which would have been gobbled up by any self-respecting grand-mother, have been catastrophically dropped, teams that have somehow managed to lose matches that only divine intervention could prevent them from winning, and run outs, the form of dismissal which creates by far the most amusement, have been allowed to disappear into the mists of time.

But here they all are, lumped together in their infamous glory and what joy Ian Valentine's accounts will bring. There is not a cricketer in the world who will not be able to identify most embarrassingly with something in this wonderfully amusing book. Since reading the first chapter scarcely a day has gone by without me going step by step through the process of being bowled first ball by Rex Neame in the 1955 Eton v Harrow match at Lord's, thereby enabling him to complete the first hat-trick taken by an Harrovian bowler in that contest. Photogaphs show that I was two paces down the pitch at the time, Heaven forfend.

This is a book which, once read, should find a permanent place on any cricket lover's bedside table. When sleep is elusive and one's head is full of grisly thoughts, this is just the answer. The embarrassment and unhappiness of Ernest Vogler, Tommy Ward, Gavin Hamilton, Mashrafe Mortaza, Scott Boswell, Roy Sheffield, Monty Bowden and a whole host of others will do the reader the world of good. By the way, hands up anyone who has heard of any of those seven and has a clue why their unhappi-ness should provide such pleasure.

Still to come are the umpiring blunders, the reason the immortal EW Swanton was not sent to Australia to cover the Bodyline tour, and a delicious cocktail of a lot of people who should have been immune from such disasters, coming up with gratifying quantities of egg all over their faces. It's good stuff from the first page to the last.

The Primary Club

Membership of the Primary Club is open to anyone who has ever been out first ball, in any form of cricket, whether the best batsman in Test cricket or the most useless tailender in a village XI. Few who have played the game for any length of time are spared the desolation of a golden duck. That surge of disappointment is a bond that transcends all nationalities and levels of ability.

The Primary Club was formed on the 31 July 1955, following a match between Beckenham CC and the Old Olavians in Kent. Its founder members were four Beckenham cricketers – Ralph Lilley (who designed the Club's distinctive shattered wicket logo), Keith Patterson, Keith's brother Norman (who died in 1975) and Mike Sheeres (who was a trustee of the Club until his death in 2005). It is not immediately clear why this particular match led to the formation of a club to mark the achievement of being out first ball, because Keith Patterson scored 80 and the others didn't bat. But many good ideas are spawned in the relaxed bonhomie of a cricket match and this soon proved to be a very good idea indeed.

In those early days, life membership cost 10/6d (52.5p) and a tie £2. The equivalent figures in today's money would be about £10.50 and £40 so the Club's current tariff of £7.50 and £12.50 is something of a bargain. Initially, membership was only open to those who were out first ball playing for or against Beckenham so it is, perhaps, unsurprising that in its first nine years it raised only £46.

From the start, the Primary Club supported the cause of blind cricketers. In those early years, the money raised was donated to FR Brown's Fund for Blind Cricketers (Freddie Brown was England's captain on the 1950-51 Ashes tour). Subsequently, most of the money raised was donated to Dorton House, a specialist school near Sevenoaks in Kent, which is run by the Royal London Society for the Blind.

In the early 1970s, the popular BBC radio cricket commentator Brian Johnston learned of the existence of the Club. He began to mention it on *Test Match Special*, in particular on the Saturday of home Test matches (on which day members not wearing the club tie are liable to a fine!). The Club's membership duly expanded rapidly. On 31 August 1982 it was registered as a charity with the Charity Commission and its current objectives are 'to provide for the sporting and recreational needs of the blind and partially-sighted, especially young people in the care of the Royal London Society for the Blind'.

After the Club had expanded, the trustees decided to distribute its funds more widely. By the late 1980s net income was around £35,000 and grants were made not only to Dorton House but also to such clubs and organisations as the Metropolitan Sports & Social Club for the Visually Handicapped, British Blind Sport, Birmingham Sports & Social Club for the Visually Handicapped and St Vincent's School in Liverpool – all of them still flourishing (and in receipt of Primary Club grants) to this day.

The Club's income has grown steadily, reaching a record £363,570 in the year to 31 March 2006 when, in addition to the funds raised at various functions to mark the Club's Golden Jubilee (including a dinner at Lord's, when Richie Benaud was the guest speaker), a legacy of some £117,000 was received from the estate of the late Ronald Lockwood, a Club member and retired violinist. In the year to March 2010, the total sum raised by the Club went through the £3 million mark – a vast leap from £46!

The majority of the funds raised are donated by the 8,300 members on its active mailing list, most of whose donations – usually between £10 and £50 – are made on receipt of the Club's annual newsletter at the beginning of each new season. Grants, averaging about £4,000, are made each year to between forty and fifty schools and clubs providing sporting and recreational facilities for the visually handicapped. The Club has also funded two large projects for Dorton House: in 1993-94, it made grants totalling £162,000 for a swimming pool and, ten years later, provided £94,000 for a purpose-built canal boat, *The Golden Duck*, which was officially launched on the Regent's Canal on the day when Britain was awarded the 2012 Olympics.

The Club has always relied exclusively on volunteers for its fund-raising and administration. It is fortunate to have as its Patron Derek Underwood MBE, one of England's finest bowlers, who played his early cricket at Beckenham CC. Its trustees include Mike Brace CBE, until recently Chairman of the British Paralympic Association (who was heavily involved in the 2012 Olympics bid and who has great knowledge of the various sports in which the visually impaired participate), Peter Baxter, recently retired as producer of TMS (who did much to maintain the Club's profile on the programme following Brian Johnston's death in 1994) and John Stern, editor of *The Wisden Cricketer*, who have been great supporters of the Club.

In 1998, the Club introduced a new rule, under which members were liable to pay a fine of £2 each time an England player was out first ball in a Test match; the rule had to be modified rapidly when there were eleven such instances in 1998 and now it applies only to home Test matches. The biggest fund-raiser under the rule has been Kevin Pietersen, who has been out first ball three times. In 2009, Graham

Onions (later to play a notable part in saving two Test matches against South Africa, with England's last pair at the wicket) was out first ball twice.

In 2006, Andrew Strauss MBE, the current England captain, became the first President of the Primary Club Juniors. He did not record a 'primary' in a Test match until he was out to the very first ball of the deciding match against South Africa in Johannesburg in January 2010. His diamond duck arrived amid a rich vein of batting form, proof that nobody can escape fickle fortune in cricket.

That test of character is one of the reasons we love cricket so much. But a golden duck is a piffling setback compared with the loss of one's sight. With your help, we can ensure that many visually-impaired sportsmen will develop the love of cricket that unites us all.

For more information visit www.primaryclub.org or e-mail secretary@primaryclub.org

Paul Larlham,
Secretary

A Brief Glossary

Duck – dismissed without scoring a run (possible derivation: a duck's egg).

Golden duck – dismissed first ball, without scoring a run.

Diamond duck – dismissed first ball of the team's innings, without scoring a run.

Pair – dismissed for a duck in both innings (possible derivation: a pair of spectacles).

King pair – dismissed for a golden duck in both innings.

Sledging – the art of riling a batsman to break his concentration in the middle, usually with insults. It works on some batsmen and backfires with others. The Aussies prefer to call it 'mental disintegration'.

A Nelson – when the score is 111. Believed to be named after Admiral Horatio Nelson, who ended up with one arm, one eye and one leg. A Double Nelson is 222; Triple Nelson 333 etc. For English batsmen, it is an unlucky number, which made superstitious umpire David Shepherd hop on one leg.

The Devil's Number – The Australians are equally wary of the number 87 (13 shy of a hundred), although it can also help them concentrate as they near a ton.

To walk – rarely seen in the modern game, but when a batsman concedes he is out before the umpire triggers him. Occasionally a batsman will walk on an lbw when it is obviously plumb.

ODI – One Day International. Usually a match with 50 overs a side, often played over an afternoon and evening, so becoming a 'day-nighter'.

T20 – Twenty20 cricket: 20 overs a side.

IPL – Indian Premier League: a T20 competition which brings the best cricketers of the world together, paying out generous dollops of cash for their services.

Cow corner – a fielder at deep midwicket for an agricultural mow across the line. A useful position for tail-end sloggers and crazy-eyed village cricketers.

Minefield – a terror track for the batsman and a boon for the bowlers. Less common nowadays with covered pitches and lucrative television rights.

Burner – rhyming slang for a 'turner' or pitch that takes spin. (Also known as a 'Bunsen' for obvious reasons.)

Chinaman – a ball from a left-arm unorthodox wrist-spinner, who tweaks the ball from off leg to right-handers. This technique mirrors that of the right-arm leg-spinner. The term was first used pejoratively by Englishman Walter Robbins in a Test match against the West Indies in 1933, when he was beaten in flight by Puss Achong, who was of Chinese origin. Robbins trudged back, grumbling: 'Fancy being done by a bloody Chinaman!'

Googly – a ball that is spun from off to leg to right-handers, but without using an off-spinner's action. A surprise variation, but it often ends up in the stands if dragged short or the batsman picks it. Also known as a 'wrong-un' or 'Bosie' after its inventor, Bernard Bosanquet.

Doosra – literally the 'other' or 'second' one in Urdu, it is the off-spinner's version of the wrong-un, in that it spins like a leggie, but with an off-break action. Popularised by Saqlain Mushtaq, although probably invented by Sonny Ramadhin, its use sometimes leads to accusations of chucking.

Bump ball – when the ball slams into the pitch and flies into the hands of a fielder. The bounce is often missed (or ignored), leading to claims for a catch. Gives rise to 'crowd catches' in which the crowd cheer, believing a clean catch has been taken.

Bumper – a short-pitched bouncer.

Throat ball – when the ball rears up sharply from a length or just back of a length, or when a batsman is slow to pick up the length of a bumper.

Snicko – abbreviation for Snickometer, a televisual aid, triggered by soundwaves captured by the stump microphone. It indicates whether the ball has edged or snicked the bat.

Hot Spot – an infrared imaging system that reveals the 'hot spot' where the ball has hit the bat, gloves, pad or batsman.

Hawk-Eye – another tool for the broadcasters (and sometimes the umpires) which can track the path of a ball and therefore predict its likely path.

Belter – a flat pitch that favours the batsmen. Also called a featherbed.

Chin music – when the batsman is getting nothing but bumpers and throat balls.

Dilscoop – invented by Sri Lankan batsman Tillakaratne Dilshan in T20. The plucky batsman flicks the ball off his nose and over the head of the keeper. A dentist's delight.

Mankad – the unsporting practice of running out a batsman who is backing up. Made infamous by Vinoo Mankad in 1947, when he dismissed Aussie batsman Bill Brown. Outlawed when batsmen were allowed to back up before the bowler has completed his delivery stride.

Dolly (drop) – an easy catch (that is grassed), also called a sitter.

A Zero – no runs, no wickets, no catches, no run outs in the match.

Lollipop – a bad ball that asks to be hit. Often called 'buffet bowling' by Geoff Boycott, i.e. help yourself.

Rabbit/bunny – a tailender who is a 'walking wicket': easy to send back to the hutch. Can also mean a batsman who has been dismissed several times by the same bowler, e.g. JP Duminy was Graeme Swann's bunny, etc.

Duckworth/Lewis (D/L) – a mathematical formula for calculating a fair target in case of delays, usually caused by rain. Notoriously complicated, it can lead to the more academic captain winning.

Bodyline – short-pitched bowling at the body with the aim of forcing the batsman to fend off to fielders waiting in close on the leg side (also called leg theory). Used by the dastardly Douglas Jardine to thwart Don Bradman in the 1932-33 Ashes series. Now illegal.

Chucking – throwing the ball with a bent arm instead of bowling with a straight arm.

Plumb – to be rapped on the pads right in front of all three. Not always given out though.

Supersub – a brief but flawed experiment by the law-makers to allow teams to sub a player off during an ODI.

Double teapot – a fast bowler standing with both hands on hips after a misfield, dropped catch or not-out decision with which he disagrees.

Triggered – given out wrongly by the umpire. It often implies a certain relish in the umpire's finger-wagging. Sawn off means the same.

Shooter – When the ball shoots along the deck. If bowled straight and fast, the batsman hasn't a prayer.

Chapter One:
Famous First Ballers

No matter the level of cricket, every batsman breathes a little easier after surviving his first ball, whether he scores off it or not. But if his wicket falls to that delivery, the surge of disappointment is acute, as there is no worse batting performance than a golden duck. Even the very best batsmen at the height of their powers have suffered the pain of a primary, falling prey to good bowling, poor umpiring, over-confidence or plain bad luck. By the next innings, the memory is banished and the runs flow again.

Commentator's curse

Archie MacLaren

On the 1897-98 England tour of Australia, Lancastrian Archie MacLaren swept all bowling attacks before him, scoring six first-class hundreds in total, including three in Tests, and passing 1,000 runs on tour at an average of nearly 55. No doubt an astute captain and a dependable bat, MacLaren could be stubborn as a sucking tick, waging war against selectors as though for the fun of it. Career highlights included a record-setting 424 against Somerset at Taunton in 1895 and a partnership of 309 with CB Fry inside three hours for the Gentlemen against the Players. But the start to his Test career in 1894 was far from glorious. He barely contributed to the remarkable turnaround in Sydney in the first Test, which England won having been forced to follow on (*see* Chapter Seven **From the Jaws of Victory**.) Worse was to come at Melbourne in the second Test, when MacLaren was caught at point by Harry Trott off the first ball of the match. The delivery was sent down by Arthur Coningham in his first and only Test. MacLaren's was the first diamond duck in Test cricket, as England rolled over for just 75 runs, although they quickly rallied to win the match by 94 runs.

Ernest Vogler

The South African leg-spin/googly bowler Ernest Vogler was a feared opponent before the start of the First World War, contributing to memorable defeats against England with his ability to mask his variations. He tended to bat at eleven, although that did not stop him from top-scoring with a rapid 62 in Cape Town in 1906. But more often than not, Vogler (who was interestingly known as both Bert and Ernie, long before the Sesame Street double act) did little to trouble the scorers. His lowest moment as a tailender came in the first Test against Australia in Sydney in 1910, in which the visitors were dealt a sound thrashing. Australia amassed 528, with Clem Hill taking 191 of them. Vogler did not take a wicket, leaking nearly six runs an over. He then ended the first innings, bowled for a goldie by Bill Whitty. Following on, the match finished as Vogler bagged the first king pair in Tests, missing a straight one from Charles Kelleway.

Len Braund

The Londoner was one of the most talented all-rounders of his generation, able to shape a match with a hundred at the top of the innings or turn it back towards his side with a spell of leg breaks or a dazzling slip catch. CB Fry described him as being as 'cool as a cucumber', some praise from a man who was pretty steady in a crisis himself. After twenty years on the circuit, having three times taken 100 wickets and scored 1,000 runs in a season, Braund retired to become an excellent coach and a respected umpire. His crowning moment with the ball came in the last match of the 1903-04 Ashes series down under, a series which England had already won. Opening the bowling on a damp pitch, the leg-spinner took all but two wickets of the first innings, including that of the masterful Victor Trumper, caught and bowled. (Trumper had already scored 88 at the time, which almost counted double given the state of the pitch.)

England's reply of 61 all out was weak, although more rain had made the pitch a bowler's paradise. It would have been worse too, had numbers ten and eleven not scored the only three boundaries of the innings. Braund batted at eight, making five runs, but was promoted to opener in the second innings, after Australia had been shot out for 133 (Trumper making a primary). But he had no answer to fast bowler Albert 'Tibby' Cotter on the dicey surface, skewing his first ball into the hands of Victoria's Peter McAlister. Moustachioed off spinner Hugh Trumble then proved unplayable, running through the rest of the England side to take 7 for 28, as the total barely reached three figures (101 all out).

Victor Trumper

Australia boasted many superb batsmen during the Golden Age before the First

Another member for the Primary Club

World War, but the man who dwarfed them all was Victor Trumper. It doesn't bear thinking about how many runs he would have made in the days of covered pitches, as he was able to churn out runs against high quality bowlers on wickets that had often been torn to ribbons. He could dig in or cut loose as the state of the match dictated, so one-day internationals (ODIs) and Twenty20 (T20) would have also brought the best from the New South Welshman. He would have been a top pick in the IPL for sure. But even the best are powerless against the vagaries of fortune.

On the eve of the fourth Test in 1908 at the MCG, excitement was building in anticipation of Trumper leading Australia to the Ashes. Already 2-1 up, with two to play, victory would regain the spoils. Australia won the toss and chose to bat first on a placid pitch: there was not a spare seat in the ground. A great cheer greeted Trumper as he walked to the middle alongside his captain Monty Noble, one of the most accomplished all-rounders ever to play the game. In the first over, Noble took a single off opening bowler Arthur Fielder to bring Trumper on strike. The spectators held their collective breath as the bowler ran in, expecting a textbook forward defensive or even a flashing cut or drive. Instead, the ball caught the outside edge of Trumper's bat and flew into the grateful hands of Jack Crawford in the slips. Trumper had done well to get a bat on it. In the second innings, after the pitch had been turned into a quagmire by rain, Australia were made to face a sticky spell before stumps. The fourth ball Trumper received squirted under his bat and completed his pair.

There was a rest day on the Sunday and the hot Melbourne sun dried out the pitch for Warwick Armstrong to set up the victory with a hundred. Australia had won the match comfortably, but the superstar had contributed not a single run, catch or wicket.

Jack Russell

Charles Albert George Russell – known to all as Jack – was a gritty opener who scored hundreds against each of the county sides for Essex over three decades, alongside five Test hundreds in ten matches at an average of 56 runs. But his England career started dismally. Openers so often set the tone for the rest of a match and even a tour, and Russell's diamond duck at Sydney in the first Test of 1920 was the first faced by an Englishman in a series the team would lose 5-0. It was also his first ball in Test cricket. He made just five in the second innings. In the next Test in Melbourne, Russell was spared the opening duties, batting instead at number five, but the result was the same: a golden duck in the first innings and just five in the second. But Russell was made of strong stuff, digging in at Adelaide to score an unbeaten 135. In his last Test, against South Africa in Durban in 1923, Russell became the first Englishman to score a hundred in each innings of a Test match.

Roy Park

Known as Little Doc, on the basis that he was little and a doctor, Roy Park would have played more than his solitary Test but for the Great War. On the resumption of first-class cricket in 1919, he proved his touch again with Victoria, averaging over 80 for the season, which earned him inclusion for the second Ashes Test at his home ground in Melbourne, batting at number three. It did not go well, despite Australia cruising to an innings victory. Quick English bowler Henry Howell took only seven wickets in his career, but Park was one of them, bowled by his first delivery. Apparently, Park's wife, sitting in the crowd, bent over to pick up her knitting, and missed her husband's entire Test batting career. The doctor later admitted that he had been up all night with a patient and was not mentally ready for his debut innings. He did not take a catch in the match and bowled only a single over, which was clobbered for nine runs. Park was dropped for the next Test and drifted out of the game due to work commitments.

Sir Donald Bradman

England had won the first Test of the controversial Bodyline series, but the Australian line-up had not included the one man for whom the tactics were developed: The

Don. The New South Wales maestro had missed the match as he was 'jaded mentally', according to *Wisden*, after struggling to cope with leg theory bowling in the warm-up matches. England, under Douglas Jardine, believed he was running scared, but he returned to the fray in the second Test at the MCG. A nation bellowed for its hero to teach Jardine and fast bowler Harold Larwood a lesson, railing against what it saw as unsporting behaviour. The fact that the tactics were working didn't help either. A world record crowd crammed into the stadium to watch its white knight slay the dragon, cheering Bradman to the middle at the fall of the second wicket. His first delivery from seamer Bill Bowes was short and Bradman had plenty of time to rock back and hook. But his movement was hesitant and the ball stayed lower than he expected, taking the bottom edge and crashing into the stumps. The MCG crowd watched silently as Bradman trudged back to the pavilion for a golden duck. But on the third day, he returned to the middle to score a match-turning century, unbeaten on 103, as the rest of the batsmen struggled. Australia won the match and tied the series. Jardine was sent back to the drawing board.

Herbert Sutcliffe

The Yorkshireman remains one of England's most polished diamonds, an opening batsman with class, grit, bravery and a sense of occasion. As calm as a summer morning, when his county or country needed him most, Sutcliffe would clock in a shift. He could defend with supreme concentration or savage the opposition attack with textbook cover drives and a compulsive hook. In total, the man who played Ernie to Jack Hobbs's Eric at the top of the order, scored over 50,000 first-class runs, including 151 hundreds (nine against big rivals Lancashire) at an average of 52. In his 54 Tests, he scored 16 hundreds at over 60 runs, number four in the all-time list of averages. Yet, you can never have it all your own way. After the rigours of the infamous Bodyline Tour, where Sutcliffe had topped the aggregates and scored his Test best of 194, the England team came home via New Zealand in March 1933. The dominion was not expected to ruffle the feathers of the motherland, but nobody told opening bowler Ted Badcock. His first delivery brought Sutcliffe forward; the ball seamed, caught the edge and was gobbled up by the keeper. Out first ball of the match. Sutcliffe didn't bat again, he didn't bowl and he didn't take a catch, so his match was effectively over. Luckily perhaps, it was only a three-dayer, as bad weather ended the match prematurely.

Bob Crisp

South African mountaineer, adventurer, war hero and journalist Bob Crisp was a famously optimistic chap, so he would have recovered quickly enough from his king pair in the fifth Test against Australia in 1936. The home team at Durban were given a masterclass in batting by Jack Fingleton and Bill Brown, which they failed to learn from, subsiding to an innings defeat. Crisp, who had twice taken four wickets in four balls for Western Province, had suffered a pair in the third Test at Cape Town, undone by Clarrie Grimmett and then Bill O'Reilly. In Durban, the same happened, although this time he was bowled first ball on both occasions, as South Africa lost their last seven wickets for 31 runs. Remarkably, five of these fell to catches by close fielder Vic Richardson. It proved to be Crisp's last Test, as the war years intervened. According to his *Wisden* obituary, Crisp survived six wrecked tanks and was decorated for bravery. When King George VI asked if the injuries sustained would affect his bowling, he replied, 'No, sir, I was hit on the head.'

Denis Compton

England were expected to ease past the Indian touring party of 1946 at Lord's, which they duly did by ten wickets. However, part of the script for a country recovering from the Second World War was a fine knock from the pin-up batsman Denis Compton. Instead, Compton was bowled first ball by the plucky and crafty medium pacer Lala Amarnath, who had already dismissed Len Hutton. Cyril Washbrook and Wally Hammond soon followed to the same bowler, leaving England teetering on 70 for 4, with their mainstays back in the shed. The crowd had to make do with the elegance of Joe Hardstaff, who stroked a double hundred to take the match beyond India's grasp. Alec Bedser, on debut, took eleven wickets in the match. For Amarnath, the five-for at Lord's – including Hutton, Compton and Hammond – was a special haul after being so badly treated on India's last tour in 1936. (*see* Chapter Five **Captaincy Woes**.)

Vinoo Mankad

India's efforts against Sir Donald Bradman's exceptional team in the 1947-48 series in Australia could be compared to England's flounderings against Ricky Ponting's thoroughbreds in the 2007-08 whitewash. The one-sided nature of the series in the 1940s, however, would have been less of a satisfaction for the home nation, as India were yet to win a Test match and stood very little chance of making an impression. Bradman was still piling on the runs, while the new ball pairing of Ray Lindwall and Keith Miller was a match for a line-up far stronger than India's. One batsman who had the potential to keep the Aussies honest was the all-rounder Vinoo Mankad, although the series started poorly for him. Bradman cracked 185 from a total of 382 runs in the first innings of the first Test on a flat deck. But then it rained for two days and crusted under the hot Brisbane sun. India were lambs to the slaughter and Mankad was first to the block, caught behind first ball of the innings for a diamond duck, to Lindwall. India were all out for 58. Following on, on the same minefield, India again surrendered, this time for 98, as Ernie Toshack took eleven wickets in the match. Mankad was again snared by Lindwall, having made just seven.

Lindwall made it four from four in the second Test, but Mankad eventually found his feet in the third Test with his maiden Test hundred. Australia took the series 4-0, though Mankad made another hundred (in the fifth Test) but suffered two more ducks to Lindwall. Yet, India were showing signs of improvement under their visionary captain Lala Amarnath, which would soon culminate in their first Test win, against England at Madras in February 1952. Mankad would be at the heart of any triumph for the next ten years.

Sir Frank Worrell

Cricketers can be a superstitious bunch, refusing to swap chairs in the pavilion during a long partnership or wearing the same jockstrap for days if it will help their team. Sachin Tendulkar put his left pad on first, for example, while Steve Waugh had his lucky red hanky. Englishmen get nervous on triple Nelsons (111, 222 etc) and Aussies try to avoid 87 (13 less than a hundred). Frank Worrell was especially superstitious, according to his *Wisden* obituary. Being the Windies' 13th captain didn't help his nerves, although he did a fine job of coping. In a tour match against South Australia in 1951, Worrell was dismissed first ball in the first innings by the local quick bowler Geff Noblet. In a similar position to the talented West Indian bowlers of the 1980s, the Australian Noblet (who kept the Christian name Geffrey after the misspelling on his birth certificate) would have played many more Tests had he not been next in line to Miller and Lindwall. In the second innings, Worrell replaced all of his clothing, his pads, gloves, shoes and bat, in a bid to exorcise his bad luck. But Noblet got him again, first ball, to complete a famous king pair. Next man in Sir Clyde Walcott passed Worrell at the gate and joked: 'Why do I have to face a hat-trick every time I follow you?'

Sir Conrad Hunte

Barbadian Sir Conrad Cleophus Hunte was knighted as much for his contribution to West Indian cricket on the field of play, as his fine work off it as a champion of social change. He started his Test career in emphatic fashion against the Pakistan touring side of 1957-58, batting through the whole of his first day to score 142, alongside Sir Everton Weekes. A big double hundred in the third Test at Kingston was overshadowed by Sir Garry Sobers's famous 365 not out, but Hunte added another ton, as did Sobers and Sir Clyde Walcott, in the fourth match of the series, at Georgetown. In that West Indies top order, only the brilliant Rohan Kanhai failed to scoop a knighthood. But the batsman who gets carried away with his own success, as Hunte modestly admitted he had, is only a delivery away from looking foolish. In the final Port-of-Spain Test, the opener nudged the first ball of the match into the grateful hands of Hanif Mohammad. Kanhai quickly followed for a duck too, and the West Indies were in trouble for the first time in the series. They duly lost the match by an innings – Pakistan's first win against them – and Hunte went on to suffer a horror tour of the sub-continent.

Eddie Barlow

The cricket mistress is too tough a dame to consider whether a cricketer deserves misfortune or not. She just dishes it out and waits for the reaction. Eddie Barlow – known as 'Bunter' on account of his chubby cheeks and round spectacles, reminiscent of the storybook Billy – was one of cricket's good guys. His enthusiasm, combined with no little skill, turned him into a leading all-rounder in the 1960s and the ticking heartbeat of South Africa's greatest team, which gubbed the visiting Australians 4-0 in 1969-70 (*see* Chapter Thirteen **One-Sided Affairs**). But for the consequences of apartheid, a regime against which he campaigned vociferously, Barlow would surely have added to his six hundreds and 40 wickets (almost all were against Australia), as he was still playing cricket to a high standard ten years later. Yet no cricketer's blushes are spared and Barlow could only wander back to the pavilion during the Durban Test of 1967, having looped the first ball of the match back to the bowler Garth McKenzie. Typical of the man, he soon recovered and helped his team fight back to an emphatic win. You couldn't keep Barlow down for long and he remains the idol for any South African searching for inspiration against Australia.

BS Chandrasekhar

Chandra liked a duck. In his Test innings for India during the sixties and seventies, he was out for nought on 23 occasions, just creeping into the top ten of the most prolific duck hunters. Within that top ten, only arch bunny Chris Martin from New Zealand has a lower average. Chandra was once asked to bat higher than another batsman in his team, Umesh Kulkarni (average 4.33), but the experiment was quickly shelved when he made another duck. It is perhaps a surprise to find that a mere four of the 23 were first-ballers, although two of them arrived in the same match, the third Test at the MCG against Australia in 1977-78. Not that he would have been downhearted, as he led his country to a resounding victory in Melbourne, taking 12 for 104 in the process. In total the leg-spinner took 242 wickets and played his part in one of the most effective spin attacks to play the game. Alongside Martin and Australia's Bruce Reid, he is the only other meaningful Test bowler to have more wickets than runs to his name.

Graeme Watson

Australian all-rounder Graeme Watson never quite made it in the international arena, as either a bowler or a batsman, playing just five Tests and two ODIs. As a state player, however, he was an effective medium pacer and an adaptable batsman who could deliver in the middle order or open as required. It was as an opener that he was selected on the 1972 Ashes tour in the first ODI match to be played on English soil. Australia won the toss and chose to bat, immediately thrusting Watson into the limelight. His stay did not last long, one ball in fact, as he was bowled by Geoff Arnold. Not only was this the first golden duck in ODI history, but it was also the first duck, full stop, as all the batsmen in the inaugural ODI in Melbourne the year before had made at least one run.

Sunil Gavaskar

Some openers relish facing the first ball of an innings, while others avoid it. Many are too phlegmatic to care either way. Sunil Gavaskar, certainly one of the greatest openers of all time, wore the first ball as a badge of honour. For all but 28 of his 214 Test innings for India, he fronted up to the first delivery of the innings for his country. As India's rudder for so many of those matches, the five-foot-five-inch technician carried the responsibility with remarkable ease. His fearless (and helmet-less) resistance to the West Indian quicks earned him a staggering 13 hundreds in 27 Tests at over 65 runs, as he amassed over 10,000 runs and 34 hundreds. But when you face the first ball of an innings every time, your golden ducks are upgraded (or is it downgraded?) to diamonds. Gavaskar therefore is unfortunate to share the record for most diamond ducks in Test cricket. Geoff Arnold had him caught behind at Edgbaston in 1974; Malcolm Marshall did the same at the Eden Gardens in 1983; and in 1987, he managed a thicker edge through to Javed Miandad in the slips off the bowling of Imran Khan. Interestingly, Gavaskar batted at number four in his greatest innings in Madras in 1983, when he scored 236 not out against the full speed of the West Indies, including Marshall, Holding, Roberts and Winston Davis. But given that two wickets had fallen with the total on zero, it was business as usual!

Hannan Sarkar

Hannan Sarkar will be desperate to regain his spot in the Bangladeshi team; otherwise he will be remembered more for his trio of diamonds rather than any other batting accomplishment. That they were all executed by the West Indian bowler Pedro Collins makes Sarkar a favourite of sports triviaistas. Life in the fast lane had started well for the teenager, stroking a fifty against Sri Lanka on debut and then another in the following series, against South Africa. When his nemesis arrived in Dhaka in 2002, Bangladesh were looking to prove they could mix it with a team that was rebuilding without Lara, Walsh and Ambrose. Sadly, Sarkar helped set the wrong tone, missing a perfect yorker: out to the first ball of the series. Two years later, at the alluringly-named Beausejour Stadium in St Lucia, Sarkar had an opportunity to make amends with the sun shining on a flat pitch. Again, Collins pinned him in front, first ball of the match, adjudged lbw. His team secured an honourable draw and he retained his place for the second Test in Jamaica, only for lightning to strike for the third time. How did he feel when his skipper won the toss and elected to bat? Probably not as bad as when the first ball thudded into his pads and the umpire's finger rose. A duck in his next Test against New Zealand ended the selectors' patience.

Sir Ian Botham

When you are one of the team's frontline bowlers, batters and fielders, it is rare that at least one of those suits will not come good during a Test match. In truth, it was rare for Ian Botham that even one of these disciplines deserted him. But in the second Test against New Zealand at Christchurch in 1984, the wheels came off. Botham had scored a century in the first Test at Wellington and taken a five-for in the first innings to win man of the match, which made the slump all the more surprising. New Zealand won the toss in bowler-friendly conditions, but chose to bat first. England bowled badly, including some friendly long hops by Botham, which Richard Hadlee enjoyed, smashing 99 from just 81 balls. Botham went at five an over, as New Zealand reached 307, at least 50 runs more than they should have done. In reply, England slumped to 82 all out in 50 overs, with Beefy making 18. Following on, they again capitulated, all out for 93. Botham was out first ball to slow left-armer Stephen Boock. In just twelve hours, England had surrendered, out twice for under a hundred for the first time that century. Hadlee added eight wickets in the match to his 99 runs, comprehensively winning the battle of the all-rounders.

Allan Border

If there was a cabinet marked 'greatest living Australian', then you'd probably find a whole drawer dedicated to Allan Robert Border. As determined a batsman as ever wore the baggy green, Border insisted that the opposition throw everything at him and he threw it back with interest. Although not a born leader, instead he led by example, dragging an ailing nation from the doldrums to a World Cup win in 1987 and Ashes dominance by sheer willpower. The icing on the cake, towards the end of his career, would have been victory over Richie Richardson's West Indies in the 1992-93 series in Australia. The deal had so nearly been sealed in the fourth Test at Adelaide, before the last wicket fell just two runs short of victory (*see* Chapter Nine **Umpiring Howlers**). In the deciding Test at the WACA in Perth, the man for a crisis was Allan Border. But the match turned into a shocker for the great man. His decision to bat on a fast, bouncy wicket back-fired, as Curtly Ambrose bowled one of the great spells of pace bowling, eviscerating the Australian line-up with seven wickets inside 32 balls for just one run. Border was caught behind first ball. With a lead past 200, the whole nation cried out for its captain, but Border's well was empty. For the first time in his career, he bagged a pair, inside-edging a ball from Ian Bishop on to his stumps. In a match where he needed to face 500 balls, he had perished twice in just four. He was quickly forgiven.

Jimmy Cook

Jimmy Cook's Test record is proof that mixing cricket and politics can lead to misfortune. Undoubtedly one of South Africa's premier batsmen and fielders throughout the 1980s, Cook was denied Test cricket because of his country's exclusion as a consequence of the apartheid system. Not that it stopped him setting records for Transvaal and then Somerset, for whom he belted a remarkable 7,500 runs in just three summers, including 28 hundreds. Surely, he would have delivered at Test level too. He finally got his chance in South Africa's first home Test after re-admission, at Durban in 1992 against India. Cook was nearly 40 years old. The first ball he received from Kapil Dev found the edge and flew to Sachin Tendulkar at third slip, who took a smart catch. The veteran batsman was out to the first ball of his first Test. (Incidentally, Tendulkar in that match was the first player to be given out, run out, by the third umpire in Tests.) Cook made 43 in the second innings, but never made a fifty in his three Tests, ending on an average of just 17.83 – a measly return compared with his first-class average of over 50. But the stats tell only a fraction of the story.

West Indian Leon Garrick mirrored Cook in 2001, when he smacked the first ball of his first match straight to gully, off the bowling of South African Allan Donald: out for a debut diamond duck. He made 27 runs in the second innings as the West Indies won the match on his home island of Jamaica, but he never played another Test.

Dave Richardson

The cricketing gods have an eye for weakness. When a batsman thinks he has it sussed, they dive on him like a Bermudan policeman. South African wicket-keeper Dave Richardson was enjoying the form of his life in the 1994-95 season. Scores of 93 and 109, his only Test hundred, had earned him the player of the series award against the touring New Zealanders. When they were replaced by Pakistan, the gritty competitor must have been licking his lips. South Africa, at 325 for 6, were comfortably placed when Richardson came to the middle. The bowler was Aamer Nazir, who had travelled 14 hours the day before to cover for an injured player. Suffering from cramp, Nazir managed only a couple of balls in the afternoon, but his first to Richardson was good enough to break the stumps. In the second innings, after Nazir had made a golden duck of his own, Richardson fell lbw first ball to complete the king pair. It was not the first time a keeper had suffered a royal booby in Tests, and it wouldn't be the last either.

Adam Gilchrist

Certain batsmen hear noisy celebrations from the opposition when they are dismissed cheaply, such is the threat they pose. Adam Gilchrist, beyond question one of the greatest wicketkeeper-batsmen to play the sport, was one who would leave the middle to the sound of near-hysterical jubilation, unless he had done his usual one-man wrecking job. In his illustrious Test career (17 Test hundreds and an average of just under 50), he made only four golden ducks, with two of them coming in a winning cause. But the other two arrived in quick succession, in the same match, handing Gilly a king pair. To make matters worse, this blip coincided with the crippling defeat in Kolkata in 2001, after India had followed on (*see* Chapter Seven **From the Jaws of Victory**.) For a while, it looked unlikely that Gilchrist would have to bat again, as Australia took total control of the match. A century in the previous Test in Mumbai was business in usual, so the first goldie, lbw to Harbhajan Singh, was not going to prove relevant. But after Laxman and Dravid combined to give India a healthy lead, Gilchrist was called back into the firing line. He was again dismissed first ball, this time by Sachin Tendulkar, as the Indian spinners ran through Australia in the final session. With the Eden Gardens crowd at fever pitch, it would have been a brave umpire who turned down Tendulkar's appeal. The wild celebrations that followed the raising of the finger were a tribute to the fallen.

Wasim Jaffer

The Mumbai-born opener has enjoyed some stellar moments for India, most notably double hundreds against the West Indies and Pakistan. The lowest ebb, however, came in 2007, against Bangladesh at Chittagong. With competition always tight at the top for India, who had developed a habit for juggling openers, a decent showing against their whipping-boy neighbours was expected. Having won the toss and chosen to bat, Jaffer could have been forgiven for entertaining thoughts of a long stay at the crease. The first delivery he received from Mashrafe Mortaza pitched outside the off stump and the opener shouldered arms to let it fly through to the keeper. Except that it didn't. Instead, it jagged back and hit the top of off, sending the pole cart-wheeling. In the second innings, Jaffer did do better, surviving until his third ball, before edging to the slips. Four balls faced in the match, no runs. No catches either. Zip! A week later, in Dhaka, Jaffer made a hundred, as India won by an innings.

Javed Omar

Having watched the first four batsmen for India make hundreds (including Wasim Jaffer, *see above*) on a flat pitch in Dhaka in five sessions, declaring on 610 for 3, veteran Bangladesh opener Javed Omar would have been confident of making a

When it's not your day...

score. Omar was renowned for his ability to occupy the crease, even if the runs were slow to come by. Against Zimbabwe in 2001, he had become just the third player to carry his bat on debut and he had shown his stickability on several occasions since. He now had more than three days to bat if he wanted them. Instead, his first ball from Zaheer Khan flicked the outside of his bat and arrowed into the hands of Dinesh Karthik. There wasn't much time for Omar to mope, as his team were skittled for 118. The next morning, he was back out in the middle and history more or less repeated itself: same bowler, same first ball duck, but this time the catcher was Mahendra Singh Dhoni. Poor Omar had made a king pair at the top of the order – and an unwanted entry in the record books.

Ajit Agarkar

Like a jug-eared convection fan, the Indian all-rounder could blow hot and cold. Sadly for his captains, Ajit Agarkar appeared to have no thermostatic control to ensure that he remained at his optimum setting. His talent is writ large on the record boards at Lord's (109 not out in 2002) and the Adelaide Oval (6 for 41 to set up victory in 2003). But they represented the only time he passed fifty in Tests and his only five-for. However, the statistic that is perhaps most astonishing is his batting record against Australia. He made seven consecutive ducks over four matches between 1999 and 2001, including three consecutive pairs. The first four ducks were first ballers, including a king pair in Melbourne in 1999. Four years later at the same venue, Agarkar was keen to avoid the same fate, so he took off for a single on his first delivery, chancing the arm of Brad Williams. He lost the race and duly added another golden duck to his tally.

Tillakaratne Dilshan

Here is further proof that the cricket gods target a cricketer when he is at the top of his game. The flamboyant Sri Lankan opener, Tillakaratne Dilshan, had endured a stop-start career for his country, failing to deliver consistently on his abundant talent. The advent of Twenty20 cricket appeared to release any inhibitions he may have felt in the past, leading to a run-filled 2009 that propelled him into the category of 'world's best batsmen'. His improvisation in the T20 arena – especially the kamikaze 'Dilshan scoop', or 'Dilscoop' as it has become known, where he flicks the fast bowler's delivery over the wicketkeeper's head just before the ball hits his nose – has made him a favourite with the IPL brokers. Dilshan's skills undoubtedly helped Sri Lanka to the final of the 2009 Twenty20 World Cup. Agonisingly for him, though, and despite being named player of the tournament, he bagged a five-ball duck in the final as Pakistan won.

A clutch of exhilarating hundreds in ODIs and Tests proved he is so much more than a T20 specialist, including his 112 as Sri Lanka piled on 760 against India in Ahmadabad in the first Test of the November 2009 series. At Kanpur, in the second Test, Dilshan had to stand by and watch as India eased to 642 runs in just under two days, before inviting Sri Lanka to have a go before stumps. For a man in such rich form, any opportunity to bat on a flat pitch is a blessing, but he must still play himself in. Dilshan, however, chased his first delivery, a gentle leg-side loosener from Zaheer Khan. Too eager, too early, he succeeded only in chipping the ball to Pragyan Ojha at mid on. Out for a diamond duck. Had he left that first ball alone, he would probably have scored a big hundred, such was his form. Sri Lanka lost the Test by an innings and 144 runs.

Mike Hussey

Watching a fine batsman in a trough of form can be excruciating or delightful, depending on your loyalties. Every batsman goes through a lean patch, so there is sympathy aplenty, but he is only likely to get that from the opposition once he has notched another low score. When the confidence goes, a top-class batsman will gasp for life like a goldfish on the kitchen floor. England's recent Ashes victories were greatly aided by two of Australia's best batters struggling for touch. In 2005, Matthew Hayden had the potential to bully the English bowlers into submission, as he had done before and would do again. He had filled his boots against the county sides, but the English fast bowlers never gave him the licence to impose himself, even when he made a start. In the second Test at Edgbaston, captain Michael Vaughan scored a telling blow over the big Queenslander by placing a fielder at short, straight mid-off, challenging the batsman to drive down the ground. Hayden picked up the gauntlet, but only succeeded in mishitting the ball into the hands of the fielder Andrew Strauss: done first ball, like a kipper. With no fifties in the first four Tests, a patient hundred arrived in the fifth Test at The Oval, but it proved to be too late. Mike Hussey, another left-hander with a record of taking matches away from the opposition, followed a similar path in 2009. The warm-up matches were fruitful, but he looked at sea in the Tests. His nadir came at Edgbaston in the third Test when he left a straight delivery from Graham Onions, which cannoned into his off-stump. Usually so assured at leaving the ball, he was made to look like a prize plum, to the delight of the home crowd. But, gritty competitor that he is, Hussey scored an obdurate fifty in the second innings and then finally a back-to-the-wall hundred in the second innings of the last Test, after another duck in the first. Despite struggling for form, he still ended the series with an average of 35, higher than all but one of the England batsmen.

Adam Gilchrist (2)

For the best pinch-hitters in ODI cricket – Adam Gilchrist, Matt Hayden, Sanath Jayasuriya, Chris Gayle etc – it is not always the number of hundreds that point to their value at the top of the order. Gilchrist *only* hit 16 ODI tons in his 287 matches for Australia, on top of 55 fifties. But even five or six overs from the opening batsman were guaranteed to have the opposition playing catch up, as he rarely progressed at less than a run a ball. A quick-fire 30 from Gilchrist would allow the next batsmen time to set themselves for a long innings. Selflessness combined with quick eyes and hands made an explosive combination. But the flip side is that the opposition can feed off any failure. In the second match of the 2005-06 VB Series against the South Africans, at the 'Gabba, Gilly tried to smash his first delivery, a wide swinger from Shaun Pollock. On this occasion, the luck was against him, and the ball edged back on to his stumps. A diamond duck! Immediately the Aussies were struggling, managing only 228 runs all out. Although Jacques Kallis was run out the first ball he received in the reply, the visitors made it home comfortably through a typically nuggety fifty from their own keeper-batsman, Mark Boucher. If that first delivery to Gilchrist had inside edged past the stumps for four, instead of crashing into them, the path of the match could have been so different…

Sachin Tendulkar

Even the very greatest are not spared the occasional calamity. And let's not be in any doubt that Sachin Tendulkar is the greatest ODI batsman to have joined the pyjama party. Surely, no other will come close to his tally of 17,000 runs and 46 ODI hundreds (his world record 200 not out proves there is plenty left in the tank), made over the last four decades. That he has coped with the expectations of a cricket-bonkers nation such as India, fulfilling the dreams of millions, is testament to his heart and humility, as well as his astonishing eye and technique. Yet, that was all in front of him when he started his international career as a callow 16-year-old in 1989. After his first two ODIs, his record read: no runs, no wickets, no catches, no wins. His figures improved, but it still took the Little Master 70 innings to score his first ODI hundred, which was promptly followed by three consecutive ducks. The lowest moment of these formative years arrived in the final of the tri-nations tournament in Sharjah in 1991 against old foe Pakistan. Put in to bat, Pakistan had made a splendid 262 from their 50 overs, despite Zahid Fazal being carted off with cramp just two shy of what would have been his only ODI hundred. India started steadily enough, reaching 47 for 1, before the rug was pulled from beneath their feet by seamer Aaqib Javed, also a teenager. Opener Ravi Shastri was adjudged lbw, before Mohammad Azharuddin suffered the same fate first ball. Tendulkar took guard on a hat-trick, with the crowd at fever pitch and he was struck on his big pads. Despite a suspicion that he had shuffled outside the line of off-stump, the umpire raised his finger for the third time in a row to signal the rare feat. Aaqib finished with figures of 7 for 37, the best figures by any bowler in ODIs until 2001. Sachin has not had a golden duck in ODIs since then.

Hannan Sarkar (2)

In the 2003 World Cup in South Africa, Sri Lankan opening bowler Chaminda Vaas ended the pool match against Bangladesh as a contest inside the first over. Bowling fast, full, left-arm in-swingers that dipped late at the Bangladeshi batsmen, he took a hat-trick in the first three balls of the match. Poor old Hannan Sarkar was bowled for another diamond duck; Mohammad Ashraful then chipped back to the bowler; before Ehsanul Haque was snaffled at second slip. Bang, bang, bang, game over. The number five batsman, Sanwar Hossain, at least had the presence of mind to hit the fourth ball of the innings to the boundary, but he was dismissed on the fifth, leaving Vaas with 4 for 4. In the circumstances, Bangladesh did well to reach 124 all out, but they soon lost the match by ten wickets.

JP Duminy

At the time of writing, South Africa's talented left-hander JP Duminy was enduring a torrid run of poor form. His Test career started with a fanfare, as he guided his side to glorious victories in Australia, whilst deputising for an injured colleague. His 166 runs at the MCG in the 2008-09 series, when South Africa looked dead and buried (the score included a partnership of 180 with number ten batsman Dale Steyn), was the stuff of boyhood fantasy. Runs at ODI and T20 flowed in unison, until Duminy was being touted as the next big noise in world cricket. He may yet be, but first he must regain his self-confidence against off-spin. On England's tour of South Africa in 2009-10, Duminy became Graeme Swann's bunny, picking up two golden ducks on the bounce. Indeed, Swann – who has made a habit of snaring wickets in his first over – dismissed Duminy almost at will. India's off-spinner Harbhajan Singh took up the baton, trapping the left-hander first ball during the decisive second Test at the Eden Gardens in 2010, as South Africa collapsed on a flat pitch (*see* Chapter Eight **Team Collapses**). Another Indian off-spinner Yousuf Pathan then produced a carbon copy in the ODI series: Duminy's fourth primary for South Africa in three months. His averages have dipped alarmingly, but no doubt they will be remembered as a blip in a brilliant career. Similarities could be drawn with England's Kevin Pietersen who was also suffering a trot of cheap dismissals to slow left arm spin bowlers, who were soon queuing up to take his wicket. While both batsmen have an opportunity to rank among the best of the sport, they must first prove their ability to master bowlers of all varieties in all conditions.

Chapter Two
Horror Debuts

A call-up to the national side is a proud moment in a cricketer's development. But will his technique stand up to sterner scrutiny? Will he have the bottle to cope with the nerves? Many successful cricketers have recovered from a lousy start. For others, however, torrid experiences on debut have proved to be their last.

Fred Grace

WG Grace and his excellent bushy beard are well enough known. But Fred (FG) Grace and his equally splendid mutton-chop sideburns were eclipsed by his brother's fame. A quick-scoring batsman for Gloucestershire, he toured Australia in 1873, enhancing his reputation as an all-rounder. When the Australians arrived in 1880, Fred lined up for England's first home Test match, alongside WG and their older brother EM Grace (also with mutton-chops) at The Oval. Only the three Chappell brothers for Australia have since matched this fraternal display. WG helped himself to 152 runs in the first innings, but Fred was out for a second-ball duck. In the second, with England chasing just 57 runs to win, Fred was bowled without scoring, again to the second delivery. EM also fell for a duck before WG took his side home. Fred had bagged the first pair in Test cricket, although he is also credited with taking one of the most impressive catches of that or any other era. He pouched a steepler by the gas towers, which had travelled for 155 yards, while the batsmen turned for their third run. Sadly, within a month Fred was dead, having developed pneumonia after sleeping on a wet mattress. EM Grace more than made up for this waste, siring 18 children with four different wives.

Fred Tate

Medium-pacer Fred Tate played only one Test for England during his career, but it will forever be associated with his name. That it proved to be one of the most exciting matches ever between England and Australia was scant consolation. As are the whims of the cricketing gods, Tate suffered his darkest moment at the peak of his powers. The summer of 1902 was his best, at the grand old age of 35, taking wickets against all-comers on the first-class circuit: 180 of them in total. This form won him a place in the England Test side against Australia in what proved to be the deciding match of the summer at Old Trafford. Heavy rain had given the selectors an age-old dilemma: do they give a debut to the specialist bowler, Tate, to make the most of conditions or go with the all-round skills of a reliable bits-and-piecer like Geoff Hirst or Gilbert Jessop? They gambled on Tate. By lunch on the first day, it seemed a poor punt, as Tate bowled too short to Victor Trumper, who crashed a hundred before lunch. Tate ended the innings wicketless, although an Australian lower-order collapse caused by Bill Lockwood gave the hosts some hope.

Stanley Jackson (128) and Len Braund (65) set up the reply with a stand of 140, yet the Australians still enjoyed a lead of 37 runs. Within a blink of an eye, however, that lead looked thin, as the top three batsmen were dismissed for 10. Then came Tate's first dance with destiny. Lockwood, who had taken all three, induced a lofted flick from Australian captain Joe Darling, which looped into the hands of Tate at square leg. At 16 for 4, the match was in England's grasp. Or it would have been if Tate had held on. 'Doubtless,' the hacks scribbled, 'either Hirst or Jessop would have caught that behind his back.' Darling, reprieved, reached 37, battling out another hour with Syd Gregory (24). Nobody else managed more than four, so their partnership of 54 was gold dust. (It should not be overlooked that Tate took 2 for 7 in that innings and also held a catch.)

More heavy rain meant that England's attempt at 124 for victory was always going to be tight, but at 92 for 3, with the great Ranji at the crease, Tate had every right to sit more comfortably. But then six wickets fell for 24 runs and Tate was summoned to the middle for the last tango. Rain again fell, delaying the denouement. Eventually, Tate faced up to Jack Saunders and glanced him for four past the keeper. Four more to win! But the next ball slid under his bat and the match was lost by three. With ball, bat or in the field, Tate could have won it for England. But he fluffed it and the Test has been named after him ever since. Happily for the Tate family name, son Maurice soon made amends.

Tommy Ward

The South African wicketkeeper made the worst possible start to his Test batting career, becoming the only player in history to record a king pair on debut. The opening match of the 1912 Triangular Test series, against Australia, started promisingly enough for the gloveman, as he completed two stumpings. But Australia made 448 before South Africa struggled in reply, despite a fine unbeaten hundred by Aubrey Faulkner, batting at number five. Although Ward was the last man in, he was no mug with the bat, later scoring two Test fifties as an opener. But the modest crowd at Old Trafford saw none of that ability. His bat missed the first ball he faced from leggie Jimmy Matthews and he was adjudged lbw, giving Matthews a hat-trick. Following on, Ward was soon back in the firing line, as South Africa collapsed to 70 for 7 (Faulkner, who opened this time, made a duck). For some reason, Ward had been promoted up the order to number nine, but he was confronted with the same situation: Matthews on a hat-trick. This time, he got his bat to the ball, but it chipped back to the bowler, who ended Ward's miserable batting performance. Matthews took both hat-tricks on the same day and they were the only wickets he took in the match. Ward played another 22 Tests for South Africa before being tragically electrocuted in a gold mine at the age of 48.

Jack MacBryan

Winning a Test cap for England would have been just one more of life's little adventures for Somerset sportsman Jack MacBryan, who had won an Olympic gold medal for hockey at the 1920 Antwerp Games and represented his county in both rugby and golf. During the Great War, Jack (born in a village called Box...) was wounded in the battle of Couteau and spent the rest of the war in a Dutch POW camp, where the prisoners were able to play cricket regularly. His sporting achievements are even more remarkable given that his war injuries limited the use of one arm. Yet it was an injury to batsman Jack Hearne that gave MacBryan his chance, although his Test debut at Old Trafford in 1924 against South Africa was over almost as soon as it had begun. With just 116 on the board, the visitors were forced to abandon their innings for rain, which did not stop for the rest of the match. Hearne returned for the final Test and MacBryan never played in another, having failed to take a catch, bat or bowl in his only Test.

Sir Donald Bradman

The selectors were so disenchanted with the great man's debut match for

A warm welcome

Australia in 1928, won by England at the 'Gabba in Brisbane, that Don Bradman was demoted to drinks carrier for the next Test. The 19-year-old had watched England pile on 521 runs, and then Australia's top order crumble to 71 for 5, unable to repel Harold Larwood and Maurice Tate. Batting down at number seven, Bradman did score 18 from 40 balls, before being adjudged lbw by Tate. In the second innings, chasing an absurd 742 (after England had made the first declaration ever in a Test match in Australia), the home team were skittled for 66, Bradman joining the freefall with a five-ball one. The selectors had seen enough for now, dropping Bradman for the only time in his career, although he returned for the third Test at the MCG, where he compiled watchful scores of 79 and 112 (the first of his 29 Test hundreds) at number six. The teenager spent much of the series chasing leather in the outfield, as the visitors won with ease 4-1. How quickly the roles were reversed!

Dennis Smith

Twenty-year-old Dennis (HD) Smith's head was spinning after bowling the first ball of his Test career. Playing in Christchurch against Douglas Jardine's England team, which had just regained the Ashes in 1932-33, all his wildest expectations were being exceeded. Say what you like about the bowling tactics during the Bodyline Series, but they would have been irrelevant without one of the most effective batting line-ups to leave England. Yet any batsman is vulnerable first up and the Test debutant, who had played only a handful of first-class matches, pitched the perfect late in-swinger to the left-hander Eddie Paynter, rocking his castle for a golden duck. In the previous over, Herbert Sutcliffe had been removed first ball of the match by Ted Badcock (*see* Chapter One **Famous First Ballers**). Wally Hammond had been dropped in that same over. The score was 4 for 2. It could have been 0 for 3, with three of the world's best batsmen dismissed. Instead, Hammond went on to make 227. Smith did not take another wicket. Indeed, that wicket was the only one of his career, as he was dropped for the next match and never played Test cricket again.

Sir Leonard Hutton

Yorkshireman and opener Len Hutton was one of the finest batsmen to don the England badge, his name often being uttered in the same breath as Hammond, Hobbs, Compton and Sutcliffe. Equally capable of playing a swashbuckling innings to turn a match or digging in to carry it, England would have many more entries in the 'Team Collapse' chapter of this book were it not for the skill and concentration of Hutton, whose stout technique scored a glut of runs on uncovered pitches. But his curtain-raiser did not indicate the great feats that were to follow. Played out against the visiting New Zealand in 1937 at Lord's, Hutton blocked 29 balls before being bowled for a duck by Jack Cowie, who was enjoying a far more successful debut. Wally Hammond, who was nearing the end of his illustrious career, gave the 21-year-old fledgling a masterclass in Test batting, knocking 140 runs. In the second innings, Cowie again snared Hutton early, this time for 1. Hutton would add another 6,970 runs to that single, reaching an average of 56.67. His first hundred came in the next match and in his sixth, he broke Hammond's world record to score 364 against Australia.

John Warr

While the 1990s in England are remembered for selectors picking bowlers from relative obscurity, giving them a match, and then dropping them back on to the county treadmill, they did not invent the policy. In the 1950-51 Ashes series down under, medium pacer John Warr was tossed to the wolves at the age of 23, having played most of his cricket at university level. At that time, the wolves had very sharp teeth, including Invincibles such as Arthur Morris, Lindsay Hassett, Neil Harvey and Keith Miller. The first two matches lost, the beleaguered MCC decided to give Warr his first cap and the new ball. In different conditions against a lesser line-up, Warr bowled well enough to take several wickets; but on a true SCG pitch in blazing sunshine, against an experienced top order who knew that time was their friend, the debutant was sorely tested. Keith Miller, who dismissed Warr in the first innings, batted for just under six hours to amass 145 not out, combining with number eight Ian Johnson (77) to put on a match-winning 150-run partnership. Warr conceded 142 runs from his 36 eight-ball overs, for no wicket, before England lost by an innings, with Warr last man out, for a duck. He did retain his place in the next Test at Adelaide, again comprehensively won by the hosts, despite Len Hutton's defiant 156 not out. The Aussies took another 139 off Warr in the match, although he did at least get a wicket in the second innings: Johnson caught behind by Godfrey Evans. Johnson apparently walked out of sympathy, even though he had not hit the ball. Later in the match, Johnson bowled Warr for a duck to complete his pair. Warr was dropped for the fifth Test (in which Alec Bedser took ten wickets to win the match), and he never played again. His average of 281 runs per wicket with a strike rate of 584 balls per wicket is still the worst for any Englishman.

Jeff Thomson

The shaggy-haired speedster from Sydney made his debut for Australia against Pakistan in the second Test at the MCG in 1972-73. He had already caused waves in state cricket with his unorthodox slingy action and express pace, which could hurry up the best batsmen from just short of a length. In the days before speed guns were commonplace, there was no way of saying for certain whether Thomson regularly touched the 100mph mark, but he was certainly one of the fastest and most intimidating bowlers that the game has seen. But, unknown to the selectors, Thommo carried a broken bone in his foot into the match and bowled accordingly. On a flat deck, the Pakistani bowlers took him for 100 runs in the first innings with nothing in the wicket column. In the second innings, skipper Ian Chappell gave him only two overs, which stretched his arrears to 110 runs for the match. He was dropped for the last match of the series, but returned as an unknown package against the visiting England side in 1974-75, ripping out 33 wickets and writing himself into Aussie cricketing folklore.

Graham Gooch

England's highest ever Test run scorer (8,900 runs in 118 matches at 42.58) had yet to get off the mark after his first match. The 21-year-old had forced himself into the line-up against Ian Chappell's touring Australians in 1975 after a string of impressive innings for Essex had caught the eye of the board. Most of his teammates were at least a decade older than the debutant, who was tipped to be able to cope with the searing pace of Dennis Lillee and Jeff Thomson. Yet, in the first innings, he did not face either of them, as he was quickly wrong-footed by the dependable support bowler Max Walker, nicking one to Rod Marsh behind the stumps for a duck. Marsh gobbled up the next edge in the second innings, as Gooch did well to avoid injury from a fast delivery from Thomson that spat off a length. Gooch had faced just ten balls in the match, although he was not alone in his struggles against express bowling on a damp pitch (*see* Chapter Five **Captaincy Woes**). After a relatively modest contribution in the next match, the youngster was dropped and he did not return until 1978. Even then, Gooch did not score a Test hundred until his twenty-second match in 1980, nor a one-day hundred until his twenty-seventh match. But he soon made up for lost time, carving attacks from all nations until his last appearance at international level in 1995.

Malcolm Marshall

The Barbadian fast bowler became one of the most feared and effective weapons in the West Indian arsenal during the 1980s, able to swing the ball both ways or intimidate the batsman with extreme pace. He even used the relative shortness of his stature to send the ball skidding on to the victim at break-neck pace (or break-nose pace, in the case of Mike Gatting), giving scant time for evasion. Capable of bowling on all surfaces, Marshall was arguably the best in the West Indies stable of quicks; perhaps even the best fast bowler of all time. His return of 376 wickets in 81 Tests at an average of 20.94 with a strike rate of 46.7 is all the more impressive given that he was competing with his fellow fast bowlers for a share of the spoils. He could bat too, lifting his blade ten times for Test fifties, often in trying circumstances. But in his debut Test series in India in 1978-79, when so many of the regular fast bowlers had hooked up with the Kerry Packer carnival in Australia, Marshall looked far from the finished article. In the three Tests he played, the popular 20-year-old took only three wickets at a cost of 265 runs, averaging 88.33. In five innings, five runs came off his bat, including a duck on his first attempt. Sadly for the rest of the world's batsmen, these experiences only served to make him a stronger player.

Graeme Fowler

Foxy Fowler will be well known both to followers of BBC Radio 4's Test Match Special and Lancashire, all of whom he entertained for many seasons. Like Kent's Robert Key, he scored a Test double hundred for England and was soon dropped. Fowler's ODI career was more stop than start, playing only five matches for his country. His debut innings in Sydney against New Zealand in a tri-nations tournament was a gruesome spectacle, as he laboured at the wicket for 20 balls against some fine bowling from Richard Hadlee and Ewen Chatfield, before eventually he got enough bat on ball to find the hands of a fielder. Hadlee bowled David Gower soon afterwards, leaving England in trouble at 10 for 2. But if Fowler had only managed to see off the opening bowlers, he might have found the going easier. Allan Lamb (108 not out) and Chris Tavare (82 not out) certainly did, sharing an unbeaten partnership of 190 to win the match.

Dave Houghton

A hard-hitting batsman with a sharp cricketing brain, Dave Houghton was one of Zimbabwe's finest run-getters in its formative years. He would surely have scored many more Test runs, had his nation not begun Test cricket until late in his career. Even then, he made up for lost time, scoring four hundreds, including one in Zimbabwe's inaugural match and a double hundred against Sri Lanka. His debut ODI, however, was a different matter. Picked as wicketkeeper in Zimbabwe's opening match of the 1983 World Cup, Houghton was caught behind first ball by Rod Marsh off the bowling of Graham Yallop. The minnows were left squirming on the hook at 86 for 4, but Houghton's dismissal brought Duncan Fletcher to the crease, who almost single-handedly turned Australia over with both ball and bat (*see* Chapter Fourteen **Minnow Mayhem**). In hindsight, was it perhaps a blessing that Houghton had nicked off so quickly?

Saeed Anwar

Twenty-two year old opener Saeed Anwar of Pakistan must have gulped when he saw the pitch at Faisalabad in his debut Test match against the mighty West Indies in 1990. The curator had prepared a track that would help the home team's pace duo of Wasim Akram and Waqar Younis, who were the key to winning the match. But with an opposition attack that included Curtly Ambrose, Ian Bishop, Courtney Walsh and Malcolm Marshall, the visitors were unlikely to be dismayed. Pakistan captain Imran Khan won the toss and is believed to have ignored his senior batsmen's plea to bowl first. Anwar was thrust into the firing line and duly pocketed a duck, snared by Ambrose. The next day, Anwar was again trudging back from the middle without scoring, this time lbw third ball to Bishop. His team set a target of just 130 runs, which the West Indies knocked off with ease, despite a diamond duck by Dessie Haynes. It was a temporary setback for Anwar, who had soon scored a big ton against New Zealand and established himself as one of the classier stroke-players in his country's large portfolio of attractive batsmen. He also crafted 20 ODI hundreds and held the all-time record for the highest ODI score (194 versus India) for many years, until Sachin Tedulkar doubled up in 2010 (200 not out against South Africa at Gwalior).

Gavin Hamilton

It is rare for any player in a Test match to return a 'zero' – no runs, no wickets, no catches, no run-outs – but even more so for an all-rounder. That it should happen in a player's first and only Test match, turns it from quirky to tragic. Scotsman Gavin Hamilton had forced his way into the England tour party for South Africa in 1999, following some blockbuster performances for Scotland and Yorkshire. He could hit quick runs and swing the ball in favourable conditions. But in Johannesburg he did neither, as England were blown away by an innings in just over three days. Fast bowler Allan Donald accounted for him both times for a duck, exposing a weakness to the 'throat' ball; while Hamilton's 15 overs yielded 63 wicketless runs. In fairness to the Scotsman, few of the England batsmen covered themselves in glory, as Donald and Shaun Pollock shared 19 wickets. Only Alec Stewart scored a fifty (after his golden duck in the first innings). Michael Atherton also bagged a pair, including a first-baller in the second innings. But it was all that the selectors needed to see as they lost faith in Hamilton, who later returned to the Scottish fold with a Test batting and bowling average of scratch.

Nilesh Kulkarni

After bowling just one delivery, Test cricket seemed easy for Nilesh Kulkarni, a tall left-arm spinner from Mumbai. His team-mates had already hammered the Sri Lankan attack for 537 runs during his debut match in Colombo in August 1997, including a masterful hundred by his captain Sachin Tendulkar. When Kulkarni was brought on to bowl the last over of the second day by his skipper, the Sri Lankan openers were looking ominous on a flat pitch. But Kulkarni dismissed Marvan Atapattu with his first ball, caught behind by the wicketkeeper Nayan Mongia, becoming just the twelfth Test player in history to take a wicket with his very first ball. That night, he must have dreamt of cutting through the rest of the Sri Lankan line-up. But the reality was more of a nightmare. Not only did Sanath Jayasuriya (340) and Roshan

Mahanama (225) bat throughout the third day, but they did not fall on the fourth either, posting a partnership of 576 runs, before both fell with the score at 615. Sri Lanka carried on to record a monster 952 for 6, as the match was drawn. Kulkarni finished with figures of one wicket for 195 runs off 70 overs, now fully aware of the rigours of the game at Test match level.

Marvan Atapattu

When Kulkarni got rid of Atapattu, the Indians' celebration might have been quieter than some, as the opening batsman was hardly striking fear into the hearts of opposition bowling attacks. The selectors had clearly seen potential, which would eventually be vindicated with 16 Test hundreds, six of which were doubles. But the start to Atapattu's career was abject. A pair on debut against India in 1990, in which his side were dismissed for 82 and lost by an innings, was followed up two years later by a first ball duck against Australia in Colombo, while batsmen about him made hundreds. He did at least open his account in the second innings, but with just a single. By the end of his third Test, again two years later, it was still his only run, as another pair followed in Ahmedabad: one run, in six innings, over four years. Atapattu would eventually notch up four pairs in his career, the highest number for a front line batsman. Yet, he is fourth alongside Ricky Ponting in the list for all-time double hundred makers, behind only Bradman, Hammond and Lara. Vulnerable first up, but when he's set…

Ken Rutherford

The enigmatic right-hander did slightly better than Marvan Atapattu in his first three Tests for New Zealand, although not by much. In fairness to the 19-year-old, he had been plonked in the Caribbean by the selectors after just one first-class season, to face the combined talents of Marshall, Holding and Garner in their 1985 pomp. Marshall got him for a duck in his first innings in Port of Spain, before he was run out without facing a ball in the second. A four, edged through the slips, found him his first runs in the next Test in Georgetown, but Garner kept the same line and soon had him caught behind. Martin Crowe's exemplary 188 meant Rutherford didn't need to bat again. In Bridgetown, the youngster was pushed down to three, but he was caught first ball by Viv Richards off Marshall, as the rot continued. Marshall nabbed him in the second innings too, after he had scored just two. The fourth Test in Jamaica gave Rutherford some leeway, as he came in at number six, and he survived 21 balls, but only scored a single (Marshall again). He was in long enough to be smacked on the head by Garner. Inevitably, Marshall grabbed the ball in the second innings to take Rutherford for the fifth time in the series, although he did last 33 balls for his five runs. Twelve runs in seven innings at an average of 1.71. To make matters worse, Courtney Walsh had equalled his series aggregate in just one innings.

Shane Warne

It seems more in keeping with the rest of his illustrious career to designate Shane Warne's 'debut' as the match at the MCG in the Christmas Day Test of 1992, when he ran through the West Indians in the second innings to claim seven wickets for just 52 runs. Or even the wonder ball against Mike Gatting, his first in Ashes cricket, at Old Trafford in 1993. But Warne had already suffered a few scars before then, most notably in his real debut matches, against India in Australia in early 1992. Ravi Shastri and Sachin Tendulkar took a liking to the maverick leg spinner at the SCG, milking him for 150 runs in his 45 overs. Shastri eventually provided the young Australian with his first wicket, having made 206 in 477 balls. Warne was duly dropped for the seamer-friendly Perth pitch, but recalled in Adelaide, where he returned figures of 0 for 78, albeit that quick Craig McDermott took ten wickets and bowled his team to a tight series-clinching win. None the less, after his first Test series, Warne had a bowling average of 228 and a strike rate of 408. Fifteen years of bamboozling the best batsmen reduced that to 25.41 and 57.4 respectively, with the small matter of 708 wickets, before we even look at ODIs or first-class cricket.

Alan Wells

The cricket gods can act like spiteful theatre critics, demanding that you rise to the challenge when the spotlight beckons, casting you back into the shadows when you don't. Sussex stalwart Alan Wells had played out 15 seasons in the wings of county cricket, waiting for his moment to star on the biggest stage. His consistency as a middle-order batsmen had deserved an opportunity sooner, causing him to join the 1990 South African rebel tour in frustration. As captain of England A tours, he had excelled, earning credit for nurturing young talent such as Michael Vaughan and Nick Knight. His moment to shine finally arrived in the series decider against the West Indies at The Oval in 1995, batting at number six against Ambrose and Walsh. But again, he was made to wait throughout the first day, as the top five dropped anchor. And then Ambrose took the new ball at the end of the day. Graham Thorpe was caught behind and the curtain rose for Alan Wells. Ambrose steamed in, found the perfect length and the ball seamed towards the inside edge of Wells's bat, thumping into his pad. On another day, it would have dropped short of Sherwin Campbell at short-leg or deflected to the boundary rope for four and Wells might have survived until stumps. It didn't, and he was caught first ball. An unbeaten three runs in the second innings, as the match petered out, were a relief, but no consolation. He never played for England again.

Bryce McGain

Few professionals will admit that the taking part means more than the winning, which it often does at amateur level and especially in English village cricket. As an IT worker in Melbourne at the age of 35 years, the notion of playing Test cricket for Australia must have been fanciful to Bryce McGain, if not laughable. But opportunity knocked when Shane Warne retired and resident Victorian spinner Cameron White was called away on international duty. Tweaker McGain was plucked from club cricket and soon impressed at state level. When Stuart McGill hung up his baggy green, McGain found himself as the best leg-spinner in the country. Never afraid to pick on form rather than age, at either end of the spectrum, the selectors took McGain to India, but he was soon on the plane home with a shoulder injury. His chance seemed to have gone. But in the last Test in South Africa in 2009, with the series already in the bag and off-spinner Marcus North injured, skipper Ricky Ponting welcomed McGain into the Test ranks. The South African batsmen were pleased to greet him, smashing him for 149 runs in just 18 overs at 8.27 runs an over, one of the most expensive returns in Test history. He was run out for a duck in the second innings to end an ignominious debut. But at least he had gained a cap for his country.

Malinda Warnapura

It is bad enough making a first ball duck on debut, but when four of your mates go on to score hundreds, you know it is not your day. Malinda Warnapura's first match for Sri Lanka, against lowly Bangladesh in Colombo in 2007, had started well enough, as he clutched on to a catch in the deep to remove the opposition's captain and best batsman, Mohammad Ashraful. Bangladesh's collapse to 89 all out brought the opener Warnapura to the crease just after lunch, much earlier than he might have expected. The nerves quickly took over though and he went back to a ball to which he might ordinarily have pushed forward: leg before wicket for a golden duck. Sri Lanka were 1 for 1, but they soon recovered, reaching 227 for 3 by stumps. Fortunately for Warnapura, the selectors gave him another go and he scored 82 in the next Test, a week later.

Tharanga Paranavitana

Warnapura would have had every sympathy for his opening partner in the first Test against Pakistan at Karachi in 2009. He was watching from the other end as Tharanga Paranavitana faced his first delivery from skiddy right-hander Umar Gul. Had he taken a more deliberate stride, rather than propping half forward, he might not have edged the ball to second slip. Hesitancy is costly in a game that rarely gives second chances. To make matters worse, the rest of the batsmen filled their boots on the friendly surface, scoring over 1,500 runs in the match. Paranavitana managed just nine of them, in the second innings, before being run out attempting a quick single.

Michael Atherton

The future England captain and mainstay of the batting line-up during the torrid 1990s, made his debut in the fifth Test of the 1989 Ashes series at Trent Bridge. David Gower's side had already handed back the urn and were fighting for pride against a dominant Australian side. Atherton's first job was to watch Mark Taylor and Geoff Marsh bat out the first day and into the second, setting up a total of 602 for 6. Despite fielding for nearly seven sessions, confidence was high for the 21-year-old, given the flatness of the pitch and his own good form. He was eventually thrust into the firing line, as Allan Border declared before lunch on the third day. Opener Martin Moxon fell early to Terry Alderman, who was enjoying a golden series, to bring the debutant to the crease. The second ball he faced nipped back off the seam and struck him in front of the sticks, causing the dreaded finger to rise. In the second innings, however, he showed his tenacity, delaying the Australian celebrations for nearly three hours with his knock of 47 runs in 127 balls, top scoring for his side. His debut innings would not be Atherton's last mauling by the Aussies.

Devon Malcolm

England's fast bowler Devon Malcolm also made his bow in that match and he succeeded in making the batsmen uncomfortable with the new ball. However, his first wicket did not arrive until the score was 553 (Steve Waugh for a duck). His figures of 1 for 166 from 44 overs were scant reward for his efforts. Merv Hughes dismissed him cheaply in both innings, although he did manage to launch one delivery into the stands, an indicator of the occasional lower order fireworks that were to follow in his career.

MS Dhoni

The Indian captain is currently ensconced as the best ODI batsman in the world after a series of important knocks for his country over the last two years. Capable of rebuilding an innings or launching withering attacks on the opposition, Dhoni can play accumulator, destroyer or finisher as the situation demands. He has also developed a knack for reaching his hundred at the end of an innings or match, leading to seven tons and an average of over 50. The superstar wicketkeeper is lightning fast between the sticks and leads a new brand of Indian batsmen who will look for quick singles and turn twos into threes. However, this enthusiasm cost him dear in his debut match for India, against Bangladesh of all teams, in Chittagong in 2004. Dhoni had faced just one ball, when he was run out attempting to pinch a run. Happily for India, this setback was a temporary one. Time will tell whether Dhoni carries on to become that huge nation's greatest ever captain.

Suresh Raina

An aggressive left-hander who can strut at the wicket between boundaries with the best of them, Suresh Raina is finally beginning to fulfil the potential he has shown on the Indian domestic circuit. It has been a tortuous path on the international scene, however, since the fresh-faced 18-year-old first donned the blue of India in a one-day match against Sri Lanka in Dambulla in 2005. The experience was an unhappy one for Raina. His first task was to negotiate Muttiah Muralitharan, not an easy one for a veteran, even less so for a teenager on debut. He failed to pick the doosra, went back to cut the ball through point and choked with shock as the ball jagged in to trap him plumb in front of all three. Out first ball. His day improved, as he ran out Marvan Atapattu with a direct hit from midwicket, confirming his ability as an exciting fielder. But the match ended on a low note, as he was thrown the ball in the 49th over, with just one needed to win. Sanath Jayasuriya walloped his second ball for four and the match was lost.

Jonathan Trott

There are certain venues where you might fantasise about making your ODI debut as a number three batsman for England. A full house at Lord's, Eden Gardens or the MCG, for example, with your team on 150 for 1 on a flat track against tired bowlers. A soggy Stormont in Belfast against Ireland in a one-off match, where any success may well be written off as routine, is probably not high on the list. Jonathan Trott had perhaps envisaged his debut at Newlands, having been brought up in Cape Town, but with his colours firmly pinned to England's mast, he needed to get off to a good start. However, lbw to his fifth ball for zip, as the Irish gave their bigger neighbours a fright in 2009, was not the display of assurance the selectors had hoped to see. Trott did not make the ODI squad against the Australians later that summer. But it had already been a decent week for the fidgety right-hander, as he had scored a superb hundred on his Test debut in the decisive match of the Ashes series at a packed-out Oval in London. That experience must have exceeded his boyhood dreams. The fifth Test at The Oval has so often been a delivery room for England one-Test wonders, but Trott wowed the selectors, earning his spot on the winter tour to South Africa.

Shahadat Hossein

Opening the bowling for Bangladesh as they gain a foothold on the Test ladder is a poisoned chalice and quick bowler Shahadat Hossein has drunk the deepest from that cup. His strike rate of a wicket every ten overs is by no means the worst around, while he has taken 60 wickets in his 25 matches, including five-fors against South Africa, India and Sri Lanka. But for all those wicket-taking balls, there are too many that ask to be smacked to the boundary. His lowest moment came on his debut at Lord's in 2005, when Bangladesh were mauled by England. It was the young nation's first outing at the home of cricket, but the match was over halfway through the third day. Hossein had impressed the selectors with his raw pace, but this was always going to be a gamble, as his radar could waver. The moment proved too much for the teenager, as he was smashed for 101 runs off only 12 overs: 8.41 runs per over. It remains the most expensive innings economy rate for any bowler to have sent down six overs in a Test. His career economy rate has still to recover fully, languishing at 4.12 runs per over, the highest for any frontline bowler in Tests.

Tony Pigott

Journeyman all-rounder Tony Pigott had probably never entered the England selectors' thought processes during his career, but he did gain a cap by virtue of being a professional cricketer in the right country at the right time. He was moonlighting for Wellington in 1983-84, as the touring England side suffered a run of injuries and poor results. When the management realised they were struggling to find eleven fit players for the second Test at Christchurch, Pigott was sent an SOS. Famously, he answered his country's call by postponing his wedding ceremony, which was scheduled for the Monday, the fifth day of the Test. As

One-cap wonder CC.

it transpired, he would have made it down the aisle with time to spare, as New Zealand thrashed the wayward visitors, dismissing them twice for under a hundred (*see* Chapter One **Famous First Ballers**). Pigott started brightly and took a couple of wickets, but was punished by Richard Hadlee (99 from 81 balls), as he joined the malaise of half-trackers and half-volleys on a favourable pitch. The match was over after twelve hours playing time, leaving Pigott to begin a charm offensive on his fiancée. He was not asked to play in the third Test, so joining the ranks of one-cap wonders.

Chapter Three
Battered Bowlers

For every batsman who scores a hundred, and for every dropped catch or mis-field, there is a disheartened or angry bowler left shaking his head. The modern laws, pitches and equipment give an edge to the batsman, demanding ever more toil and sweat from the hapless bowlers. As a result, *Wisden's* pages are scarred with painful bowling figures, including the names of the leading exponents.

Maurice Tate

One of England's very finest bowlers of his or any era, the jovial and lion-hearted Maurice Tate was a favourite among players and spectators, at home and abroad. His ability to keep running in and delivering the ball at a reasonable pace on a decent length, often swinging it in late, made Tate a formidable opponent for more than ten years. His father Fred had a brief and inglorious career for England (*see* Chapter Two **Horror Debuts**), but Maurice enjoyed the opposite. He could bat a bit too, scoring one Test hundred and ending his Test career with an average of over 25 runs. He often completed the double of 1,000 runs and 100 wickets for his county, Sussex. He was another who would have made the Indian billionaires twitchy at the IPL auctions. He loved locking horns with the best of the Australians, relishing the contest with a broad grin. England were dealt a hiding in the 1924-25 Ashes series, losing 4-1, but Tate took 38 wickets, the most for any Englishman in a series in Australia. In the first Test at Sydney, he showed his stamina and class by taking eleven wickets and bowling 89 eight-ball overs (712 balls). Four years later, on his return down under, the series scoreline was reversed, but Tate took a mere 17 wickets, as the spoils were shared about. The sole Australian win came in the final Test at Melbourne, with the spectre of a home whitewash looming large. This timeless Test lasted eight full days before the result arrived, like cats and mice playing chess. Jack Hobbs and Maurice Leyland traded hundreds with Bill Woodfull and Don Bradman, but England blinked in the second innings, making just 257, after Douglas Jardine perished for a first ball duck. The Aussies reached the requisite 287 runs over a week after the match had started. Needless to state, the burden fell on the bowlers, who toiled on a flat pitch. Tate ran in 100 overs in the match – 600 balls and at least five miles – but ended the match wicketless. Nevertheless, his pace, accuracy and good humour did not waver.

Norman Gordon

The highest fourth innings total ever chased down was by the West Indies at Antigua in 2003, when they reached a dramatic 418 for 7 (*see* Chapter Seven **From the Jaws of Victory**). No doubt this performance will be bettered soon. But for remarkable circumstances, though, this record total might well have been 696, which even modern scoring rates would never have threatened. As war clouds gathered in Europe in March 1939, England were playing out the fifth Test against the South Africans at Kingsmead in Durban. With a 1-0 lead to the visitors, the authorities agreed to play a timeless Test, which would later become known as *The* Timeless Test. The flattest of pitches was kept flat by overnight rain and rolling, allowing the batsmen to accumulate runs without pressure of time. The hosts won the toss and gained a 214-run lead after four days' play. Quick runs never entered their thinking, as they carefully built a target of just under 700 to win. In total, Yorkshire left-armer Hedley Verity bowled 766 deliveries in the two South African innings, taking just four wickets for 184 runs.

Surely, England would not get close? Bill Edrich, who had endured a miserable tour, including a low score in the first innings, was upgraded to number three on a whim by skipper Wally Hammond and he responded with a fluent double hundred. Paul Gibb and Hammond himself added hundreds, bringing the total within grasp. But the match proved not to be timeless after all. On the eleventh day, England needed to board a train for Cape Town and the boat home. With 42 runs needed and the tenth afternoon still available, the heavens opened and the match was declared a draw. Eddie Paynter was out for 75 runs, not long before stumps were drawn. His was the only wicket of the match taken by quick bowler Norman Gordon. Gordon had already bowled over 700 deliveries, without success, and finished with match figures of 1 for 256.

For many of the players it was their last Test match, as the war called time on their careers. The English pair of Verity and Ken Farnes, as well as South African bowler Chud Langton, were all killed in the war. Gordon is the sole survivor of the 22 players at the age of 98 (in 2010).

Chuck Fleetwood-Smith

Through little fault of his own, Chuck Fleetwood-Smith's Test career started under a cloud, as many Australians would have preferred to see the veteran Clarrie Grimmett play instead, but Don Bradman insisted on the Victorian's left-arm chinaman. In the 1936-37 Ashes, however, he played his part in the series turnaround, taking ten wickets in the fourth Test at the Adelaide Oval, as Australia came from 2-0 down to win the series with victory in the fifth Test at the MCG.

In England in 1938, Fleetwood-Smith bowled well enough in tandem with Bill O'Reilly to retain the urn, but the fifth match of that series would be his last in Australian colours. Against an inspired Len Hutton, who batted over two days to reach a then world record of 364 runs (still England's highest individual score), the double-barrelled Australian was found wanting on a flat track. Two other batsmen scored big hundreds, as England reached a staggering 903 for 7. The left-armer bowled 87 overs and went for 298 runs, the most expensive innings ever by any bowler. His single wicket in the match was barely a consolation, although Hutton was given a life on just 40, when the keeper Ben Barnett fumbled a stumping opportunity off Fleetwood-Smith's bowling. At the other end, the wily O'Reilly's 85 overs went for *only* 178, taking three wickets in the process.

Khan Mohammad

Early in 1958, at the age of 21, a certain G. St A. Sobers broke Hutton's world record, at Sabina Park in the third Test against Pakistan. The young West Indies player made 365 not out – his first three-figure score in a Test for his country. Inevitably, the Pakistani bowlers' figures read like a car crash. Their plight was not helped by the oft-forgotten detail that Conrad Hunte reached 260 from a partnership of 446 with Sobers and might have passed Hutton quicker, had he not run himself out. In total, just two wickets fell to the bowlers in the total of 790, both of them to Fazal Mahmood, a fast-medium seamer who showed great heart in sending down 85 overs, conceding 247 runs. His opening buddy, Mahmood Hussain, another warrior for Pakistan in their early years, broke down after just five balls, so he missed out on the fun. Medium pacer Khan Mohammad took up the slack, bowling 54 overs for fully 259 runs, the most expensive figures for a Test bowler without a wicket. Not surprisingly, the exhausted Pakistanis lost by an innings (and 174 runs).

England

The bowlers shared the misery around during both of Brian Lara's epic knocks at the Antigua Recreation Ground, where he scored 375 in 1994 to break Sobers's record and then 400 not out, almost exactly a decade later, to regain the record from Matthew Hayden. The 400 run effort was probably the more notable, given that Lara had struggled for runs in the series against a dominant English attack. Spare a thought, however, for England batsman Graham Thorpe, who was the only fielder to be on the pitch throughout both innings. Having watched Lara pile on a total of 775 runs over five days, he himself made only 42 runs in three innings. Still, there are worse places to watch history unfolding.

Malcolm Nash

Some cricketers will be forever remembered for their failures rather than their successes and Welshman Malcolm Nash is one of them. A capable batsman, a safe pair of hands and an attacking bowler, Nash was a useful player for Glamorgan for seventeen years. But of his thousands of overs bowled, two will remain in the memory for posterity. Most famous is the over that was carted by Garry Sobers in a championship match between Nottinghamshire and Glamorgan at Swansea in 1968. The season was drawing to a close and the great batsman was in need of a challenge. Usually a seamer, Nash was experimenting with slow left-arm tweakers. An aggressive bowler at heart, Nash did his best to get the batsman out, but every ball flew off the middle of Sobers's bat for six. The only wobble came on the fifth delivery, when the boundary rider, Roger Davis, caught the ball but stepped over the ropes. The sixth ball was hammered into the street outside the ground and history was written. Nine years later, bowling from the other end to Lancastrian Frank Hayes, history nearly repeated itself, as Hayes took 34 off a Nash over, scoring a four off the second ball.

Sonny Ramadhin

In village matches, the bowler will usually give the skipper a nod after five or six overs to say he's getting a bit tired and could do with a blow. Some old pros will bowl eight or even ten on the trot, as to stop would mean stiffening up irreparably, but that's about the most you can hope for. The notion of bowling 98 overs in an innings is beyond comprehension, but then it would be for most professionals too. However, that was the feat achieved by West Indies off-spinner Sonny Ramadhin in the second innings of the first Test at Edgbaston during the summer of 1957, as Peter May and Colin Cowdrey overhauled a huge first innings deficit. The Trinidadian's usual partner in crime, Jamaican Alf Valentine, was not picked for the match, a mistake in hindsight, as Ramadhin took nine wickets in the match. Yet, a mixture of fine batting – or rather padding – and eventually fatigue, resulted in England easing to a draw. In total, Ramadhin bowled 774 deliveries in the match, the most by anyone in Tests, even more than those who had the misfortune of bowling in timeless Tests. Was his effort a triumph or a heroic failure?

Tony Lock

Jim Laker's remarkable (never to be emulated?) feat of taking 19 wickets of the 20 on offer in the Old Trafford Test of the 1956 Ashes, inevitably led to accusations of skulduggery by the Australians. The groundsman, said the critics, had prepared a dry, crumbling pitch that would help England's Surrey spin twins, Laker and Tony Lock, rather than Australia's pace pairing of Ray Lindwall and Keith Miller. England, who won the toss and batted first, therefore had the best of the conditions. Any truth in the accusation (the heavy rain was probably a more telling factor) would be scant consolation to left-arm spinner Tony Lock, who finished the match with just one wicket on a burner. Not that Lock bowled atrociously, conceding only 106 runs in 69 overs. He spun the ball sideways at times, but it took the ball away from the right-handers, who could leave it with comfort. Laker, an off-spinner, attacked the stumps with devastating effect. The bare fact remains, however, that Lock bowled more overs than Laker in the match, yet ended up 18 wickets shy of his partner. And there was no question of easing Laker's path to the ten-for, as foul weather threatened to end the match as a draw. The pair were not bosom buddies and Lock apparently tried too hard to get a wicket, angrily sending down an increasing number of faster deliveries, with his suspiciously crooked action. Had Lock bowled better, or had more luck, then Laker's moment would never have arrived.

Harbhajan Singh

An 18-year-old Harbhajan Singh, in just his fourth Test for India, played the Tony Lock role in the second Test against Pakistan in 1999. Anil Kumble performed the Lakeresque heroics, taking all ten wickets in the second innings to win the match. On a turning pitch, with uneven bounce, the rookie diplomatically took 0 for 51 from his 18 overs, as the veteran cleaned up. Despite three wickets in the first innings, this was an uncertain match for 'Bhaji', as he was run out first ball, attempting a crazy second run, and then bowled by Saqlain Mushtaq for a golden duck, avoiding a king pair by an onion skin. Saqlain, incidentally, ended the match with ten wickets, which was largely overlooked, as they came in two innings and not one!

Tony Greig

In the era of power plays and Twenty20, it is not uncommon to see a bowler bullied for multiple boundaries in the same over. In Tests, cavalier assaults still remain a rarity. In 1977, they were a revelation. Picked for a full strength Australian side to play England in the one-off Centenary Match in Melbourne, David Hookes was a carefree 21-year-old with the world at his feet. A string of hundreds at state level – including consecutive double hundreds – had earned his call-up at a packed MCG in front of some of the biggest names in Ashes history. With long blond hair and luxuriant moustache, he wowed both the guys and the girls in the crowd, especially when he laid into the occasional off-spin of Tony Greig, as Australia sought to set a target. Greig served it up – half-volleys, half-trackers and full-bungers – and Hookes smashed him for five fours in the over, all round the wicket. The cameo was sufficient to earn him a contract with Kerry Packer's World Series, although it was to prove the defining moment of his career. He later became a successful coach, but was tragically killed at the age of just 48, punched by a bouncer during a post-match party.

Sir Ian Botham

Entertainers, team-mates and now fellow knights of the realm, Ian Botham and Viv Richards were always likely to cause fireworks when they met in international

Buffet bowling

matches. Given the respective strengths of the two nations at the time, Richards tended to be on the winning side, although Botham was one of a very few English-men who could have held down a place in the West Indies side during the 1980s. In April 1986, Viv strolled out to face the England bowlers in the second innings of the last Test of the series, played at the ARG in his home town of St John's in Antigua, an island he had helped bring to the cricketing world's attention. The five-match series was already decided 4-0 and the match was all but decided too, with the West Indies needing quick runs to set up a daunting target. But nobody expected them to come quite so quickly! Viv smacked his first delivery for three and his second for six to make his intentions clear. The field spread and braced itself for the barrage. Botham, never shy of a challenge, did his best to restrict the Master Blaster, often bowling wide of the wicket with nine men on the boundary, but there was no dictating terms to Richards that day. Botham even tried to bounce the helmetless batsman, but the ball ended up in the prison outside the ground. (Appropriate perhaps, given that Viv's father Malcolm was governor there for several years.) Off-spinner John Emburey went the distance too, as the Antiguan skelped seven fours and seven sixes to reach his hundred in 56 balls, still the fastest in Test history.

Courtney Walsh

The thoroughbred Courtney Walsh was the West Indies' saviour so often in his exceptional career that it seems almost churlish to point out his low moments during the group stages of the 1987 World Cup in India and Pakistan, which his team were-expected to pass through by right. But against both England and Pakistan, Walsh leaked runs at the death, with the opposition searching for a miracle to win on each occasion.

In the match against England, Allan Lamb stood between the Caribbean side and certain victory, needing an improbable 35 runs from the last three overs. After Walsh's penultimate over was taken for 16, Patrick Patterson allowed just 6, leaving the deficit at 13. Walsh took the responsibility of bowling the last over, only to see Lamb hit a two and then a four. Four leg-side wides followed, then a single off a no-ball and finally a full-toss that was hammered to the boundary by Neil Foster.

Against Pakistan, the West Indies again seemed to be coasting to victory, until a string of dropped catches allowed Saleem Yousuf to stage a fight-back with a half century. But when he fell, it was left to the tailenders to flail the willow. Walsh had taken 4 for 26 in his first nine overs and it needed a leap of faith to believe that Abdul Qadir would hit the 14 needed for victory from the final six balls. One, one, two, left him ten short with three balls to come. The spinner then moved to leg and launched the quick bowler inside out over the mid-off boundary for six. The batsmen scrambled two off the fifth, before Walsh chose not to 'Mankad' (*see* Chapter Twelve **Expensive Run Outs**) the non-striking batsman Saleem Jaffar for backing up too far. This act of sportsmanship ultimately cost the West Indies the match and qualification, as Qadir hit another two for victory. Yet Walsh left for home with his integrity intact.

Eddie Hemmings

One of the many joys of cricket for the supporter and spectator is the 'game within the game' that allows even the most one-sided of contests to become a gripping spectacle. It could be a batsman approaching a milestone or facing a particular bowler who has dismissed him regularly in the past. The follow-on target is one such intrigue, often sparking mini-battles despite the bowling side having complete control of the match. At Lord's in 1990, India were never going to win after Graham Gooch had led England to a score of 653 for 4 (*see* Chapter Four **Costly Drops**). Reaching the follow-on target of 453 alone needed a sound team effort after several days in the field and hundreds by Ravi Shastri and Mohammad Azharuddin took them close. All-rounder Kapil Dev added a fifty of his own, but the total was still 23 runs adrift with nine wickets down. Number eleven took the shape of Narendra Hirwani, who was good for two or three at the most. In short, Kapil would have to do it himself. The first two balls of the next over from the genial, but ageing off-spinner Eddie Hemmings were studiously blocked back to the bowler, giving no indication of what would follow. The third ball disappeared over long-on's head and into the Nursery Ground. As did the fourth and the fifth. Never one to shy away from a challenge, everybody at the ground knew that Kapil would go again, no matter the delivery. With men back on the boundary, Hemmings dutifully dangled the carrot, only for Kapil to biff it once more over the ropes for six. Four sixes in a row; problem solved. 'I suppose it's logical,' said Richie Benaud on commentary. 'If you need 24 to avoid the follow-on, why wouldn't you get it in four hits?' Hirwani was out to the first ball of the next over.

Asoka De Silva

Much better known as a member of the ICC's elite panel of umpires, Ellawalakankanamge Asoka Ranjit De Silva represented a developing Sri Lankan side in ten Test matches between 1985 and 1991 as a leg-spinner. Although his economy rate of 2.65 stacks up well enough, his potency as a wicket-taker was found wanting, as he snaffled just eight wickets in total. He never managed more than two wickets in a match, which added up to a weighty average of 129 runs per wicket, the highest of any Test bowler to have sent down more than 2,000 deliveries. He also bears the chagrin of having the highest strike rate of any meaningful bowler, needing 291 balls to take each wicket. Notable scalps included Javed Miandad and Ken Rutherford (twice), but he watched plenty of batsmen reach three figures.

Bob Willis

In their pomp (which lasted most of their careers) Glenn McGrath and Shane Warne appeared to take pleasure in identifying the batsman they would make their bunny in the forthcoming series, often with alarming accuracy. The pre-series chat was all part of their mental disintegration tactics, as well as keeping the media sweet. Whether they would have singled West Indian wrecking ball Sir Viv Richards out for special treatment is idle speculation. Indeed, the opposite might have been true, as the Antiguan used to enjoy rocking an opposition attack to its core, by hounding its best bowler into submission and leaving the rest rudderless. In the early eighties, Bob Willis was one of England's most potent weapons. On an overcast day at Old Trafford, during the 1980 series, that had offered assistance to Roberts, Garner, Holding and Marshall in causing England to collapse from 126 for 3 to 150 all out; Willis was most likely to cause similar problems, having already taken 12 wickets in the series. Three quick West Indian wickets fell, including one, Haynes, to Willis. The Master Blaster would not sit quietly by and wait for more to follow. Instead, he launched himself at Willis – and Willis alone – sending him to all parts of the ground, until his old mate Ian Botham snuck one through his defences. From his knock of 65, fully 52 runs were made in boundaries, with 53 in total coming off the bowling of Willis. When Clive Lloyd started laying into him too, en route to a hundred, Willis was allowed to brood in the outfield. His 14 overs cost 99 runs, at 7.07. Fellow new ball bowler Graham Dilley conceded only 47 runs from twice the number of overs.

Shane Warne

When two juggernauts clash in a Test series, the pre-match media hype is ratcheted up. In the three-match series of 1998 in India, Sachin Tendulkar and Shane Warne were at the height of their powers. Their showdown would go a long way towards deciding the outcome, especially as Warne would be carrying the Aussie attack without the assistance of an injured Glenn McGrath. Some hosts will ensure that their top batsmen are not exposed to the visiting bowlers before the start of the first Test, for fear of losing the psychological battle. But the opposite can also be true, if that batsman smashes his adversaries round the park. Playing for Mumbai in a warm-up match, Tendulkar tucked into the Australian spinners with relish, hammering Warne to reach a rapid double hundred as the state side won by ten wickets. In the build up to the first Test in Chennai, the Little Master then practised for hours against leg-spinners bowling into thick rough, preparing himself for Warne to bowl at him from round the wicket. But the champion bowler had his own plans too and they worked, tempting Tendulkar down the pitch in the first innings and inducing an edge to slip. Tendulkar was out for just four and all India groaned. By the second innings, the match was on a knife-edge just after lunch on the fourth day. Sachin had reached fifty and the blond Victorian leggie gestured to the umpire that he was coming round the wicket. Two sixes and two fours in quick succession made him move back over. The battle had been won. Tendulkar finished unbeaten on 155, while Warne went for 122 runs from his 30 overs. India won the match comfortably the next day. In the second Test, India again dominated, creaming 633 runs for 5, while Warne leaked 147 runs for no gain. Tendulkar took another brilliant 177 off the Australian bowlers in the third Test, although the visitors won the dead rubber to end the series 2-1. Tendulkar's mastery of Warne had been the difference.

Chaminda Vaas

In the first of the 2008 three-match ODI series against the West Indies in the Caribbean, Sri Lanka had completed a Houdini act, recovering from 49 for 5 (opener Mahela Udawatte made a duck on debut) to reach a competitive 235 for 7. The day then improved further for the visitors to the Queen's Park Oval in Trinidad, as the West Indies batsmen struggled to stay with the rate. Two run outs and a golden duck for middle-order batsman Marlon Samuels left any hope of victory on the slight shoulders of Guyanan Shivnarine Chanderpaul, a responsibility that he has relished on so many occasions. Capable of both digging in for hours or unleashing a brutal assault, no opposition captain can truly relax while Shiv is at the crease, especially if he is batting with the tail. But with ten runs still needed off the last two balls, only one wicket left and the dependable Sri Lankan left-armer Chaminda Vaas bowling yorkers, the contest appeared to be over. Vaas had dug the Sri Lankans out of many deeper holes in the past, but that night he got it badly wrong. The fifth ball of his over was over-pitched, outside the off stump, allowing Chanderpaul to hammer it past mid-off for four. A six was still needed for glory. Vaas again delivered a freebie, this time a floating leg-side knee-high full-toss that just asked to be whacked. Shiv accepted the gift, launching the ball into the night air and the stands beyond the mid-wicket boundary. His team ran on to the pitch, the crowd went bonkers and Shiv rushed about like a mad thing. A shell-shocked Chaminda Vaas had to be dragged back to the dressing-room.

Ian Salisbury

England craved a leg-spinner to match the menace of Shane Warne and for 15 matches in the 1990s the selectors' hopes were pinned on Ian Salisbury. His career started brightly, as he picked up five wickets in his debut innings against Pakistan at Lord's in 1992, but he struggled thereafter to take wickets consistently or control the scoring rate. County batsmen, who were less well-versed in picking leg-spin bowlers, often fell to his turn and bounce. Quality Test batsmen, who had faced Warne or the subcontinent spinners on turning pitches, were not so easily tamed. His career ended as it began, against Pakistan; although this time he bowled on tour in 2000. England won the series, but Salisbury picked up only one wicket for 193 runs, as he played second fiddle to Ashley Giles (17 wickets). Saqlain Mushtaq took 18 wickets, while even part-timers Graeme Hick and Marcus Trescothick appeared above Salisbury in the bowling averages. He has not played since for England, although he continued to take wickets for Surrey and Warwickshire until his retirement in 2008. His Test bowling average of 76.95 is the highest by any English bowler to have delivered over 2,000 balls.

Mashrafe Mortaze

All bets were off concerning Bangladesh winning the third match of their ODI series against Zimbabwe in Harare in 2006 after medium-pacer Shahadat Hossain completed his nation's first international hat-trick. He removed Tafadzwa Mufambisi and then both Elton Chigumbura and Prosper Utseya (first ball) to rip out the Zimbabwean's middle-lower order, with another 89 still needed for victory. Wicket-keeper Brendan Taylor was set at one end, but the new man, Tawanda Mupariwa, was only batting at number nine because the two below him were so hopeless. Surely, the Bangladesh win was simply a matter of time? Taylor managed to keep the scoreboard ticking, while Mupariwa played the innings of his career. Yet, with an over to go, Zimbabwe still needed 17 runs, to be bowled by Bangladesh's best, Mashrafe Mortaze. A huge six from the second ball made the crowd start to hop, but with Taylor turning down singles, more boundaries were needed. Mortaze was helping the cause, sending down a raft of full tosses and a wide. Taylor hit another four, but when his partner was run out, the equation was five runs off the last ball.

Again, Mortaze obliged with another full toss, which Taylor gleefully hammered high into the bleachers. Whilst Taylor's knock had been sublime, Mortaze trudged off knowing it should never have been allowed to happen.

Stuart Broad

Of course, Yuvraj Singh was not the first man to dispatch all six balls of an over for six in senior cricket. Sir Garry Sobers, Ravi Shastri and Herschelle Gibbs all achieved the feat, although their efforts were against lesser bowlers. Yuvraj, on the other hand, was facing one of England's premier seamers, Stuart Broad, in the Twenty20 World Cup in 2007 at a packed Kingsmead. Although Broad was still finding his feet at international level, he still backed himself to bowl a yorker-length delivery that would restrict the left-hander's ability to loft the ball. Sadly for the Nottinghamshire man, each one was either a half-volley or a full toss. Broad's bowling colleague, Andrew Flintoff, had not helped the situation, sending a few choice words in Yuvraj's direction in an attempt to wind him up. Instead, it fired him up, as he smashed the first delivery over mid-wicket and out of the ground. The second was a nonchalant flick over backward square-leg, followed by an inside-out carve over extra-cover. By now the pressure was showing on Broad's face, but he kept to his plan. The idea was good, but the execution was lousy, as a waist-high full toss outside the off stump was dismissed for six over point. England called a huddle, while the spectators bayed for more, but any new strategy proved ineffective as the fifth ball was thumped into the midwicket stands. Yuvraj could probably have engineered a six from whatever Broad threw at him, so a juicy length delivery on leg stump was easily deposited over mid-on. So thirty-six came off the over, as Yuvraj reached his fifty in only 12 balls.

Steve Harmison

If the theory is that the early exchanges of a match or series define its course, then Steve Harmison's opening delivery at the 'Gabba on England's 5-0 drubbing down under in the 2006-07 Ashes series is ample evidence. Long gone are the days when the bowlers could hit their straps against state sides. Indeed most modern players are dead against elongated tours, especially the tall Northerner, who is a devoted family man. Harmison was clearly undercooked as he took the new ball, sending his first delivery to his old mate Andrew Flintoff at second slip. The facing batsman Justin Langer needed a moment to work out where the ball had gone. It was only one run and one extra ball, but it set the tone. During the 2005 win, Harmison had shaken up the Aussie batsmen in his opening burst at Lord's, striking Langer on the elbow, Matthew Hayden on the helmet and scarring Ricky Ponting on the cheek. They knew they were in for a fight. Harmison had the potential to be England's danger man, but after just one ball in the first Test at the 'Gabba, that threat had passed. He returned figures of 1 for 123 from 30 overs, as Australia made 602.

Glenn McGrath

Other bowlers could end an innings with figures of 0 for 86 off 25 overs and it would not elicit comment. But for Glenn McGrath, Australia's premier pace bowler for a decade and one of their very best, these meagre returns in the third Test at Old Trafford against England in 2005 were his worst ever. Extenuating circumstances, such as the fact that he had rushed back from injury having freakishly sprained his ankle just minutes before the start of the second Test (*see* Chapter Eleven **Insult to Injury**), were dismissed by this fearsome competitor. He had his chances too, especially against England skipper Michael Vaughan, who edged through to Adam Gilchrist whilst on 41. The keeper spilled it, causing McGrath to chunter all the way back to the start of his run up. The very next ball, a superb in-cutter, which cleaned the batsman up, was rendered irrelevant as McGrath had overstepped the front line, straining for a bit extra. Vaughan continued, to make 166 before being caught on the boundary by McGrath himself. The tall bowler finished the match on a high, however, taking five wickets in the second innings and blocking out for the draw. But any hopes of victory had diminished in that earlier spell.

RP Singh

There's no great surprise in learning that the worst figures for career economy rates in Tests are held by bowlers from the current era. Shorter boundaries, better bats, covered pitches and the T20 revolution have all conspired to make it easier for the batsman to score more quickly. Test matches are now more exciting or predictable, depending on your viewpoint. Strike bowlers like Shane Bond, Brett Lee, Dale Steyn, Jimmy Anderson, Lasith Malinga and Fidel Edwards have all leaked three and a half runs an over throughout their career. In a different era, perhaps, those figures would have been nearer those of Ray Lindwall (2.30 runs per over), Sydney Barnes (2.36), Maurice Tate (1.94), Fred Trueman (2.61), Michael Holding (2.79) or Wasim Akram (2.59). Only two bowlers in Test history, of those who have bowled more than 2,000 balls, have an average in excess of four runs an over. Bangladesh's Shahadat Hossein (*see* Chapter Two **Horror Debuts**) tops the pile with 4.12, but more surprisingly is the appearance of the name of left-arm Indian swing bowler RP Singh (4.02). Only six times in 24 innings did he go for less than 3.5 an over. In the three-match Test series against South Africa in 2008, he took no wickets for 235 runs in the opening two matches and was replaced by the young hope of Indian fast bowling, Ishant Sharma.

Roger Wijesuriya

The tall Sri Lankan off spinner might have been better off *not* taking the wicket of Pakistan tailender Abdul Qadir in the third Test against Pakistan in Karachi in 1985. It was the first Test wicket of his career, a proud moment for any bowler. But it did mean that Roger now had an average and a strike rate. Sadly, he did not take another in his four-match career, which left him with the worst bowling record in the history of Test cricket. On average, he needed 294 runs to buy a wicket or 586 balls (97.4 overs) for each scalp. Therefore, hypothetically, if he was to bowl an opposition out twice to win a match, he would need over 21 days, whilst his batsmen would have to score nearly 6,000 runs…

Michael Atherton

Being a batsman who bowls occasional spin is an unfortunate tag, as it usually means you are asked to turn your arm over against two set batsmen on a flat deck when the regular bowlers have run out of ideas. Any credit, if you do manage to take a wicket, is given to the captain for an inspired bowling change, or the batsman is criticised for throwing his innings away. The only hope for the part-timer is that the batsmen are so worried about getting out to a nobody that they milk singles rather than smashing boundaries. England skipper Michael Atherton was not the worst of leg-break bowlers, taking three five-fors in first-class cricket, before back problems robbed his bow of that string. He did bowl the odd over, in his early Test career, picking up the talented Indian batsman Dilip Vengsarkar at The Oval in 1990, although his seven overs went for 60 runs. After eleven matches, he had achieved a bowling average of 282, which edged out John Warr's all-time low for England of 281. Atherton did not bowl again until 1996, when he brought himself on against his old Lancashire buddy, Wasim Akram, at Headingley, once the match had petered out into a draw. It was a brave gamble: 15 runs conceded would give him the highest average in Tests ever. A wicket would halve his tally. As it happened, Akram played round a ball that was straight enough for Steve Bucknor to slowly raise his finger. Atherton's average plummeted to 151 and he never bowled again.

Kevin Pietersen

For all that KP started his first-class career as a bowler in South Africa – once taking four top order wickets against a touring English team for Kwa-Zulu Natal – his Test record is underwhelming. There is usually plenty of bluff and bluster when the tall off-spinner takes off his sweater to bowl – and plenty of ostentatious celebration for any success – but the results are a far cry from his batting achievements. His four wickets have arrived at a cost of 548 runs (4.16 an over), leaving an average of 137, the highest for any bowler who has taken more than two wickets in Tests. Pietersen also wallows in tenth position of the worst career bowling averages for those who have bowled 5,000 First Class deliveries. (Interestingly, Sachin Tendulkar sits third.) Food for thought for any selector tempted to use him as a genuine all-rounder: but as a partnership breaker, he will surely continue to have success. After all, how many batsmen can resist the urge to swing out when Pietersen is goading them from 22 yards away?

Allan Donald

The South African paceman was often the scourge of opposition batting orders, taking 330 wickets at just 22.25. When pundits start talking about 'the great fast bowlers', Donald's name usually gets a mention and rightly so. Haring into the wicket, often daubed with white war-paint on his cheeks, he could hurry up the most adept players of speed. Tailenders rarely stood a chance. Many of his most memorable performances came against England, and he took 86 wickets in the process. The spoils were probably shared by the end, as he suffered the occasional failure amongst the successes. One such aberration was the demolition job administered by England in the third Test at The Oval in 1994, the first series in England after South Africa's readmission. Donald had taken seven wickets in the win at Lord's and had peppered the batsmen at Headingley, albeit without much success. England duly needed to win the deciding Test to draw the series, a task that looked unlikely after surrendering a first innings deficit. Donald had taken three wickets, but along with Fanie De Villiers, he had riled England's fast bowler Devon Malcolm with some short-pitched bowling. Malcolm reacted by running through nine of the South Africans in one of the finest spells of controlled hostility ever delivered by an England bowler. Donald was his last victim, castled by a searing yorker. Yet, on the same pitch, with a tricky target of 205 runs still needed, Donald then endured his worst figures in an innings, as England belted him for 96 runs from only 12 overs. Gooch, Atherton and Hick played him with ease, as the home side charged to an eight wicket victory. The eight runs an over conceded were the third worst by a bowler to have delivered six overs, and they came from one of the game's greats.

Pommie Mbangwa

The likeable and well-spoken Zimbabwean, Pommie Mbangwa, has won plenty of plaudits for his commentary skills since hanging up his boots. As a fast-medium seamer, however, he was popular with the opposition opening batsmen, especially in ODIs. Unfortunately for Mbangwa, he often found himself bowling against some of the most destructive batsmen of the modern era – Sanath Jayasuriya, Sachin Tendulkar, Saeed Anwar and Shahid Afridi – who all took a liking to his fare, usually on good pitches with a lightning outfield and short boundary. On several occasions in his 29 ODIs, Pommie disappeared for more than seven an over, including a painful 59 runs from six wicketless overs against Sri Lanka in 1999 as Jayasuriya teed off. Mbwanga's figures improved towards the end of his career, but the Zimbabwean remains the only ODI player to have bowled more than a thousand balls and returned an average in three figures (103.63). His strike rate of 124.4 is also the highest for a frontline bowler. Ouch!

Dale Steyn

During his first outing in an ODI for South Africa, in a steamy Melbourne, the 22-year-old Dale Steyn showed little potential as the world's premier quick. His sole Test series to date against England had proved erratic and expensive, so he needed a sound performance against a tough Australian outfit in 2006 to prove himself. The match was being played at the Telstra Dome with its roof closed, which turned the stadium into a greenhouse. The conditions ought to have helped Steyn's natural ability to swing the ball, but instead it turned him into a spray gun. While experienced seamers like Shaun Pollock and Andrew Hall returned tidy figures, the youngster was creamed for a volley of boundaries by Phil Jaques, who hit a fine 94 on debut. After five overs were taken for 58 runs, skipper Graeme Smith had seen enough and invoked the experimental 'super sub' law, replacing Steyn with all-rounder Johan van der Wath, who conceded only 20 runs from his five overs. Steyn's match lasted all of 18 overs. Australia cruised to victory.

Mick Lewis

In fairness to the burly Victorian quick, none of the bowlers on show enjoyed success at the Wanderers in the ODI played on the 12 March 2006, the fifth of the series. All the South African bowlers were mauled by Ricky Ponting (164 from 105 balls) as Australia posted a world record 434. Likewise, Lewis's colleagues were hammered by Herschelle Gibbs (175 from 111 balls) as the hosts defied all belief to chase the total down with just a ball to spare. Lewis felt the wrath of both Gibbs and Graeme Smith in the initial powerplays and then got worked over a second time as Mark Boucher and the tailenders scrambled to the win. His only consolation perhaps was that Ponting had enough faith in his ability to let him bowl out his full ten overs, while others were cut short. Had he stopped at just eight or even nine overs, then Lewis would not hold the record for the most runs conceded in an ODI by a bowler: ten overs, no maidens, no wickets for 113 runs. Those figures proved to be a gravestone on his career, as he lost his contract soon afterwards and never played another ODI for Australia.

Stuart Clark

The ODI against the West Indies in Malaysia in 2006 seemed to be going as usual for the Australians, posting a big total of 272 on the back of stand-in skipper Michael Hussey's hundred. The West Indies in reply were falling well behind the rate, albeit that they had wickets in hand. A quick squeeze by the fast bowlers and the customary collapse was bound to ensue. So Hussey turned to one of his most dependable bowlers, Stuart Clark, who had spent the last year confirming himself as the heir to Glenn McGrath. However, Chris Gayle and Brian Lara did not show him quite the same respect. Clark's non-threatening pace, on a predictable line and length, was just right to allow the left-handers to heave through the line and launch the ball to the boundary. As the batsmen began toying with Clark, so the tall bowler lost his shape, dropping in the odd half-tracker and full-bunger that went the same way as his conventional efforts. Gayle and Lara smashed 151 from 20 overs, all the more remarkable given how slowly they had started. The Windies chased down the target with 16 balls to spare. Clark's seven overs flew for 87, more than 12 runs an over. None of the other bowlers went for a run a ball. Had Hussey not spared Clark those last three overs, then Mick Lewis might have been pushed off the top of the dung heap.

Muttiah Muralitharan

One man who would have been most delighted to see Mick Lewis concede so many runs was Muttiah Muralitharan, the brilliant Sri Lankan off-spinner. In further proof that even the very best in the game cannot avoid moments of cricketing despair,

Murali had been hammered for 99 runs from his ten overs against the same Australians just a month previously. The little Tamil has taken over 500 ODI wickets, on top of his 700 plus Test scalps, but he did not add to that list at Sydney in the second final of the 2006 VB Series. Sri Lanka had won the first match and seemed to have taken a stranglehold of the second, as Australia slumped to 10 for 3 after Chaminda Vaas's opening burst. Ordinarily, this would be an invitation for Murali to control the middle overs, allowing no more than four or five an over. But Ricky Ponting (124) and Andrew Symonds (151) recognised the need to press on if they were to win the match. Whenever the off-spinner came on to bowl, the pair smacked him out of the attack, forcing captain Marvan Atapattu to search out a different solution. For Murali, it was a chastening experience, having leaked more than 60 runs in an innings on only five occasions in 269 matches. The 237-run partnership was further enhanced by a late barrage of strokes from Michael Clarke and Mike Hussey, rubbing more salt into Murali's wounds. Australia made a staggering 368 for 5 and won the match easily, before wrapping up the series with a nine-wicket win in Brisbane.

Scott Boswell

There are moments on a cricket pitch when you wish the ground would swallow you up. At least if the batsman is having a shocker, then he'll probably be dismissed soon. He can hide among friends with a cup of tea in the pavilion. For the bowler who has lost his radar or developed a bad case of the yips, then he is terribly exposed, especially if the meltdown comes at the start of an over. The simple exercise of completing six legal deliveries suddenly becomes a Herculean task. In a league or village match – or even a first-class match given the size of the average crowds – the matter is soon forgotten. In the final of a one-day tournament at a packed-out Lord's, with the cameras charting the bowler's painful demise, the moment is captured forever.

Scott Boswell, opening bowler for Leicestershire, entered the final of the 2001 C&G Trophy against Somerset full of confidence, picked instead of veteran fast bowler Devon Malcolm (who was deemed a liability). Boswell had taken four wickets in the semi-final against Lancashire, all of them prize England scalps – Michael Atherton, Neil Fairbrother, Graham Lloyd and Andrew Flintoff. Perhaps he might join them in the national set-up, if he could put in a similar performance in the final? But any such dreams turned to dust in his second over, as Boswell's compass was upset by the Lord's slope. Nerves manifested themselves as sweat in his palms, which further affected his control. His unorthodox action relied on timing, so when that left him, the wheels came off.

His first over was not a disaster – just the one wide, although two half-volleys were crashed to the boundary. His second over was a calamity. Six of the first eight deliveries were wides and big ones too, five of them coming on the trot. The crowd (and some of his grinning team-mates) entered the fun, cheering every blooper as Boswell wiped his hands on his trousers and shortened his run-up. The umpire looked like he was learning to fly. The only man to show him any sympathy was the opposing batsman, Marcus Trescothick, who hit a couple of wide full tosses to make them count. The 14-ball over cost 14 runs and Boswell was sent to the boundary for the rest of the afternoon. His final act of the day was to be bowled out, as Somerset easily won. Boswell only ever bowled one more over for Leicestershire, in a Sunday League match, which went for 18 runs, before he hobbled off with a calf strain. His professional career was finished.

Darren Gough

Almost every Ashes series during the 1990s and early 2000s started the same way – lots of English pre-match optimism, which was quickly deflated by an emphatic Australian statement of intent. The opening day of the first Test of the 2001 series at Edgbaston ended no differently for the home side, although they had at least owned the momentum for part of the early exchanges. A second wicket partnership of 104 between Michael Atherton and Mark Butcher gave hope, but it was soon nipped in the bud after lunch by Jason Gillespie, who had Atherton caught at slip. Then the perennial destroyers of England, Glenn McGrath and Shane Warne, found their rhythm, running through the makeshift batting line-up. But at 191 for 9, Alec Stewart and Andy Caddick delighted the crowd with an hour of fireworks, racing along to 294 before Stewart was trapped in front. This was hardly a match-winning total, but at least the tanked-up Brummies had something to work with, especially as Darren Gough could be a match for any batsman on his day. But if the crowd was pumped, so was the opening Aussie Michael Slater. The first two deliveries from the popular Yorkshireman were hammered behind square for four. Two more fours were struck in the over and suddenly Australia were 18 for 0. Business as usual. Along with Matthew Hayden, Slater raced the score to 98 off 97 balls, before Hayden was caught brilliantly by Craig White. As the dust settled at the end of a frantic day, the unavoidable truth was that Australia were in a dominant position yet again. Hundreds for Steve Waugh, Damien Martyn and Adam Gilchrist confirmed that the next day, as Gough's 33 overs went for 152 runs. England then collapsed from 142 for 2 to 164 all out, by which time Gough had completed his pair with a first ball duck.

Chapter Four
Costly Drops

'Catches win matches' is the slogan learned by every English-speaking cricketer from an early age because it is true: they do. Missed chances, on the other hand, linger long in the memory, especially when the lucky batsman makes the butter-fingered fielder pay. Is there a worse feeling on the cricket field than grassing an easy catch?

England

In the exciting Ashes series of 1907-08, which must have matched the 2005 series for tense finishes, England had pushed themselves into a position of ascendancy in the third Test at Adelaide. They had lost the first Test by two wickets and pinched the second by just one, due to some dogged tailending by Sydney Barnes and Arthur Fielder (*see* Chapter Seven **From the Jaws of Victory**). Now those two new ball bowlers had been instrumental in reducing the hosts to 285 in Adelaide. England had then gained a 78-run lead, which looked even stronger after Barnes had removed Victor Trumper for a duck. Wickets continued to fall regularly and soon Australia were teetering on the edge of defeat at 180 for 7, a lead of just 102. Time was not an issue in a timeless Test. However, Australia had one last ace up her sleeve. Clem Hill, one of the finest batsmen the country has ever produced, was lurking down at number nine, as he had been suffering from 'flu. Rising from his sick bed,

A good catch

he joined debutant Roger Hartigan in the middle for one last desperate push. Their eighth wicket stand of 243, as the English wilted in the South Australian heat, became the stuff of Aussie legend. Hartigan made 118 and Hill a towering 160, as he sweated out his fever. Unfortunately for England, Hartigan was dropped at point by Fielder on just 32, while Barnes spilt a gilt-edged chance at mid-off when Hill was on 22. Would either of those catches have won the match and the series? Possibly. But they were dropped and Australia charged to an emphatic 245-run win, with poor old Fielder the last wicket to fall.

Walter Robins

'Oh, don't give it another thought, Walter,' said the English captain Gubby Allen at the MCG during the third Test against Australia in the 1936-37 series. 'You've just cost us the Ashes, that's all.' Walter Robins had dropped Don Bradman first ball in the second innings, after a cleverly engineered piece of bowling and field placing by Bill Voce had tempted the great man into a lofted pull shot. Bradman had also been imaginative with his captaincy, flipping his batting order to let the pitch dry out (*see* Chapter Seven **From the Jaws of Victory**). Had he been out for a golden duck, then the match would almost certainly have been lost and with it the rubber, which England were winning 2-0 at the time. Allen's pessimism proved prescient. Bradman scored 270, adding a partnership of 346 runs with Jack Fingleton, who made 136. England eventually lost the match by 365 runs and were hammered by Bradman in the final two Tests, as Australia retained the urn. Oh dear.

Roy Sheffield

When the keeper spills a catch behind the stumps, the fielders are usually fairly supportive. A tap on the shoulder or a friendly 'chin up' helps him move on. But fielders have long memories. If the spared batsman carries on to score a bundle, keeping them out in the hot sunshine when they could be munching scones in the pavilion, then sympathy quickly wanes. The chatter dries up. Throws to the guilty keeper become lower and harder. The collective sulk is on. For Roy Sheffield, wickie for Essex in 1932 against the mighty Yorkshire, all chances needed to be snaffled if his bowlers were to make inroads. Morale was low anyway, after a drubbing from Surrey the day before. The team needed a boost. Opening bowler AG Daer provided it early in his spell, catching the edge of Yorkshire mainstay Percy Holmes, who had scored just three. The ball flew through to Sheffield, at a difficult height, and he launched his gloves at it. But it did not stick. 'Chances are coming, lads, we'll get the next one.' The next one arrived with the score at 555 the following day. (*see* Chapter Ten **Chasing Leather**.) Holmes had scored 224 and his partner Herbert Sutcliffe 313. Daer, not amused, ended on figures of 0 for 106 and then bagged a pair.

Jack Crapp

The Cornishman held many fine catches at first slip for Gloucestershire in his career, but he is another who will be remembered more for a failure than any success. Picked for the third Test of 1948 to play Sir Don Bradman's Invincibles on the back of a hundred against them for his county, Crapp had played well enough at Old Trafford, scoring 37 and 19 not out, and pouching a catch in each innings. He kept his place for the fourth Test at Headingley and although he did not contribute much with the bat, England were in a dominant position by the fifth day, setting Australia a target of 404 runs to regain the Ashes. Even with the Don in their ranks, it was surely beyond the visitors. In truth, it ought to have been. Bradman twice edged to Crapp, off the left-arm chinaman of Denis Compton. Both shots were catchable, but both were grassed. Wicketkeeper Godfrey Evans, so often Mr Reliable, could offer no advice, as he was suffering his own spell of butterfingers, missing two clear cut stumping chances against Bradman's partner Arthur Morris, who went on to score 182. Bradman was unbeaten on 173 and Australia had won by seven wickets. Crapp played the two drops over in his mind for the rest of his life, wondering if it was the sun in his eyes or Godfrey's gloves in the way. Would he have given all his 385 first-class catches for just one of those Bradman chances?

West Indies

At its peak, West Indian fielding will rival any other nation in its intensity and accuracy. When the wheels come off, however, and the focus blurs, then the circus comes to town. Sir Garry Sobers's 1972 side, which unexpectedly drew with the touring New Zealanders, learnt the hard way that dropped catches are costly. In the first Test at Kingston, in which Glenn Turner carried his bat to score 223 in the first innings, Joey Carew put down a dolly at extra cover when the Kiwi opener was on just 47. At the time, New Zealand would have been six wickets down and 400 runs in arrears. Instead, the drop released Turner to play a hero's knock. In the following Test, at Port-of-Spain, New Zealand owed its parity to captain Bev Congdon, who scored a nuggety 166 not out, batting at three. No less than three chances were spilled before the team innings reached 100, by which time the New Zealanders were six down anyway and struggling. Congdon was dropped twice more as he guided the tail to 348. Had the West Indies taken just one of the catches on offer in the first two Tests, they would have surely snatched a 2-0 lead. Instead, the series resulted in a stalemate.

New Zealand

Sadly for New Zealand, they were equally charitable in that series! In the third Test in Bridgetown, a wet pitch and an unwise decision to bat helped the visitors to run through the West Indies for only 133 runs. Lawrence Rowe, who had taken a double hundred and a hundred off the Kiwi bowlers in his debut Test in Kingston, suffered a first ball duck, edging through to the wicketkeeper. As the pitch dried out, in-form Bev Congdon and Brian Hastings both scored hundreds to give the visitors complete control of the match with a 289-run lead and plenty of time to force a win. The advantage appeared to be terminal, when Maurice Foster was trapped lbw by Bruce Taylor for four runs, leaving his side five down for just 171 runs. But it is one thing to get in a position to win and quite another to cross the line. Glenn Turner, of all people, spilled a straightforward catch at first slip when number five batsman Charlie Davis was finding his feet. Terry Jarvis had smeared his fingers with the same butter, putting down a gift, again at first slip, from Garry Sobers himself, soon after the West Indies had drawn level at the start of the fifth day. Either catch would have won the match, no doubt about it. Instead, Davis made 183, Sobers 142, sharing a stand of 254 for the sixth wicket that earned a draw.

England

The first Test of the 1972 Ashes series at Old Trafford was eventually won comfortably by England, but they made heavy weather of it with some sub-standard catching. The unfortunate Geoff Arnold could only kick the turf in frustration as three edges were dropped by the slips off consecutive balls. England's captain, Ray Illingworth, tore into his fielders, accusing them of ineptitude. The barrage of abuse ended later that day when Illingworth himself grassed a chance, leading to endless grumblings about how Old Trafford was a poor seeing ground. Amidst the drops, Aussie skipper Ian Chappell was caught brilliantly first ball on the boundary by MJK Smith off a Tony Greig long hop. When it is not your day...

Clive Lloyd

The 1979 Prudential World Cup final at Lord's was always tipped to go the way of Clive Lloyd's West Indians, who had the perfect balance of attack and defence, whether batting or bowling. Their fielding was pretty special too. But, having been inserted in the 60-over affair, the Windies buckled to 99 for 4. Derek Randall, the host nation's premier fieldsman, threw down the stumps to dismiss the dangerous Gordon Greenidge, before the English seamers removed Desmond Haynes, Alvin Kallicharran and the skipper Lloyd. Only Viv Richards and Collis King were left before the wicketkeeper and bowlers. But England had a problem. Fast bowler Bob Willis had withdrawn on the morning of the match, leaving skipper Mike Brearley to gamble on filling the extra twelve overs with part-time bowlers, such as Geoffrey Boycott. The pumped-up King was not going to sit quietly while the buffet car was open and he launched a ferocious attack that turned the match on its head. Even Richards was left stunned, as King pummelled 86 runs from 66 balls with 10 fours and three sixes. The part-timers' twelve overs were clattered for 86 runs as the West Indies sped to 286. After King departed, Richards opened his shoulders to reach 138 not out. England started their reply steadily, indeed too steadily, as Brearley and Boycott put on 129 for the first wicket in 48 overs. Lloyd, who later denied it, was accused of dropping an easy chance from Boycott on purpose to keep him in the middle. Any hopes of a T20-style run feast were then squashed as Joel Garner and chums ran through all ten wickets for the addition of only 65 runs. David Gower made a duck, while Wayne Larkins and Bob Taylor were dismissed first ball. Lloyd's drop proved to be a calamity for the batting side!

Rodney Marsh

The third Test against the West Indies at Adelaide in early 1982 ought to have ended on a satisfying note for the rugged, moustachioed wicketkeeper, Rodney Marsh. The match was his 80th for his country, passing the record held at the time by Neil Harvey, in a successful career as a fine gloveman and an obdurate batsman. His 255 Test dismissals – 95 catches off Dennis Lillee alone – are testament to his ability, and contradict his nickname, Iron Gloves. Batting first, 1-0 up in the three-match series, Marsh had an opportunity to show his worth with the bat, putting on 50 runs with Allan Border before being sconed on the helmet by Colin Croft and forced to retire. Typically, he returned to the middle and was eventually out for 39. Larry Gomes then scored an unbeaten hundred for the visitors to give them a useful lead of 151 in a game they had to win. But in the second innings, Border withstood Michael Holding, Andy Roberts, Joel Garner and Croft to score a ton of his own, which took Australia to relative safety by the end of the fourth day. Marsh (38) was batting with Kim Hughes (84) the next morning and looking comfortable until a probing spell from Holding and Garner took the last six wickets for 24 runs. The West Indies were suddenly back in the match, needing 236 runs in four and a half hours. Marsh caught both Gordon Greenidge and Desmond Haynes off the bowling of Jeff Thomson and when Viv Richards fell for an even 50, the visitors were wobbling. Captain Clive Lloyd, in his last match in Australia, gave a chance off Thomson on just 17, but the keeper shelled it. Lloyd punished the mistake, scoring a rapid 77 not out, to win the match and draw the series.

Chris Scott

Durham wicketkeeper Chris Scott completed 283 first-class catches in his career, but it is a costly drop that gives him regular airtime in sports trivia quizzes. Playing against Warwickshire in 1994, Durham had amassed 556 in the four-day match. With little chance of victory on a flat track, Warwickshire could bat for the next two days if they wished. Capturing the wicket of Brian Lara, at number three, in the form of his life after breaking the Test record against England in Antigua that spring (*see*

Chapter Three **Battered Bowlers**), would have proved vital. Opening bowler Anderson Cummins nearly caught and bowled Lara first ball. Then he did knock Lara's stumps over on just ten: but it was a no ball. Lara was on 18 when he edged through to Scott off the bowling of Simon Brown, offering a routine chance. The ball bounced out of Scott's gloves. 'I suppose he'll get a hundred now,' he commented. Lara actually made 501 not out, the highest knock ever in first-class cricket, scoring nearly 400 of those runs in one day. Four of the Durham bowlers carded over 150 runs in the innings. Crestfallen, Scott let through 28 byes, although whether he received much sympathy is unlikely.

Kiran More

English opener Graham Gooch's astounding performance for England in the first Test of the 1990 series against India at Lord's – in which he scored 333 and 123, recording the highest aggregate run total in a single Test match – should have been nipped in the bud. With 36 to his name in the first innings before lunch, Gooch feathered one through to the keeper Kiran More off the bowling of paceman Sanjeev Sharma. More fumbled it. Gooch was still going at tea the next day, having punished the drop for 297 runs. England eventually declared on 653 for 4, having been asked to bat first. Sharma did eventually get Gooch, but only in the second innings, once he had made 456 runs in the match. India lost by a margin of 247 runs. Sharma was the last man to fall, run out by Gooch. He did not play another Test for India.

Saeed Anwar

For sheer volume of runs, Pakistani fielder Saeed Anwar's two drops off Mark Taylor in the second match in Peshawar in 1998 were the most costly in Tests. A one-handed half chance in the covers on 18 and then a 'sitter' at bat-pad on 25, both off the bowling of Mushtaq Ahmed, allowed the opener to add another 316 or 309, depending how generous you are feeling. Taylor was still at the crease at the end of the second day. Mushtaq ended the innings having conceded 153 runs from 46 overs, without a single scalp. It could have been worse for Anwar too, as Taylor opted not to bat on, declaring with his score on 334. His fellow players urged him to break Sir Donald Bradman's Australian record (also 334) and then have a dig at Lara's 375, the highest Test score at the time. But captain Taylor, putting the state of the match before his personal goals, invited Pakistan to bat instead. Anwar obliged, scoring a hundred to help earn a draw, although his run ledger for the match was still deep in the red.

Graham Thorpe

Gloucestershire's left-arm swing bowler Mike Smith earned his England call-up to face

Australia at Headingley in 1997 after several consistent seasons, troubling the best batsmen on the circuit. With the series poised at 1-1, Smith had an opportunity to make a name for himself. Although Aussie paceman Jason Gillespie had ripped through England for 172 runs in the first innings, the visitors struggled in their reply, losing four quick wickets. Only opener Matthew Elliott showed resistance to the new ball. Smith came on first change and found the edge of Elliott's bat. The ball looped towards Graham Thorpe at second slip, but did not stick. Elliott eventually fell one run short of his double hundred, having shared a 261-run partnership with Ricky Ponting; Australia declared on 501 and wrapped up the match with an innings to spare. England would lose the series 3-2. Would Thorpe's drop have made a difference to the final destination of the urn? Possibly not, given Australia's overall ascendancy throughout the series. But it could have made a difference to Smith, who finished the match wicketless and was dropped himself, never to play Test cricket again.

Nathan Astle

The talk at the end of day two of the second Test between New Zealand and Pakistan at Christchurch in 2001 revolved around two occurrences – one good and one bad for the home side. On the plus side, Matthew Sinclair had carried his bat from number three to post a composed double hundred in a first innings total of 476. However, having seen both visiting openers removed in quick succession, Nathan Astle spilled a routine chance at second slip, offered by groin-strained Pakistani captain Inzamam-ul-Haq. Usually utterly dependable, Astle himself looked shocked to find he had dropped it. Would it hurt them the next morning? You bet it did. What should have been 42 for 3 became 157 for 3, as Inzi put on a hundred with Faisal Iqbal. He then added another century with Yousuf Youhana, before limping off after tea, finally dismissed for 130. Any hope of winning the match still lay on the grass at second slip. Yousuf kicked on to a double hundred, helped by a maiden ton from tailender Saqlain Mushtaq.

Lou Vincent

The following year, the two nations locked horns again, but this time in Pakistan. The Kiwis knew that they had to grasp even the smallest of chances from Inzi or there would be a long wait for the next one. Bowling first on a flat deck in temperatures that touched 38 degrees Celsius, the day had started well for New Zealand, as Pakistan's number two batsman, Shahid Afridi, was removed for a golden duck in the opening over. Another fine blade, Younis Khan, soon fell to spinner Daniel Vettori, bringing Inzi to the middle. The big man was no fan of quick singles at the best of times, but in that heat, he was even more content to occupy the crease and hit the bad balls for four when they arrived. However, he did offer one tiny chance, with his score on 40. It was not an easy one, slashed into the covers off the

Dolly drop

bowling of Vettori. But it went to Lou Vincent, New Zealand's sharpest fielder and the man most likely to cling on. The ball did not stick though and Inzi made the most of it, eventually falling for 329, more than half of his side's 643 all out. Having reached his hundred, the powerful batsman found a second wind, launching a series of towering sixes, each one a kick in Vincent's guts. Vettori did not get another wicket in the innings, as his 40 overs were punished for 178 runs. The Rawalpindi Express, Shoaib Akhtar, then blew away the exhausted Kiwis for just 73 and the match was eventually won with a deficit of an innings and 324 runs. Inzi could have beaten them on his own!

Shane Warne

The England cricketers may not agree, given the number of times that the blond-haired Victorian leg-spinner has enjoyed winning the Ashes, but there ought to have been space made on that open-top London bus for Shane Warne after the 2005 series. Without his stellar contribution with both bat and ball – 40 wickets and 249 runs – the series would have been much less memorable. England could never relax in the series while Warne was still involved, keeping the spectators and viewers on the edge of their seats for two months. It was cruel, therefore, that it should be Warne who spilled the catch which could have retained the Ashes and continued the sixteen years of Australian dominance. Trailing 2-1 in the series, Warne and Co needed to win at The Oval to break English hearts. The situation to strike presented itself on the fifth day, as Glenn McGrath picked up Michael Vaughan and then Ian Bell for a first ball duck, caught in the slips by Warne. Australia were only 80 runs behind, with plenty of time to force a result. McGrath's hat-trick ball to Kevin Pietersen struck the skunk-haired batsman's shoulder and flew to third slip, eliciting a superb 'not out' decision from Billy Bowden. Warne then found the edge of KP's bat on zero, but the chance was spurned by Adam Gilchrist and first slip Matthew Hayden. Then, with Pietersen having made just 15 runs, Brett Lee found another edge that travelled surprisingly slowly to Warne at first slip. The speed deceived him, although it was a catch he would have taken eight times out of ten. KP then hammered two sixes off Warne's next over. Throughout the years of dominance over England, chances like these had stuck for the Australians or it had been one of their batsmen who had taken the game away from the brink. Instead, Pietersen pressed on, compiling a dazzling 158. Warne took 12 wickets in the match, which petered out into a draw. But for a dropped catch, it could have been him on the balcony with the champagne.

South Africa

Australia's total of 355 in the first innings of the second Test against South Africa at the MCG in 2005-06 was several hundred more than it ought to have been. The first Test had been drawn and Australia were still looking shaky after losing to England that summer. Captain Ricky Ponting needed a hundred to boost public opinion and the opportunity seemed to have been wasted when he chipped a catch to Andre Nel on just 17. The quirky fast bowler dropped it. Ponting went on to make 117. But South Africa were still pressing. Nel eventually snared Ponting, Andrew Symonds fell next ball and Adam Gilchrist was undone soon afterwards. Mike Hussey then cut Nel towards the normally safe hands of Jacques Kallis at point, who shelled the catch. Hussey proceeded to score 122, most of those smashed in a brilliant exhibition of tail shepherding, as he added 107 with last man Glenn McGrath, who contributed just eleven. South Africa fell 184 runs short in the fourth innings, less than their net losses from the drops. More importantly, Australia had been allowed to regain their confidence, which made them dangerous to handle... (*see* Chapter Thirteen **One-sided Affairs**). Ponting hit twin hundreds in the third Test in Sydney to seal the series.

Russell Arnold

Dropping an easy catch, no matter the level of cricket you play, is a gut-wrenching experience. Not only do you have the personal pain (both mental and physical) of the ball bouncing off your hands, but then you have to square it with the bowler who has just been robbed of his moment of satisfaction. Some bowlers smile and give encouragement. Others are less charitable, reminding you about it for the rest of the season. For accomplished fielders, the desolation of dropping a catch can be much more harrowing than losing their own wicket, as it is a matter entirely within their own control. Sri Lankan batsman Russell Arnold was one of his side's best catchers, often in close under a helmet for bat-pad chances. He certainly caught many more than he dropped, but one opportunity he failed to grasp would cost the bowler a famous milestone. Muttiah Muralitharan, the highest wicket-taker in Tests, had taken nine wickets at his home town of Kandy on the first day of the second Test against Zimbabwe in 2002. With one wicket needed to equal Jim Laker's full house against Australia in 1956 and Anil Kumble's ten-for against Pakistan in 1999, half the town had turned out to see the momentous occasion. Every fielder was crowded round the bat of Travis Friend, as Murali bowled the first delivery of the day. Friend played forward and the ball caught the edge, thudded into the pads and then looped towards Arnold. A cry of anguish rose as he fumbled the ball and then sprawled on the grass next to it. No matter, Murali would get another chance soon. Until, that is, number eleven Henry Olonga had a mad swipe at the other end at Chaminda Vaas, who was doing his best not to get a wicket, and the ball lodged in Kumar Sangakkara's gloves before he had the presence of mind to drop it. The appeal was stifled, but the ball had feathered off the bat. Vaas had the wicket and Murali was denied the best innings figures in Test history.

Ashley Giles

In the Ashes Test series of 2006-07 in Australia, the English think-tank was lambasted for picking an out-of-form Ashley Giles as their spinner, rather than the exciting young Sikh bowler Monty Panesar. Loyalty can be a virtue, especially as Giles had played such an important all-round role in the 2005 victory, but it can also be blinding. The Warwickshire man had effectively been chosen for his superior batting and fielding, as the Aussies would have far rather faced him on a fourth day pitch than the enigmatic Panesar. When you tempt fate, it often jumps up and bites you on the backside. In the second Test at Adelaide, England were enjoying the upper

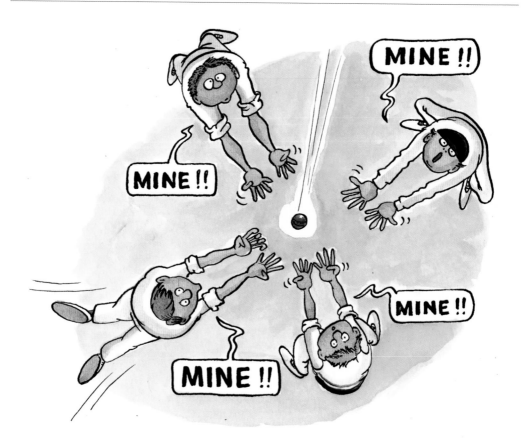

hand for one of the rare occasions in the series. The visitors had declared on a creditable 551, with Giles making an unbeaten 27. In reply, the tired Aussies had reached just 78 for 3, when the dangerous Ricky Ponting, fresh from a big hundred in the first Test, pulled a ball from Matthew Hoggard to deep square leg. He hit the ball hard and flat, but Giles should have caught it. Ponting, who had been on 35, was not out until the score was 257 for 3, having stroked 142. The wheeling spinner only managed one wicket for 103, as Australia racked up 513, before forcing an unlikely victory. Giles made a duck in the second innings collapse (*see* Chapter Twelve **Expensive Run Outs**) and did not play another Test for England.

Khaled Mashud

In its formative years as a Test nation, Bangladesh has struggled to find consistent performers, but wicketkeeper Khaled Mashud was one of the more reliable. Determined as a batsman and efficient with the gloves, he provided some ballast to a rudderless ship during the first half of the last decade. But being a benchmark in the team does have its drawbacks: when you mess up, heads start to drop.

On the third day of the second Test against the mighty Australians at Chittagong in 2006, Bangladesh were already staring down the barrel. A first innings total of 197 all out was never going to be enough to threaten Ricky Ponting and his men. Bangladesh had come close to achieving the impossible in the feisty first Test and the Aussie top order were looking to put the young upstarts back in their place. However, the lesson did not come from any of the household names. Sent in as nightwatchman, in what proved to be his swansong, Jason Gillespie was not going to give his wicket away. In a rain interrupted day, he put his head down, even running out his captain in his determination to survive. But a chance was eventually offered, an invitation to the wicketkeeper, Mashud. But he declined it. The ball fell on the ground, the batsman dropped on 44. By stumps, Gillespie had become just the fifth nightwatchman to score a ton in Tests. Worse was to follow, as Gillespie then sped to an outrageous Test double hundred, 201 not out, sharing a partnership of 320 with Mike Hussey (182). In his Test career, Gillespie made a little over 1,200 runs and one-sixth of them came in that innings in Chittagong, lifting his average from 15 to 19. And then he was dropped from the side.

Tinashe Panyangara

The depleted Zimbabwean team needed to grasp every available opening of the second Test at Bulawayo in 2004, if they were to give Sri Lanka a contest. Having been dismissed for a creditable 228 in the first innings, the young side made an encouraging enough start, snaring Sanath Jayasuriya for 'only' 48 runs. He was replaced at the crease by Kumar Sangakkara, who has since made a habit of compiling regular hundreds, most of them sizeable. But in 2004, he was enduring a comparatively lean spell, having failed to pass three figures for 17 Tests. Medium pacer Mluleki Nkala, who had dismissed Jayasuriya, drew a false drive from the new man just three balls later. The ball flew low to Tinashe Panyangara at mid-off who leaned forward to pouch the ball with both hands. Sangakkara's heart sank – a duck on a flat pitch against a modest attack. But as Panyangara tumbled forward, his elbows bounced on the turf, dislodging the ball from his grasp. If his plan was to safeguard Sangakkara's wicket for himself, then it worked, as he later dismissed the left-hander, but only after he had scored 270, including a stand of 438 runs for the second wicket with Marvan Atapattu (249). Poor old Nkala did not take another wicket in the innings and was out for a duck as the match inevitably ended in a crushing defeat.

Mohammad Aamer

Dropping one of the finest batsmen ever to don the baggy green for Australia at his home ground on a flat wicket on the first morning of a Test match is not advisable. Especially if you are going to have to bowl at him for the rest of the day. Having butchered a gilt-edged opportunity to beat the Australians in the second Test at Sydney in 2010, Pakistan ought to have been 1-1 entering the final deciding Test at Hobart. As it happened, Australia had a 2-0 lead (*see* Chapter Seven **From the Jaws of Victory**), but Pakistan could still be confident of winning the last Test. After opener Simon Katich had returned to the hutch at 28 for 1, the Hobart crowd welcomed their favourite son, Ricky Ponting, to the crease, with no less than 38 Test hundreds to his name. Like all batsmen, Ponting can be vulnerable early on, albeit that those straws are rarely clutched. Mohammad Asif bowled the first over to the newcomer, pitching three up outside the off stump, before banging a straight one in short. An expert puller and hooker, Ponting backed himself to hit the ball in front of square, but it hurried on to him, top-edging straight to the waiting fielder at square leg. It was a brilliant piece of bowling to a dangerous batsman. All that was missing was the catch. Seventeen-year-old Mohammad Aamer, a huge talent for the future, buckled under the pressure and the moment had gone. Ponting did not give another chance until he had scored 209 after lunch on the second day, having added 352 for the fourth wicket with Michael Clarke (166). Pakistan eventually lost at a canter.

Chapter Five
Captaincy Woes

More than in most other sports, the captain is the central figure throughout a cricket match, capable of inspiring victory from his men with a strategic masterstroke. Of course, he can also condemn his side to defeat with a string of sorry decisions. There is no hiding place for the skipper, as a team's failure will forever be associated with his name.

Monty Bowden

In February 2010, at the age of 25, Alastair Cook became England's youngest Test captain for several decades, but he was long in the tooth compared with Monty Bowden, who skippered his country in the second match of an unofficial tour of South Africa in 1888-89, later granted Test status. For the 23-year-old Surrey batsman, the trip was an opportunity for adventure, although the two-match series started poorly for him, as he was run out for a duck on debut. In the second match, he

A good toss to lose

took over the captaincy from his friend Aubrey Smith, making 25 in his only knock before standing back to watch Johnny Briggs take 15 for 28, most of them bowled (*see* Chapter Eight **Team Collapses**). As the tourists returned triumphant, Bowden and Smith opted to stay behind in the hope of making their fortune through gold, diamonds and the stock market. Bowden scored a hundred in the Transvaal's first Currie Cup match, before travelling north to Rhodesia. At the age of just 26, he died from a fever in a mud-hut hospital. That night, his body had to be guarded against hungry lions until it was buried in a makeshift coffin constructed of whisky cases. Smith was also pronounced dead from pneumonia a few years later, but he was able to read his own obituary in the local newspaper, having staged a remarkable recovery. He went on to become a household-name film star, playing the quintessential English gentleman in forty films. Eventually he did die of pneumonia, but not until he had reached the ripe old age of 85.

Arthur Carr

Nottinghamshire's Arthur Carr was definitely old school, even for the 1920s and 1930s. Emotion was for the weak, said he. Ruthless endeavour was a sign of strength. As a captain, he demanded respect from his charges and he was prepared to earn it, standing closest to the bat and putting his body on the line against the fastest bowlers of the age. Indeed, he was instrumental in developing the controversial bodyline theory with Douglas Jardine for the 1932-33 Ashes series, giving his Notts quicks, Harold Larwood and Bill Voce, every opportunity to practise it during the preceding English county season. He staunchly defended them on their return.

Carr played for his country on eleven occasions, although his average of 19.75 does him little credit. As captain of the team that faced the Australians in 1926, the third Test at Headingley began with the series still in the balance after two draws. Carr won the toss and chose to field first on a soaking pitch, which he hoped would become tacky in the hot sun and prove unplayable. The first ball from his premier quick Maurice Tate carried to Herbert Sutcliffe at second slip, removing opposite skipper Warren Bardsley for a diamond. So far so good. Charles Macartney, who had scored an unbeaten hundred in the second Test, replaced his skipper and got off the mark with a two. But the fifth ball of that over again caught the edge of the bat and flew to Carr at first slip. He put it down. Did he show remorse? Not he. But he must have felt a mild twinge of regret as Macartney (151) played one of his greatest hands, hammering a hundred before lunch and dominating a partnership of 235 runs with Bill Woodfull (141). What could have been 2 for 2 in the first over became 366 for 3 at stumps. England held on for the draw, drew the fourth too and eventually regained the Ashes in the fifth Test, a match that Carr missed as he had tonsillitis. In the four matches he played in that series, Carr batted only once, making just 13 runs.

Freddie Calthorpe

The English captain Freddie Calthorpe had a long transatlantic return voyage during which to contemplate his flawed decision not to invite the West Indies to follow on in Jamaica in early 1930. The fourth Test was agreed to be timeless in order to split the teams, who were tying at one win apiece. England took control, amassing 849 runs in three days, on the back of 325 scored by Andy Sandham. The hosts could make only 286 in reply, but Calthorpe decided to bat again, to give his older players a chance to recuperate. Eventually, the Windies were set a meaningless target of 836 runs. Unfortunately for Calthorpe, George Headley scored a defiant double hundred and the last two days were washed out through rain. The touring party were forced to catch their ship home, with the series still tied.

Maharajah of Vizianagram

Lieutenant Colonel Sir Gajapatairaj Vijaya Ananda, the Maharajkumar of Vizianagram – (latterly known as Vizzy) – was an immensely wealthy man who channelled huge amounts of his fortune into developing the game of cricket in India in the 1930s. He organised tours that attracted some of the biggest names in world cricket to the subcontinent, as popular then as visits by Manchester United or Cristiano Ronaldo to the Far East are nowadays. As with many over-enthusiastic benefactors, Vizzy wanted value for his money and he also fancied himself as a bit of a cricketer. Like the emperor in his new clothes, nobody wanted to tell Vizzy that he was as bad as his first-class average of 18 suggested. He did score the odd fifty, but the bowlers tended to know there would be something in it for them if they served up a series of half-trackers with nobody at cow corner. In 1932, a disgruntled Vizzy was forced to pull out of a tour he had helped finance due to poor health.

The tour had been a success, mainly because the captain, the Maharajah of Porbandar, who was equally rich and useless at cricket, had prudently stayed on the sidelines. No such discretion for Vizzy in 1936, who believed he was the man to inspire India to a famous win against England. He bought the captaincy and control of the squad. Arrogance can be useful as a skipper if you are a brilliant player – but when you bat at number nine, score 33 runs in six innings, can't field and don't bowl, then you need to be an unbelievable strategist! Vizzy compounded his error by sending home the team's best player, Lala Amarnath, on a petty point of ill-discipline. The three-match series was lost 2-0, although the margins of defeat would have been much wider without the batting of Vijay Merchant. Had Vizzy possessed the foresight to let Amarnath play instead of him, then he might have been remembered as a fine leader instead of a pig-headed toff. Yet Vizzy remains the only cricketer to have been knighted whilst *still* playing for his country. Who says money can't buy you love!

Sir Leonard Hutton

Nasser Hussain's decision to insert Australia on the first day of the 'Gabba Test in 2002 certainly backfired. But it was not the first time that such an error had been made. No less a luminary than Len Hutton did exactly the same in the opening match of the 1954-55 Ashes series, again in Brisbane. Hutton could rightly point to his stable of four thoroughbred fast bowlers and the fact that these attacking tactics had worked in the tour matches. Also, his fielders shelled no fewer than twelve catches, which could have vindicated his decision. But the buck always stops with the captain and the Aussies batted on until the middle of the third day, before declaring for 601. Australian opener Arthur Morris made 153, adding 200 runs with Neil Harvey (162). All four of the English quick bowlers each conceded more than 120 runs. Hutton eventually had his opportunity to atone, but his innings lasted just four minutes before he was caught behind. He made just 13 runs in the second knock, as England lost by an innings. Happily for Hutton, his side won the next three Tests and returned home with the Ashes. Having eased past New Zealand on the way home, the great man took off his England sweater for the last time.

Dudley Nourse

Too much time to ponder can often cloud the mind, leading to over-complication of a simple matter. For Dudley Nourse, skipper of South Africa in the third Test at Kingsmead against Australia in January 1950, the decision ought to have been straightforward. Having knocked up 311 in the first innings and then run through the tourists for only 75 runs – Morris, Hassett, Miller, Harvey et al – enforcing the follow-on was the obvious choice. His off-spinner Hugh Tayfield had caused havoc, nipping out 7 for only 23 runs. Had the last wicket fallen in the middle of a day, then Nourse might well have invited the Aussies to have another go immediately. But the innings was wound up at the end of the second day. Throughout the rest day, Nourse deliberated on the weather, the pitch and the time remaining (two more days) and convinced himself to bat instead. Quick runs on the third day, he concluded, would put the total out of reach of the Aussies, allowing Tayfield a free licence on a worn pitch. South Africa had never won a match on home soil against Australia, so perhaps Nourse was fearful of his batsmen buckling under the pressure of a fourth innings chase. His decision was quickly proved flawed, as his batsmen did indeed collapse, all out for 99. No matter – 336 runs was still a mighty ask. At 59 for 3, Nourse knew that the wickets of Arthur Morris and Neil Harvey would have all but guaranteed victory. Tayfield caused Morris to hit his wickets on 44, but Harvey played an innings of great maturity despite his 21 years, scoring an unbeaten 151 in nearly six hours. Australia eased home by five wickets, leaving Nourse to rue his decision. The visitors won the series 4-0, Harvey scoring four hundreds at an average of 132.

Sir Garfield Sobers

If a skipper takes a cavalier gamble to try to force a result, then he has to be prepared to cop any criticism that follows if his ship capsizes. There are few Test captains who would have risked a match, let alone a series, on a fifty-fifty call, like the one that tempted Garry Sobers in the fourth Test in Port-of-Spain against England in the 1967-68 series. The first three Tests of the five to be played had ended in a draw, so any attempt to break the deadlock ought to have been welcomed. Having biffed 526 runs in the first innings and dismissed England for 404 just before stumps on the fourth day, it was unthinkable that the West Indies would lose. But Sobers always played to win. He had confidence in himself and his bowlers to force the issue, especially after his part-time spinner, Basil Butcher, had taken five wickets in the first innings. Having added just 92 runs, Sobers declared, setting the England batsmen an enticing target of 215 from a possible 50 eight-ball overs. A good declaration will leave enough of a carrot for the batsmen to take some risks of their own, so giving your bowlers a chance. But this was still a good pitch and the England top order was in fine form. Openers John Edrich and Geoffrey Boycott were not renowned for pushing the scoring-rate, but they did not need to – there was plenty of time. Colin Cowdrey had already scored a hundred in the match and he was able to play freely en route to a fluent 71. Boycott, who enjoyed a stellar tour, timed his unbeaten 80 to perfection, knocking off the winning runs with just an over remaining. The West Indies duly lost the series and Sobers was largely culpable. But when you play cricket with that sort of panache and adventure, you shouldn't be too heavily criticised when it goes wrong occasionally: should you?

Mike Denness

Too often in sport, honour can be interpreted as weakness. For every batsman who walks when he nicks it, there are ten who think he's a bloody idiot. Scotsman Mike Denness was perhaps too gracious to be an effective leader, especially on an Ashes tour down under in 1974-75, where the opposition could unleash the fury of Dennis Lillee and Jeff Thomson. Like the other batsmen in the trenches with him, Denness's cultured technique struggled to cope with the incessant barrage of the fearsome twosome and he hardly made an impression in the first three matches, scoring a total of 65 runs. England were soon on the ropes, two down with three to play. Denness calculated that he was the least likely of the top order batsmen to turn the side's fortunes around. He would make way. Was this a noble gesture or an admission of defeat? Inspiring or deflating? In pure results, it proved to be the latter, as Australia reeled off a 171-run victory. One wag is supposed to have written a letter, addressed simply: 'Mike Denness, Cricketer'. 'If this letter reaches you,' it said inside, 'the Post Office thinks more of you than I do'. For the last two Tests, Denness returned to the front line, and he promptly hammered 188 runs in the final match, England's only win in the rubber. By this time, though, both Lillee and Thomson had withdrawn due to injuries.

Mike Denness (2)

The following year, the Aussies returned the compliment, staying in England after the 1975 Prudential World Cup to play a series of four matches. Denness had taken England to the semi-final of the inaugural Cup, where they were defeated inevitably by Australia, and had retained the captaincy, despite some opposition – notably from Geoffrey Boycott, who had retreated into exile, having been overlooked. Had Boycs's broad bat been available to Denness, he might well have chosen to bat first when he won the toss at Edgbaston in the first Test. Rain was forecast on days two and three, so the wicket was likely to play truest on the first day. But Denness chose to bowl. He was not alone in his thinking, as his team was full of wily old pros, who agreed that the ball would zip about under the grey skies. Or was it that they just wanted to postpone the battering from Lillee and Thomson? Or would the game be washed out before they had to face them at all? As a strategy, it failed utterly. Australia timed their innings to perfection, losing their last batsman with the score at 359 runs, just before a thunderstorm soaked the wicket. Lillee, Thomson and Max Walker did the rest, cleaning England up twice to win by an innings and 85 runs. Denness was out for single figure scores in both attempts and then fell on his sword. Again.

Bishan Singh Bedi

The intelligent left-arm spinner Bishan Singh Bedi was a wonderful servant of Indian cricket, contributing many of the nation's best moments during its developing years in the late 1960s and throughout the 1970s. As a captain, Bedi knew his own mind and he had the strength of will to stick by his decisions. This can be an admirable trait, but also a hindrance if a more pragmatic method is needed. The third Test against Pakistan, played in November 1978 in Karachi, towards the end of Bedi's career, was one such case in point. India were already one down in the series and needed to win the last match to tie the rubber. However, despite two masterful hundreds from the bat of Sunil Gavaskar, the other Indian batsmen could not propel their team into a winning position. Indeed, they seemed destined to lose comfortably until Gavaskar, Karsan Ghavri and Kapil Dev counter-attacked on the afternoon of the fifth day to set the home side a target of 164 runs from 25 overs. Realistically, his attack was never going to bowl Pakistan out, so saving the match had to be Bedi's objective. With the right fields and a bit of time wasting, this should have proved an easy enough task. But Bedi decided to set his fielders deep, inviting the batsmen to hole out. Instead, Asif Iqbal and Javed Miandad ran them ragged, haring between the wickets, scoring ones and twos at will. Ninety-seven runs came from just nine overs, with only a handful of boundaries scored. Asif fell, but the momentum was continued by Imran Khan. Still Bedi stuck to his strategy, waiting for the Pakistani batsmen to make a mistake and be caught. Instead of slowing the run-scoring down with his quick bowlers, Bedi bowled himself in order to try to buy a wicket. Imran duly smacked him for two sixes and a four in the same over, before reaching the target with just seven balls to spare. Bedi's four overs cost 33 runs and Gavaskar was appointed skipper for the next series.

Mark Taylor

The skilful left-hander Mark Taylor was already a proven performer for Australia by the time he inherited the captaincy from Allan Border for the first Test against Pakistan in Karachi in 1994. But his team had not recorded a win in Pakistan for 35 years. Against the attack of Wasim Akram, Waqar Younis and Mushtaq Ahmed, victory would be merited. Taylor had potent weapons of his own, including Glenn McGrath and spin twins Shane Warne and Tim May. The new skipper did the right thing when he won the toss, electing to bat first on a pitch that would wear down by the fourth innings. Taylor suffered only five ducks in his 186 innings for his country, but unfortunately two of them arrived in Karachi, when he needed them least. Wasim Akram took a return catch in the first innings, before Waqar Younis had him caught behind in the second. There was no shame in being dismissed by those two, but he became the first captain in Tests to record a pair in his first match in charge. Ultimately, Pakistan scraped home by a single wicket, thanks to a nerveless innings by youngster Inzamam-ul-Haq, in what umpire Dickie Bird called the most exciting match he had ever stood in. Critics queried Taylor's decision to take a new ball in the second innings when Warne was turning the old one, allowing the Pakistani batsmen to release the pressure with a flurry of boundaries. Dependable keeper Ian Healy also missed a crucial stumping. Taylor would have to wait until 1998 to exact his revenge.

Tony Greig

Tony Greig, a South African-born Scot who captained England, was never afraid of courting controversy in his playing career and was forever on the look-out for an opportunity to gain the mental edge over his opponents. There is little wrong with verbal jousting, just so long as you can back it up on the field of play. Before the West Indies arrived in England for the five-match Wisden Trophy in the blazing sunshine of 1976, Greig decided to put the boot in. 'I'm not really sure they're as good as everyone thinks,' he announced on the BBC's Sportsnight programme. 'These guys, if they get on top they are magnificent cricketers. But if they're down, they grovel, and I intend, with the help of Closey [Brian Close] and a few others, to make them grovel.' The first two Tests were drawn, although it was clear that Gordon

Greenidge, Viv Richards and the quartet of fast bowlers had the upper hand. England were then bowled out for 71 and 126 at Old Trafford (Close's last Test) and then shot down at Headingley (despite 116 and 76 not out from Greig). The series had been lost, with not a genuflection in sight. In the final Test at The Oval in South London, thousands of British West Indians turned out to jeer Greig. Richards taunted the England bowlers with a fabulous 291, before Michael Holding bowled like the wind to take 14 wickets on a flat track, twice sending Greig's stumps cartwheeling. The England captain duly sank to his knees in front of the crowd and grovelled in penance for his comments.

England

The English summer of 1988 had started well for the hosts, beating the West Indian tourists 3-0 in the ODI series. Captain Mike Gatting had been a rock with the bat, seemingly putting the trauma of the Pakistani tour and his run-in with umpire Shakoor Rana behind him (*see* Chapter Nine **Umpiring Howlers**). But, following a draw in the first Test at Trent Bridge, a tabloid scandal involving a barmaid and a hotel room gave the board an excuse to strip Gatting of the captaincy. John Emburey took over as skipper of a team that was struggling to cope with the brilliance of Malcolm Marshall. Had a vital catch not been dropped by Derek Pringle when the West Indies were struggling on the first morning of the second Test at Lord's, England could have pushed hard for victory, but the beneficiary, Gus Logie, hit fine half-centuries to set up the win. The third Test at Old Trafford was one-way traffic for the tourists, as England were skittled for 93 in the second innings. Emburey had a match to forget and was dropped for the next encounter. By this stage, the selectors were acting like French revolutionaries, axing and promoting players on a whim. The most surprising name out of the hat was the all-rounder Chris Cowdrey, son of Colin, who had played five Tests before, albeit without notable élan. He was the popular captain of a successful Kent side, so the decision was not entirely flawed, given that England craved leadership. But as godson of chief selector Peter May, he needed to do especially well to avoid accusations of favouritism. A duck and five runs at Headingley, with no wickets, was not a good start, as the West Indies cruised to the series win. Cowdrey's luck worsened when he injured himself in a county match, leaving the door open for the fourth captain of a dismal series. Graham Gooch was passed the poisoned chalice. His 84 in the second innings could not avoid an eight-wicket reverse at The Oval. England had lost 4-0 in its summer of four captains. Cowdrey never played for his country again, although he has since proved an insightful cricket commentator.

Nasser Hussein

An inexperienced England outfit was not offered much of a prayer at the start of the

2002-03 Ashes series down under, given that Steve Waugh's Australian side was nearing the peak of its powers. Visiting skipper Nasser Hussain gave several young players their first taste of the grudge match, hopeful that youthful exuberance and a lack of mental scarring would allow them to compete against a pack of grizzled performers who were used to having it all their own way. The 'Gabba in Brisbane was the customary curtain-raiser and the curator had prepared a fine batting track. If Hussain could only win the toss, said the pundits, then his young tyros could get their riposte in first with a solid total. Win it he did, but the pundits' faces dropped as Hussain asked to field. He was confident his bowlers would extract some move-ment early on. He later confessed that he had seen a look of self-doubt in the eyes of his top order that could have resulted in a collapse. As it was, the match was all but lost by the end of the first day, as Matthew Hayden and Ricky Ponting scored hundreds. Several catches were spilled and Simon Jones, Hussain's most promising bowler, was hospitalised with a ruptured anterior knee ligament (*see* Chapter Eleven **Insult to Injury**). The collapse came in the fourth innings, as England were bundled out for 79 runs in under 30 overs to lose by 384 runs.

Nasser Hussain (2)

Captain Fanatic will often be found with his head out of the pavilion skylight, staring into the distance for signs of precipitation or gathering cloud. He'll check his favourite weather websites every few hours in the week before a match for a consistent forecast or create a hotline to the national Meteorological Office. Nothing is left to chance. A more relaxed skipper will make a judgement call on his way to the wicket and probably bat anyway if he wins the toss. Nasser Hussain, England's determined leader in the late 1990s and early 2000s, developed a nose for predicting the weather, a talent which has been honed still further in his commentary for Sky Sports since his retirement. But a little bit of knowledge can be a dangerous thing. In 1999, Hussain decided to bat first in the second Test against New Zealand at Lord's, despite the ground being shrouded in heavy cloud. His sources assured him that the gloom would quickly burn off in the hot sunshine, allowing his batsmen to gorge themselves on de-clawed seamers. But things didn't work out as planned. Play was finally suspended for bad light after tea, by which time England had collapsed from 102 for 2 to 183 for 9. Number three batsman Hussain was still at the crease, but nobody else had mastered the swinging ball. His sunshine arrived the following day, inspiring the tourists to forge an emphatic lead and surge to their first victory at HQ in 13 attempts. Hussain then broke a finger and spent the rest of the match on the pavilion balcony.

Nasser Hussain (3)

Nasser Hussain's tenure as England captain had revitalised a nation which had been in the cricketing doldrums throughout most of the 1990s, but it took its toll on the man himself, especially the rigours of the 2003 World Cup in South Africa (*see* Chapter Seven **From the Jaws of Victory**). The Essex man had bared his emotions during the final of the Natwest Series against India in 2002, celebrating his only ODI hundred by pointing to the number 3 on his back and gesturing with two fingers at members of the press, who had queried his ability to bat so high up the order.

Michael Vaughan (another who never quite reached his potential in one-dayers) had already taken over as ODI captain by the time the Test series against South Africa started in the summer of 2003. Hussain needed a bright performance to reassert his credentials and he was expected to have a psychological edge over 22-year-old Graeme Smith, who had surprisingly been given the South African armband following Shaun Pollock's horror show at the World Cup (*see* Chapter Fifteen **Nearly Men**). Smith was struggling to hold down a place on merit, so Hussain attempted to undermine his confidence, apparently referring to him as 'what's-his-name' in a press conference. During the toss before the first Test at Edgbaston, the visiting captain was introduced as 'Greg Smith' by Hussain to the match referee, either through genuine absent-mindedness or possibly malicious intent. 'Greg' called correctly, chose to bat and was still batting at the end of the day. The England bowlers had sprayed the ball throughout, beckoning openers Smith and Herschelle Gibbs (179) to score a quickfire 338 partnership. Jimmy Anderson, in his third Test for England, was taken for a run a ball. Smith was eventually out for 277, adding 85 in the second innings to post a record aggregate for a South African in Tests. Vaughan had scored a hundred of his own in the draw. The strain on Hussain proved too much and he tearfully resigned the captaincy. His nightmare was not quite over, however, as he dropped a dolly from Smith in the next Test at Lord's, allowing the South African to hammer another big double hundred in the victory. Hussain resisted any urges to retire completely and scored a cathartic hundred in the Trent Bridge third Test, as England fought back to square the series. (He did not retire from all forms of cricket until May 2004, after scoring 103 not out in his final Test, against New Zealand at Lord's.)

Ashwell Prince

It was a proud moment for all involved in South African cricket when batsman Ashwell Prince was awarded the captaincy, becoming the first black player to lead the team in Tests. Regular skipper Graeme Smith was injured and Prince was charged with keeping the ship afloat in Sri Lanka in the two-match series of 2006. The Colombo pitch seemed flat as a road, so he had no hesitation in batting first, yet his team succumbed after scoring just 169 in 50 overs. The Sri Lankan openers perished quickly too, giving hope that the match would be a low-scoring tussle. Those hopes were quickly banished, as opposing captain Mahela Jayawardene and his trusted lieutenant, Kumar Sangakkara, set about forging the highest partnership score in

I won the toss, lads, and we're fielding

Test match history, batting together from tea on the first day until lunch on the third. Sangakkara was eventually out for 287 runs, a full 624 runs since the last wicket. Jayawardene did not stop until he had made 374 runs, the fourth highest individual score ever. For the neutral observer, it must have been a joy to watch these two consummate craftsmen in tandem for five sessions; but for Prince it was a lesson in helplessness. His spinner, Nicky Boje, bore the brunt, ending with match figures of 0 for 221 off 65 overs. To make matters worse for Boje, his counterpart Muttiah Muralitharan took ten wickets in the match to seal an emphatic win.

Ricky Ponting

England needed a miracle if they were to turn round the 2005 Ashes series after Australia had notched up the usual win at Lord's. Michael Vaughan's men had looked capable of giving the visitors a closer fight than in recent series, but the ease with which Glenn McGrath ran through them at Lord's in the second innings re-released that sinking feeling that had grown in English bellies since 1989. So when the metronomic fast bowler freakishly stepped on a cricket ball during a game of warm-up rugby on the morning of the Edgbaston Test, spraining an ankle that would sideline him for the match, the mood in the English dressing-room lifted. Michael Kasprowicz was competent, but he was no Glenn McGrath. More good news was to come: though Vaughan lost the toss, he learned that he would be batting first. Ricky Ponting, ignoring the advice of Shane Warne, was determined to stick to his original decision to field, even though Achilles had his heel in an ice bucket. The English batsmen were all out by stumps at the end of the first day, but they had belted 407 runs and convinced themselves that winning the Ashes was a real possibility.

Ricky Ponting (2)

When a captain's bold decision proves successful, it's the bowler who executed the plans who tends to get the credit. When a decision goes tits-up, it's the captain who wears it, no matter how poorly his team has performed. Such was the case in the pivotal match of the Ashes series at The Oval in 2009. With the series tied at 1-1, a draw would have sufficed to take the urn back to Australia. Ponting's four-pronged seam attack, including veteran bowler Stuart Clark instead of spinner Nathan Hauritz, had just dismantled Andrew Strauss's XI at Headingley inside three days. In Leeds, Clark's medium-fast accuracy had earned him figures of 3 for 18 in the first innings. But would it be so effective at The Oval, a pitch that usually offered turn? Ponting and the selectors decided to stick with the winning team. English off-spinner Graeme Swann then took eight wickets in the match, while even Aussie part-timer Marcus North snaffled four, as the surface turned to dust. Clark managed just the one wicket in the match and bagged a first-baller in what may be his last innings for Australia. In Ponting's defence, the toss proved crucial for England, while it was a seamer, Stuart Broad, who was man of the match. But would he have done the same again?

Habibul Bashar

Having secured a creditable draw against India in the first match of the two-Test series at home in 2007, Bangladesh skipper Habibul Bashar did not want to push his luck. Overcast conditions on the first morning in Mirpur for the second Test were potentially favourable for the bowlers, but a confident captain would have backed his own batsmen to cope with them. The Indian openers certainly did, stroking the ball to all parts and enjoying plenty of time on the placid pitch as they scored hundreds. Only the stifling heat and humidity checked their progress, forcing both batsmen off to rehydrate. Indeed, India did not lose a genuine wicket until the score was 408 and over 100 overs had been bowled. Rahul Dravid and Sachin Tendulkar both notched hundreds of their own – the first time ever that the first four batsmen had all scored hundreds in a Test – before India eventually declared at 610 for 3. Whether any of Bangladesh's bowlers were still speaking to their captain at that point is unlikely. Their exhausted batsmen meekly rolled over to lose by an innings and 239 runs, including Javed Omar's unique diamond pair, falling to the first ball of both innings (*see* Chapter One **Famous First Ballers**). Bashar managed just four and five in his two attempts to regain pride. Coach Dav Whatmore later accepted the blame, saying that the decision to bowl was his. Either way, Indian captain Saurav Ganguly must have chuckled all the way back to the dressing-room after losing the toss.

Chris Gayle

The languid West Indies captain Chris Gayle was another to be hoist by his own petard, during the 2009-10 tour of Australia. In the lead-up to the second Test, the Jamaican insinuated that he had never heard of replacement fast bowler Doug Bollinger, and that he was not going to watch any tapes of the left-armer before the match. Needless to say, Bollinger got him out twice in the series, although Gayle hammered two hundreds in the process. His snub came back to haunt him in the ODI series, where he was again expected to carry his side's hopes. Having playfully predicted a 4-1 win to the Windies in the five-match series, the visitors were mauled 4-0, with one match lost to rain. Gayle was dismissed on all four occasions by Bollinger, including a diamond duck in the second match at Adelaide. He averaged only 14 runs, without a single fifty to his name. But he now knew all about Doug Bollinger.

Heath Streak

The captain of a weaker team at village level may volunteer to field first, to ensure that the match at least lasts until afternoon tea. Given the importance of cake to the village cricketer, nobody bats an eyelid. At Test level, such notions ought to be foolish, although it is not unknown for a captain to choose to field for fear of being humiliated on the first morning. At least if the opposition score a bundle, then you get to bat for the rest of the match, knowing what to expect from the pitch. If a draw is your best hope, then it is not such a weak strategy, as your team will learn more about top-class Test cricket the longer the game lasts. The 2003 Test series between Australia and Zimbabwe, shorn of her better batsmen, was such a mismatch of talent that visiting skipper Heath Streak could have been forgiven for exercising damage limitation tactics from the start. On a flat Perth track in the first Test, he perhaps hoped for initial movement, as the match was being played in the October spring. But once the shine on the ball left, Matthew Hayden pushed back his shoulders, puffed out his chest and bullied the Zimbabweans for the next five sessions. Playing with a bat that must have seemed three feet wide to the bowlers, he bludgeoned 38 fours and 11 sixes to break the world record with a knock of 380 at a shade over a run a ball. Streak went for 131 wicketless runs. Australia declared on 735 for 6, the highest total in Test history by a team inserted, and won the match by an innings.

Andrew Strauss

'A good toss to lose' is a lovely cricket saying that makes no sense to the outsider, but leaves the enthusiast nodding sagely. It is possible that England would have won the decisive fourth Test of the 2009-10 series in South Africa if Andrew Strauss had lost the toss. Home skipper Graeme Smith would have batted too on a Wanderers' pitch that misbehaved more than expected. Smith and not Strauss would have faced the first ball. But Strauss called correctly and that first ball was his last of the innings, brilliantly caught at short leg by Hashim Amla. England, too often reliant on Strauss for runs, folded for just 180. Smith, on the other hand, having surveyed the pitch, was able to dig in for an excellent hundred (*see* Chapter Nine **Umpiring Howlers**), inspiring his team to 423 for 7 declared. From there, England had no reply on a wearing pitch and quickly subsided again. In hindsight, the visitors were lucky to have saved two matches, in each of them nine wickets down in the fourth innings. Twice, number eleven Graham Onions had blocked out for a last-gasp draw (*see* Chapter Fifteen **Nearly Men**). Onions had surprisingly been dropped for the final match, but then you don't pick a bowler for his ability to bat out draws. Strauss could have lost the four-match series 3-1, so a 1-1 tie was not a disaster.

Adam Gilchrist

When a captain leaves the pitch for an over or two, you can all but guarantee that the vice-captain will attempt something clever to prove his own credentials. It may be an insightful field placement or bowling change, which will leave the true captain tetchy – especially if it snares a wicket! When Adam Gilchrist took over the captaincy of Australia for the fourth Test at Headingley during the 2001 Ashes series in England, the urn was already secure 3-0. A whitewash seemed likely too, after the visitors racked up 447 before reducing England to 309 all out. Regular skipper Steve Waugh was crook with a calf tear and the attacking-minded Gilchrist opted to dangle a carrot in front of the beleaguered English batsmen. The offer of 315 runs on the final day was big and orange and juicy, especially when more cautious tactics might have secured the win anyway. The day started as expected, with Michael Atherton out to Glenn McGrath, an entry that would feature in *Wisden's* pages 19 times, becoming the most times a batsman had been dismissed by the same bowler in Tests. Marcus Trescothick fell too and a procession looked imminent. But this day would belong to one man: Mark Butcher. Only playing due to others' injuries, Butcher batted like Lara, Pollock and Sobers rolled into one, smashing a good attack on a fifth-day pitch. His unbeaten 173, made in tandem with Nasser Hussain and Mark Ramprakash, lifted the England fans who had been on the receiving end all summer. Waugh returned for the final Test, scoring 157 on one leg. Ricky Ponting was eventually crowned as his successor. Gilchrist, however, had played his part in a classic encounter.

John Dyson

Coaches and managers usually choose to sit back in the shadows, leaving the captain in the glare of the hot sun. But occasionally they do become the story. West Indies coach John Dyson reduced a gripping contest to farce during an ODI series against England in 2009, when he misread the Duckworth-Lewis tables and called his batsmen in. The crowd in Guyana were denied a tense finish, with light fading, as the Australian cast his eye down the wrong column and deduced that his team were ahead of the rate. The England captain, Andrew Strauss, who had his own piece of paper with the projected scores, quickly calculated that his side had in fact won, so he gladly followed the batsmen back to the pavilion. The error came down to an elementary mathematical cock-up: while Strauss had written '0' above the first over, Dyson had pencilled in '1', so he was always an over ahead of himself. The blunder cast a shadow over Dyson's competency as a coach, but it also further scarred the reputation of the sport in the Caribbean, where cricket suffers from increasing competition from soccer, basketball and athletics. The match had been filled with thrusts and parries, especially from local hero Shiv Chanderpaul who hammered Steve Harmison for 26 off an over, with five scything fours through the off side and an audacious paddle-swept six over fine leg. Instead of concentrating on winning the match conventionally – which they probably would have done – the West Indian batsmen became consumed with the light and the D-L totals. Ultimately, the home side got what it deserved. The momentum from its uplifting win in the Test series was lost in a sea of jumbled figures

Chapter Six
Duck Hunters

Having negotiated the first ball safely, the duck is the next pitfall to avoid. Getting off the mark is just one run on the team total, but it can be a meaningful milestone for the individual, especially if he is on debut, on a pair or enduring a pitiful run of poor form. To be out for a duck in any cricket is a gut-wrencher, no matter the extenuating circumstances.

Sir Donald Bradman

The Don hardly deserves to be in a book about cricketing failure, but his final Test serves as the most telling example that nobody, not even the finest batsman ever, is safe from the vagaries of fickle fortune. Bradman's staggering statistics are well enough known. He scored 29 hundreds in 52 Tests at an average of 99.94, including two triple hundreds and twelve double hundreds. The closest 'great', in terms of averages, is Graeme Pollock of South Africa with 60.97.

Bradman's first-class record is perhaps even more indicative of his consistency and will to grind out the runs. In 234 matches, he gathered 117 hundreds at an average of 95.14 runs: one hundred every two matches for over 20 years. On the 1948 Invincibles' tour, which he captained, his performance was beyond compare. Despite the hiatus of the war years and problems with injury, the 39-year-old from Cootamundra recaptured his best form, scoring eleven hundreds in 23 first-class matches, two of those in the Test series. Yet his last Test innings of that tour is his most celebrated. He had suffered a duck in the first Test of the summer at Trent Bridge, but that came chasing a small target after a first innings ton. By the time of the last Test, at The Oval, with the Ashes already in his suitcase, the great man's average stood at 101.39. He needed just four more runs for 7,000 Test runs and a career average of at least 100. England had been dismissed for 52 and he strode to the wicket at 117 for 1, to a standing ovation from the crowd, who knew it was his swansong. England captain Norman Yardley shook his hand and invoked three cheers from his players. The bowler, leg-spinner Eric Hollies, had forced himself into the side after taking eight wickets against the Australians for Warwickshire earlier in the month, including Bradman's. His second ball to the Don, a googly, turned past the inside edge of the bat and continued into the stumps. Again the crowd rose, this time to cheer The Don back to the pavilion.

It is scarcely believable that any other batsman will come close to matching his record. (Incidentally, Eric Hollies, the pantomime villain who denied cricket fans a fairytale ending, was himself out for a golden duck as England lost the match by an innings and 149 runs.)

Sir Garfield Sobers

With his ability to hit the ball cleanly, bowl pace and spin, field in close or on the boundary, Sir Garry Sobers was the best all-round cricketer to play the game. If he had wanted to, he could have stood as wicketkeeper for the West Indies too. There certainly would have been a scrum at the IPL auctions if his services had been put up for sale. But, for all that Sobers would have been a superstar in today's bonanza of ODIs and T20 matches, his international record for limited overs cricket is rock bottom. It was not entirely his fault, as he only played the one ODI, at Headingley against England in 1973. But it was not a golden performance. Batting first, Sobers was caught behind for a six-ball duck off the bowling of Chris Old at a critical moment, as the middle order were in the process of losing 4 for 18. Defending 181, Sobers had gained revenge over Old (his only ODI wicket), as England suffered a collapse of their own as they closed in on the target. Sobers bowled the last over of the match, with one wicket needed or four runs, depending on which side you were on. England's number ten, Bob Willis, hit two twos and the match was over. The Barbadian never played another ODI, giving him an unfortunate batting average in that form of the game of 0.00.

Mohinder Amarnath

One of India's gutsiest and most consistent batsmen during the country's formative cricketing years, Mohinder Amarnath was a man for a crisis. When his team were under fire, often abroad, Amarnath would dig deepest. The 1982-83 season brought out the best in him: he scored three hundreds and three fifties in Pakistan and then 598 runs in the Caribbean against Roberts, Holding, Garner, Marshall et al, including two hundreds and four fifties in nine innings. That summer in England, he confounded Clive Lloyd's men further, taking the man of the match award in India's shock World Cup final victory. His star could not have been burning more brightly when the West Indies were invited back to India the following year. His home fans expected more great deeds from their hero. Could he surpass Bradman's total of 974 runs in a series, made against England in 1930? A pair in Kanpur ended that fantasy, as the Windies won by an innings. In the draw at Delhi, he did get off the mark in the first innings, but that single was his only run of the match, as he was bowled for zero in the second dig. Hopelessly out of touch, 'Amarnought' missed the next two matches, but was reinstated for the fifth in Kolkota after hitting fifty in an ODI. Sadly, the poor trot continued, although few would have lived with Malcolm Marshall on that first morning, especially after Sunil Gavaskar had been dismissed with a snorter for a diamond duck (*see* Chapter One **Famous First Ballers**). In the second innings, Amarnath fell victim to a revved-up Michael Holding for his fifth duck in three matches. His name was not on the sheet for the sixth Test. One run in six innings, when expectations were so high. It's no wonder that cricket can reduce grown men to tears.

Peter Judge

The Glamorgan tailender Peter Judge is believed to have completed the quickest pair in first-class cricket. Playing in a tour match against the Indians in 1946, the Welsh outfit were shot out cheaply and invited to follow on. Judge had been the last man out, for a duck, and was surprised to see his captain Johnnie Clay gesturing for him to open the innings with his not-out partner. The batting order had been reversed, with the ten-minute break between innings waived, as time was all but up. Judge did what he was told and was duly bowled second ball, again for a duck, recording a pair within three consecutive balls and a matter of minutes.

Maninder Singh

A duck for a number eleven batsman is not normally a cause for consternation. But when a single run from that tailender's blade will win you a Test match, the teeth do start gnashing if he fails. Twenty-one-year-old Maninder Singh found himself in

Done for pace

that precarious position during the first Test of the 1986-87 series between India and Australia in Chennai. The previous five days had been filled with heroic perform-ances on both sides. Dean Jones (210 runs in five-and-a-half hours) had been hospitalised with heat exhaustion, having proved to his captain Allan Border that he was no 'weak Victorian'. Kapil Dev had scored a swashbuckling century of his own. Australian spinner Greg Matthews had bowled unchanged for the whole of the last day in temperatures above 35 degrees, wearing a sweater in a statement of defiance. Or had they all just lost their minds in the heat? Hundreds, sixes, ten-fors, golden ducks, umpiring howlers, run outs – the match had them all and the thirty thousand spectators were loving it. Eventually, the spotlight fell on Maninder. Ravi Shastri had brought the scores level in the last over of the match, leaving his partner three balls to score the winning run. He blocked the first from Matthews, as the fielders circled the bat. The next cannoned into his pads and the Australians appealed to umpire Vikram Raju. His finger rose and the match was a tie, only the second in Test history (*see* Chapter Twelve **Expensive Run Outs**). Maninder believed he had edged it, but no matter. Both teams left the field feeling disappointed not to win, after five days of physical and mental exertion. Try explaining that to someone who does not understand cricket!

Gus Logie

The lithe Trinidadian, Gus Logie, was an electric fielder in the ring and a graceful batsman who fulfilled the 'finishing role' for the West Indies in ODIs, later credited to exponents such as Michael Bevan, Graham Thorpe, Michael Hussey and Eoin Morgan. In his 133 innings, he was not out 36 times, often tidying up the loose ends after the big boys like Viv Richards and Clive Lloyd had made a mess of the opposition bowling figures. He did get out occasionally and the first four ducks of his career all arrived consecutively, against Pakistan in 1985 and 1986. A first ball duck courtesy of Imran Khan started the rot, followed up by a fifth-baller in the next match. In 1986, Logie was back in West Indies colours in Pakistan, having had a whole year to think about his last two aberrations, but a mix-up with Gordon Greenidge saw the man who ran out so many others, run out himself. He was bowled second ball in the following match, to bring his trot to four, where it ended. A measured 25 not out off 83 balls (after Viv Richards had been bowled first ball) took the West Indies home with just three balls to spare. Order had been restored.

Alan Hurst

The well-built Victorian quick bowler was not picked in the 1978-79 Australia side for his batting. Indeed, he might not have been picked for his bowling either, had Kerry Packer not made off with the best of the home team's cricketers before the Ashes series that season, won easily by England. With the ball, he was one of the rare lights in the Aussie gloom, taking 25 wickets at an average of 23.08. With bat in hand, however, he was a waddling wicket, with two webbed feet and a bill. After a pair in the first Test at Brisbane, he suffered the indignity of being dropped from number ten to eleven. Sadly, there was no place lower, as he gathered another four ducks, including a first-baller in Sydney. His haul of six ducks is the highest by any batsman in a series. But then it wasn't his job to score runs.

Pat Pocock

A tall, willowy off-spinner, who once took seven wickets in eleven balls for Surrey, Pat Pocock played 25 Tests for England over seventeen years, but never enjoyed a long run in the side. He was no great shakes as a batsman, returning a Test average of just six, although ten of his Tests were played against the pack of West Indies quicks, who didn't enjoy tailenders delaying their celebrations. A surprise call up for the fourth Test at Old Trafford against the West Indies in 1984, eight years after his last Test, thrust Pocock back under the microscope. He bowled well, taking four wickets, although he couldn't stop Gordon Greenidge scoring a double hundred. As England followed on, Pat made a pair. In the final Test at The Oval, as Clive Lloyd's team hunted a 'blackwash', Pocock did not need to bowl on the first day, as the West Indies were bowled out for 190 on a seaming pitch. But when England opener Chris Broad fell cheaply, Pocock drew the short straw as nightwatchman and bravely withstood a barrage of short-pitched bowling from Marshall, Garner and Holding, eventually perishing for a 21-ball duck. In the second innings, Pocock found himself faced with an impossible task: eight wickets down with 175 still needed. He was quickly caught and bowled by Holding for zip. Four ducks in four innings, no runs scored in the series. And yet he left the contest with credit.

Mark Waugh

Even the very best batsmen will suffer a moment of misfortune or poor form at some point in their career, which translates into a failure. But when an elegant strokeplayer like Mark Waugh, who could entertain crowds for hours on end, has a shocker of a series, you know for sure that the cricketing gods are a joyless set of Scrooges. The younger of the Waugh twins, who always seemed to have that extra bit more time to play the ball than your average Test batsman, had scored a fifty in the first Test against Sri Lanka at the Sinhalese Sports Club Ground in Colombo in 1992, where Australia had pulled victory from the fire (*see* Chapter Seven **From the Jaws of Victory**). At the time, Mark was keeping his brother out of the side, so the pressure was firmly on to keep performing. In the first innings of the second Test in Khettarama, Mark was caught second ball by a youthful Sanath Jayasuriya. The pair duly followed, as he was bamboozled by debutant Muttiah Muralitharan, lbw to the first ball he faced from the jack-in-the-box off-spinner. More misery was to follow in the third Test in Moratuwa, as he was bowled and then caught behind, again without scoring in the match. His misfortune was the first time that a top order batsman had suffered consecutive pairs in Tests. Both matches petered out into draws, allowing Australia to take the series spoils. In the next Test, the selectors made room for both Waughs and the team rarely took a backward step for the next ten years.

Ricky Ponting

For most of his career, the wicket of Ricky Ponting has been celebrated louder than any other batsman in the team and with good reason. Until he departs, the opposition faces the risk – indeed the likelihood – that the match will be taken away from them in a short space of time. The volume of runs is impressive on its own, but it is the speed with which he has scored them, often in critical moments of the match, that makes his dismissal so valuable. But it was not always thus. Throughout the late nineties, Ponting was a fixture in the ODI side, yet his Test spot – usually at number six – was far from secure. Poor form, competition for places and booze-filled night club incidents threatened to curtail the Tasmanian's obvious potential. During the Pakistan series of 1999-2000 in Australia, Ponting had managed to force his way back into the team, but he needed a score to buy some time. The first Test at the 'Gabba in Brisbane could provide only a duck, lbw, as he was undone by Shoaib Akhtar bowling at warp speed, although umpire Daryl Harper missed a faint inside edge. At his home ground in Hobart, the situation worsened for Ponting in the second Test, as he suffered the only pair of his career, undone by Waqar Younis in the first innings and Wasim Akram in the second. Australia somehow achieved the win, thanks to hundreds from Justin Langer and Adam Gilchrist (*see* Chapter Nine **Umpiring Howlers**) in his second match, but aside from a catch, Ponting had contributed nothing. With Gilchrist adding ballast at seven, the selectors might have been tempted to pick an all-rounder for the number six slot, especially now that Ponting's ability to cope with pace was in doubt. But by the end of day two in the third Test at the WACA, the decision to stick with Ponting was vindicated, as he stroked 197. Two more hundreds against India that summer put the matter to bed. His pair was soon a distant memory.

Sanath Jayasuriya

Such is the fickle nature of cricketing fortune, as we have already seen so often, it is rather neat that a man who has scored more ODI hundreds than everyone else apart from Sachin Tendulkar and Ricky Ponting, is also the holder of the record for most ducks in that format. Given his swashbuckling approach to batting, tearing into the bowling when the ball is at its hardest and the bowlers at their freshest, Sanath Jayasuriya always ran the risk of getting out cheaply. Of his 34 ducks – six more than his nearest rival Wasim Akram – the aggressive Sri Lankan made nine first-ballers. All of the greatest strikers are high on the duck list, including Shahid Afridi, Herschelle Gibbs, Chris Gayle and Adam Gilchrist, so perhaps inclusion is a badge of honour. If you go hard, you will go home quickly on a regular basis.

Romesh Kaluwitharana

The sheer weight of matches played inevitably makes a difference to your duck tally. Jayasuriya has so far played the most ODI innings with 432, giving a return of one duck every 13 innings. Tendulkar, as another example, makes the top 20 (at the time of writing) of all time ODI duck hunters, but given that his tally is a mere 20 from 429 innings, he has only suffered a duck once every 22 innings. Of the leading contenders, one name stands out: Sri Lankan wicket-keeper Romesh Kaluwitharana, who lifted the World Cup in 1996. He made an impressive 24 ducks from only 181 innings, amounting to one duck per eight completed knocks. But given that Jayasuriya and Kaluwitharana helped redefine the way that teams attack at the top of the order, perhaps the occasional sacrifice was worthwhile. The only frontline batsman to do worse than Kalu was the hapless Bangladesh skipper, Habibul Bashar, who managed 18 ducks in 105 innings: one in six.

Courtney Walsh

A fearsome and tireless competitor with the ball, Courtney Walsh never harboured pretensions of brilliance with the bat, especially as he played in an era when tailenders were not expected to hang about. If he did survive long enough, Walsh could entertain the crowd with his dancing and bobbing at the crease, very occasionally swatting a pitched-up delivery back over the bowler's head for six (he hit 17 of them in his Test career). Highlights include a studious unbeaten knock of 30 against Australia at the MCG in 1988 adding over fifty for the ninth wicket with his mate Curtly Ambrose; or the three sixes he smacked in his 18 runs not out against England in Barbados in 1994, giving the home spectators something to cheer as their team suffered a rare loss. Perhaps his most important contribution came in the epic run chase by Brian Lara in the 1999 Test against Australia in Barbados. Lara's effort would have come to naught had Walsh not survived five deliveries from a fired-up Glenn McGrath (*see* Chapter Seven **From the Jaws of Victory**). But enough of Walsh's successes! His failures were record-breaking. Nobody else has or probably ever will make more than his 43 Test ducks.

Shane Warne

Interestingly, the four highest duck makers in Tests are also four of the five highest wicket takers in the game. What you sow… etc. Of those four, Courtney Walsh, Glenn McGrath and Muttiah Muralitharan have played most of their innings at ten or eleven.

They have only two fifties between them, although Murali has often voiced his ambitions as a batsman. Shane Warne, on the other hand, has been a fairly useful striker for Australia over the years, ending on a high in his last Test match (against England in early 2007) with 71 runs from 65 balls. His return of 12 fifties, including a top score of 99, caught on the boundary (*see* Chapter Fifteen **Nearly Men**), helped make him the weightiest scorer of runs without a Test hundred. Towards the end of his career especially, Warne made a habit of digging his side out of a hole by counter-attacking. Therefore it is something of a surprise that he should have 34 ducks on his card, at a rate of one per six innings. But when you take 708 wickets, every run you score for your side is an added bonus. Anil Kumble is the exception from the top five wicket takers. He sits third with 619 wickets, but he managed a paltry 17 ducks in 173 innings, languishing in 33rd place among the duck hunters.

Mervyn Dillon

New Zealand's Chris Martin is everybody's favourite bunny, and why not? With an average of 2.28 in 56 matches, his record is a shocker. The story goes that he always cycled to nets as a youngster and had nowhere to store his bat, so he never practised. His impressive return of 28 ducks in only 81 innings translates to a duck every 2.9 innings. But his record is not the worst. Indeed, Walsh (a duck every 4.3 innings) and McGrath (3.9) are stonewallers compared with West Indian fast bowler Mervyn Dillon, who made 26 ducks in 68 innings, at a rate of 2.6. In those 68 innings, Dillon 'carried his bat' just three times!

Marvan Atapattu

Of frontline batsmen, 22 ducks is currently the highest number achieved in a career, shared by two batsmen. Steve Waugh is one, but then he did play 260 innings for his country. He copped a duck every twelve innings, which stacks up pretty well. The other is Sri Lanka's opener Marvan Atapattu (a duck every seven innings), although given that he bagged five in his first six innings, and four pairs in total, 22 ducks marked something of a recovery. Next in the list of 'proper' batsmen is Michael Atherton with 20 and then Mark Waugh with 19.

Andrew Flintoff

Apart from Marvan Atapattu (four pairs), the only other frontline batsman to reel in three pairs of ducks or more in Test matches, is English bulldog Andrew Flintoff. Despite the occasional clownish moment, history will remember Flintoff as an all-rounder capable of turning a match in a single session, whether with ball or bat, or even in the field, for example running out Ricky Ponting in the Ashes decider in 2009. His finest moments came in the 2005 Ashes series and for several seasons he provided England with an ingredient for success that so few teams enjoy: a player capable of holding down a place as both a batsman and a bowler. His tally of 17 ducks from 130 innings is high for a batsman of his quality and his first pair came in just his second match, at Leeds in 1998, as England beat South Africa to win the series. The Headingley crowd again saw a Flintoff pair, this time against India in 2002, as he survived just three balls as India swept to an innings victory. Finally, he missed out twice on a batting paradise in Antigua in 2009, but then bowled through the pain barrier as England came so close to winning (*see* Chapter Fifteen **Nearly Men**).

AB de Villiers

Replying to a competitive score of 250 all out by Bangladesh in the second Test at Centurion in 2008, South Africa were in a hole at 134 for 4. AB de Villiers walked to the crease at number six, knowing that a partnership with the set batsman, Ashwell Prince, would likely turn the game in his side's favour. A positive player, whatever the circumstances, AB (real name Abraham) decided to impose himself on the bowlers. He danced down the wicket to the second delivery from the slow left-armer Shakib Al Hasan, but missed the ball, allowing keeper Mushfiqur Rahim to complete the stumping. He was out for a duck and not a very sensible one either. No bother though, as Prince went on to make a big hundred, sharing a partnership of 270 with next man in Mark Boucher, who also made a ton. South Africa wrapped up victory by an innings and 48 runs. Remarkably, that was AB's sole duck in Tests to that date, despite batting 99 times for his country. His confidence was understandable, given that he had not been duck-egged in his first 78 hits, the current world record. Whether he finishes his career with a better duck-to-innings ratio than Sir Clyde Walcott, who fell for only a solitary one in his 74 knocks, remains to be seen. Of current players, New Zealand's Ross Taylor has yet to blank in an innings, whether out or not out, in 46 Test appearances.

James Anderson

Games within games are what keeps the cricket addict purring and swing bowler Jimmy Anderson provided English fans with endless amounts of fun as he racked up the England record for most innings without a duck between 2003 and 2009. Except it wasn't endless. Jimmy was eventually given out lbw to Ben Hilfenhaus in the fifth Test of the 2009 Ashes series at The Oval, his first duck in 54 innings. Given the importance of every run in the deciding Test, each England wicket was met by a groan, but Jimmy's demise received the deepest groan of the lot. Up and down the country, those who had followed his unlikely run felt empty inside. England went on to win the series, although it was not a golden match for Anderson, who failed to contribute a run, wicket or catch. With the pressure off, a golden duck followed three Tests later in South Africa.

Chris Read

Twenty-year-old Chris Read looked closer to a teenager when he first donned the gloves for England, which was unfortunate for the Nottinghamshire man, as it made it easier for critics to write him off as being too callow for Test cricket. Arguably the best gloveman on the county circuit for the last ten years, as well as a combative striker down the order, his county form rarely flourished on the international stage. Sadly for Read, his career may yet be defined by one dismissal, in only his second Test match at Lord's, in 1999 against New Zealand. Good form, as well as his youth, had brought him into the side, giving him an extended opportunity to prove he had what it takes to succeed at that level. A single run on his debut in the first Test of the series had not calmed the jitters, as he went out to face a rampant Chris Cairns in overcast conditions. England were mid-collapse and with his skipper Nasser Hussain set at the other end, Read had a chance to make a name for himself. But fellow Notts player Cairns had an ace up his sleeve, learnt from West Indian quick Franklyn Stephenson, another servant of Trent Bridge. Read had clearly missed that seminar and a slower-ball yorker was the last delivery the batsman expected to see. Believing it to be a fast beamer, he ducked. The ball looped under his feet to hit the stumps, leaving Read to wander off, bemused and out of his depth, for a duck. Graham Thorpe was made to look equally muggish a year later by Courtney Walsh at Old Trafford, turning his back on a floater to be plumb lbw first ball. But, such was Thorpe's pedigree at the time compared with Read's, the dismissal was deemed masterful bowling and not clueless batting.

Vasbert Drakes

In village cricket, if the timed-out dismissal (which stipulates that the next batsman in must cross the boundary within three minutes of the fall of the last wicket) was regularly enforced, it would be a common entry in scorebooks across the land. The fielding captain might appeal half-heartedly to the umpire, as old Charlie is fished out of the pub or searches for his lucky bat, but such a complaint is rarely upheld. If it is, then the batting captain may nominate which batsman is sacrificed, so it need not be his star player, should he be the tardy party. Surprisingly, given all the stories you hear about the professional cricketers of yesteryear and nightclubs, there have been only four occasions in first-class history of batsmen being timed out for a duck. All four have happened in the last thirty or so years. None were in Tests or ODIs.

Most recently, Nottinghamshire seamer AJ Harris was dismissed timed out against Durham University in 2003. Struggling from a groin strain, he was halfway down the pavilion steps when the umpires sent him back up again. Perhaps the quirkiest was the case of West Indian all-rounder Vasbert Drakes, who was a long-term servant of the Border club in South Africa. Drakes was due to fly in to East London on the morning of a match against Free State in 2002, so his club picked him, prepared to play with ten men until he arrived. The gamble appeared to have paid off when the captain won the toss and chose to bat, giving Drakes plenty of time to take his place in the order. But Border crumbled to 172 for 9. Drakes's plane was delayed, so he was given out, as he was currently in a different country from the one where the match was being played!

Keith Arthurton

The Nevis islander Keith Arthurton was undoubtedly a talented batsman, cracking an unbeaten 157 against Australia in the Brisbane Test in 1992 and then 126 against England at Sabina Park in 1994. However, Arthurton had a habit of giving his wicket away when a big score looked assured, scoring fewer runs than batsmen far less gifted. He was out first ball five times in his 105 one-dayers, but his nadir came during the 1996 World Cup, when he managed just two runs in his five innings. He faced a total of 21 balls and returned home with an average of 0.4 runs. A duck in the semi-final, when defeat looked almost impossible (*see* Chapter Eight **Team Collapses**), concluded his horror show.

Mark Vermeulen

The wild child of Zimbabwean cricket could certainly bat, when his mind was on the job at hand. But all too often it seemed to wander, perhaps towards how he was being wronged, rather than to what he could do to put things right. His Test career lasted for only eight matches, with occasional highlights such as a hundred against the West Indies at Bulawayo in November 2003. But he had also completed a pair of ducks on the same day against England at Chester-le-Street earlier that year, becoming only the 13th Test player to achieve the feat. He reacted by storming away from the ground, rather than leaving with his team-mates, which earned him a ticket home on the next plane. Before he could grow out of this petulance, Vermeulen was struck a sickening blow on the side of the head by Indian pace man Irfan Pathan early in 2004, an injury that required life-saving surgery. This accident and its aftermath appeared to send Vermeulen off the deep end psychologically and he was soon banned from English cricket for throwing his bat into the crowd (nearly hitting a young girl) and attacking spectators with the sharp end of a boundary marker. Worse was to follow back home, when he burned down his board's headquarters in a fit of rage at being overlooked for selection. The courts showed him leniency on account of his injuries and subsequent imbalance, so a stiff jail sentence was avoided. He has since returned to Zimbabwean colours, scoring an excellent 92 in his comeback match in 2009.

Chapter Seven
From the Jaws of Victory

If you really want to annoy a spectator at a cricket match, ask him who is winning. He might patiently explain that one of the teams is ahead, but that the match is not lost until the final wicket is taken or the winning run scored. More likely, he will just growl. After all, it ain't over till it's over.

England

In the match that reputedly signalled the death of English cricket, a one-off Test at The Oval in 1882, Australia won the toss and batted first on a minefield. Just over two hours later, the decision seemed flawed, as the visitors were all out for 63. However, it did allow fast bowler Fred 'the Demon' Spofforth a chance to spoon back some of the same medicine to the English batsmen that afternoon; he collected seven cheap wickets as WG Grace's team collapsed to 101 all out by stumps. If Australia could only give Spofforth enough runs to play with in the second innings, then an unlikely victory was still possible. The next morning, as the English bowlers slid about on a wet pitch with a slippery ball, Hugh Massie played one of the great counter-punching innings of that or any other era. He skelped 55 runs from 60 deliveries, including nine precious fours, which could well have been worth 150 runs on a flat track. However, once the England bowlers regained control, the procession of wickets restarted and Australia were soon dismissed for 122. The meagre target of 85 looked like a cakewalk, especially when Grace found his timing, leading the chase to 51 for 2. But as the fat lady cleared her throat to sing, Spofforth shoved a green and gold sweat sock down her gullet, scattering any England batsman in his path. He added another seven wickets to his match tally, while Harry Boyle chipped in with three, including Grace's valuable scalp. Suddenly, England were all out for 77, seven runs short. The body of English cricket was pronounced dead by the Sporting Times. Its lifeless body was metaphorically cremated and shipped across the seas to Australia.

Australia

Within a year, these Ashes were regained by Ivo Bligh's touring Englishmen, who won a three-match rubber 2-1. The first Test in Melbourne was claimed convincingly by the hosts, but England came roaring back in the second, again at the MCG, inspired by off-spinner Willy Bates (*see* Chapter Eleven **Insult to Injury**), who took 14 wickets and snared the first England Test hat-trick. The deciding Test in Sydney attracted crowds that were to become commonplace over the next 130 years, as interest in the duel escalated. Australia were in the box seat entering the fourth innings, needing 153 runs to win under clear blue skies. Spofforth had again been England's destroyer, taking eleven wickets for 115 runs to set up a likely victory. But the Aussie batsmen fluffed their lines. Captain Billy Murdoch was out for a duck, as the total slumped to 33 for 6. Fred Morley and Dick Barlow bowled unchanged for 70 four-ball overs, with Barlow the more successful, taking 7 for 40. Australia were all out for 83. A group of Melbourne ladies presented Bligh, who scored just 33 runs in his five innings, with a small terracotta urn containing a burnt bail, to signify his success in winning back the Ashes. They have been see-sawing between the two nations ever since, although more saw than see from an England point of view.

Australia (2)

The wounds from the 1882 humiliation at The Oval were further soothed when Australia threw away a golden opportunity to win the first of two Tests at Sydney in early 1887. England lost the toss and were inserted on a pitch that offered uneven bounce. Spofforth was still playing for Australia, but he was not called upon to bowl, as debutants Charlie Turner and JJ Ferris combined unchanged for 35 four-ball overs, dismissing the tourists for just 45 runs, which remains England's lowest total in Tests. Although Australia's reply of 119 was sub-par by ordinary expectations, a lead of 74 on that track was mighty. By the end of the second day, it appeared to be conclusive, as England again slipped, to 103 for 7. But with a rest day to contemplate his position (probably from the comfort of a local bar), Johnny Briggs, so often the hero with the ball, turned up trumps with the bat on a pitch that had dried out. He added 33, as the tail wagged, eking out a lead of 111 runs. A number unlucky for some, but not Nottinghamshire's Billy Barnes, who dug deep to record his finest figures for his country: 6 for 28. Spofforth, the executioner at The Oval, was the last victim off the Sydney scaffolding, as Australia lost by 13 runs. Unlucky indeed.

Australia (3)

Australia boasts the record for the most consecutive matches without following on (190 Tests between 1988 in Karachi and 2005 in Nottingham). Conversely, on the three occasions that a team has won after following on, Australia has been on the losing side. The first incident came in the first Test of the 1894-95 Ashes series in Sydney, when George Giffen (161) and Syd Gregory (201) propelled Australia to a total of 586. England reached 325 in reply and were invited to bat again. The England batsmen managed 437 runs second time around, thanks largely to Albert Ward's only

Test hundred (117). But with 177 runs needed and the pitch holding true at stumps on the fifth day, Australia looked set to romp home at 113 for 2. South Australian Joe Darling had overcome his primary in the first innings and was unbeaten on 44 that evening, alongside Giffen on 30. In today's five-day Tests, Australia's batsmen might have pushed harder for the win or the match would have subsided into a draw. Yet, with all next week to score 64 runs, the batters could take their time. That night, the heavens opened, soaking the uncovered pitch. Slow, left-arm Yorkshireman Bobby Peel, who had slept through the storm after a skinful, awoke to find the ground bathed in strong sunshine. He could barely believe his eyes when he saw the soggy wicket. 'Gi'e me t' ball,' he said, after his skipper had revived him in a cold shower. He then ran through the Australians with fellow leftie Johnny Briggs, as the pitch proved unbattable. For reasons of their own, the weather gods clearly did not want Australia to win that match. Giffen scored over 200 runs in the match and took eight wickets, yet left the ground a loser.

Australia (4)

The 1902 Ashes had already been lost by England, as the two old foes met for the fifth Test at The Oval. Fred Tate, who had suffered a torrid time in the fourth Test (*see* Chapter Two **Horror Debuts**), was replaced by Gilbert Laird Jessop. Tate was a better bowler, but Jessop was the finest cover fielder in the land and a dangerous batsman who revelled in taking games away from the opposition. Known as 'Croucher' due to his unorthodox technique, Jessop was a whirlwind at the crease, going for his shots early and not stopping until he was out, like Virender Sehwag in creams and necker-chief. But for his assault in the last innings of the match, Australia would have won at a canter. They ought to have won anyway, after Hugh Trumble took eight wickets for just 65 runs, but a dolly drop by star batsman Clem Hill allowed England to avoid the follow-on.

Another Aussie colossus, Victor Trumper, ran himself out in the second innings, thus inviting his team-mates to stutter to just 121, albeit the pitch was cutting up. With England set 263 to win, any thoughts of victory were all but erased as the first five wickets fell without 50 on the board. 'Croucher' strode to the middle with nothing to lose. He started slowly by his standards, surviving several half-chances as he tried to gauge the pitch. Then he went ballistic. Five sixes and 17 fours leapt from his swinging bat, as he reached his hundred in 75 minutes. Yet, despite the carnage, Australia were still favourites to win, with only the tailenders left and 75 runs still needed. But George Hirst took up Jessop's baton and skilfully farmed the strike to take the hosts close. Even then, England needed another dropped catch, this time by Warwick Armstrong in the slips, to reach the finishing line, with one wicket remaining. Would Australia have been so sloppy had the rubber not been dead? Nobody at the ground that day seemed to care.

England (2)

The final analysis of the 1907-08 Ashes series in Australia, 4-1 to the home team, looks like a drubbing. But this was nothing like the whitewashes of 1920-21 or 2006-07. Indeed in this instance England had their opportunities to win by the same margin. The first Test at Sydney was a typically tense affair that the English did well to lose. George Gunn, on holiday at the time, was called into the England line-up and he scored a hundred on debut. Despite shipping a 27-run deficit in the first innings, due to a fine knock of 87 runs by the classy Australian left-hander Clem Hill, England scored an even 300 in the second to set a target of 274. A day was lost to rain, juicing up the pitch, although it would play better than expected. All the same, Australia had lost their first three batsmen cheaply, including Hill and Victor Trumper, so the force was with the visitors. Even though the middle order each contributed, nobody could kick on, leaving the Australians reeling at 124 for 6. Peter McAlister and keeper Sammy Carter scored 41 and 61 respectively under intense pressure, but when they both fell, Australia still needed 56 with just two wickets in hand. But England hopes were quickly dashed, as bowlers Tibby Cotter and Gerry Hazlitt nonchalantly knocked off the remaining runs. England were one down in the series and could scarcely believe it.

Australia (5)

The tables were soon turned in the next match of the series, the New Year Test at Melbourne. This time it was England's opportunity to take a first innings lead, which the Aussie openers Victor Trumper and Monty Noble soon wiped out in the second innings. Sydney Barnes eventually bowled the home team out for 397, leaving a testing 282 for victory. Jack Hobbs had scored 83 in the first innings on debut, but when he was bowled by Noble, Gunn quickly followed for a duck. Wickets kept falling in clutches, adhering to the adage 'get one, get two', until England were teetering on the edge of a two-nil precipice at 243 for 9. Barnes was at the crease with number eleven Arthur Fielder, who was not renowned for his batting. But, showing all the debonair coolness of the age, Barnes (38) chipped away at the target, inspiring Fielder to excel in scoring 18. The scores drew level and the batsmen called through a risky single to win the match. Gerry Hazlitt, fielding close, had a chance to throw down the stumps and secure the tie, but he missed. Test cricket would have to wait more than 60 years for that sort of opportunity to present itself again (*see* Chapter Twelve **Expensive Run Outs**).

Warwickshire

In 1922, Hampshire CCC subsided for 15 runs in just nine overs in reply to Warwickshire's 223 in a three-day match. Fifteen! Seven batsmen made a duck, including the first three with the score on zero. Hampshire's captain, Lionel Tennyson, grandson of the poet, smacked his first ball for four to get the innings going, but then was caught next ball to continue the rot. Only Phil Mead (who would score a staggering 48,892 runs for Hampshire in his career, the highest first-class total ever by a batsman for a single county) showed any form of resistance, reaching six not out from twelve deliveries. Hampshire's total was the seventh lowest score for a completed first-class innings and they were duly asked to bat again. The top order fared better second time around, but at 177 for 6, still trailing by 31 runs, the game looked up. But George Brown, a man so strong apparently that he could rip a whole pack of cards in half with his bare hands, was not about to concede defeat. He bludgeoned a score of 172, ably supported by the wicketkeeper, Walter Livsey (110 not out), as the last four wickets added 344 to set a target of 314 runs for victory. Shell-shocked, Warwickshire never came close, capitulating for just 158 as Hampshire recorded one of the most unlikely victories in history. Fifteen remains the lowest total (all out) ever posted by a winning team in first-class cricket.

England (3)

The 1936-37 Ashes series took its place in history as the only five-match Test series to have been won after the eventual victors had fallen 2-0 behind. Again, the touring England side were 'Bradman-ed', but like an expert hustler, he waited until the odds were at their highest before showing his true hand. The Aussies had been outplayed in the first two matches, although England had enjoyed the best of the conditions, with Gubby Allen winning the toss on both occasions. The home team suffered a collapse in all four innings played, although this was largely due to the unfortunate rain showers and drying pitches. Bradman had chalked up two ducks already – second and first ball respectively – while his great rival, Wally Hammond, had a double hundred to his name and several wickets (as well as a goldie of his own).

The third Test at the MCG was again heavily dependent on the toss of a coin, which this time went in Bradman's favour. Heavy rain allowed Australia to gain a useful first innings lead, as England were dismissed for just 76. Yet the game was still in the balance, as the pitch would take time to recover. A rest day certainly helped, but Bradman, who was suffering from 'flu, cannily switched his batting order so that his better batsmen would have their hit on a drier pitch. His nightwatchmen did their job, hanging about until the pitch had dried out into a day-one featherbed. Bradman (270), who was dropped first ball (*see* Chapter Four **Costly Drops**), and Jack Fingleton (136) – usually batsmen three and one – came together with the score at 97 for 5 and scored a record stand of 346 runs. Imagine watching numbers six and seven bat all day, knowing that the number eight is Stan McCabe with an average in the high forties! England, who had probably been three wickets away from regaining the Ashes, were now staring at certain defeat, in this match at least. But Bradman went on to boss the last two matches as well, scoring 212 in Adelaide and 169 in Sydney, with McCabe also feasting on a glut of runs. Spinners Bill O'Reilly and Chuck Fleetwood-Smith, who had opened the batting in that decisive second innings at the MCG, were hugely influential in Australia's winning of the series and the retention of the Ashes.

West Indies

The script appeared to have been written as the fourth Test between Australia and the West Indies neared its climax at the MCG in 1951-52. The hosts, who had dominated the first two Tests of the series, had allowed the visitors back in at a soggy Adelaide in the third. The West Indies now seemed destined to take the rubber into a decider at Sydney, having reduced Australia to 222 for 9 in the fourth innings, chasing a target of 260. The headlines ought to have been hogged by Sir Frank Worrell, who had made a gutsy hundred in the first innings and then a crucial 30 in the second, often batting one-handed after being injured by Keith Miller. Neil Harvey and Lindsey Hassett had compiled excellent knocks for the hosts, but they seemed to have been made in vain. The two remaining tailenders – Doug Ring and Bill Johnston – were no mugs with a bat. Ring liked to give it a thump, while Johnston could hang about if needed. Both were Victorians and Invincibles. But neither was offered a prayer against Alf Valentine and Sonny Ramadhin. In these modern daysof computer profiling and team statisticians, the West Indies skipper John Goddard would have known that Ring liked to hit the ball inside-out over cover. A fielder set at deep extra cover would have won the match quickly and nothing more would have made of it. But Goddard waited for a mishit that never came. Ring carved out a brilliant 32, while Johnston did his bit with seven precious runs, flicking the winning single off his legs. The series was won.

England (4)

Some of the most exciting matches of the Ashes series have come when the sides are evenly matched. These tense affairs rely on virtuoso performances to tilt the advantage one way or the other. The 1961 series in England would surely have been won by the home side but for career-defining efforts by two Australians, both of whom would go on to become giants of cricket commentary. Firstly, Bill Lawry's maiden Test hundred (130) in the second Test at Lord's was double that of anyone else's score in the match. With the ball spitting from a venomous ridge at the Nursery End of the pitch, Lawry displayed courage and sound technique to defy the pace of Brian Statham and Fred Trueman for six hours in his match-winning knock. England had thundered back in the third Test, as Trueman inspired two dramatic collapses to take eleven wickets.

With the momentum firmly with the home side, the fourth Test at Old Trafford was England's to lose, having taken a lead of 177 runs after the first innings.

Just one more wicket

They bottled it. Statham and Trueman managed just one wicket between them for nearly 200 runs, as Lawry hit another hundred, although three crucial slip catches were dropped off their bowling. But even with Lawry's 102 and 67 from Norm O'Neill, Australia's lead was only 157 runs, with one wicket left to fall before lunch on the fifth day. Alan Davidson (77 not out) was a late order striker (in the Mitchell Johnson or Graeme Swann mode nowadays), the sort of menace whom the opposition captain is delighted to see depart. At Old Trafford, the risky strokes paid off, as he took 20 runs off an over by off spinner David Allen (whose other 37 overs in the innings went for just 38 runs), frustrating the England bowlers with a last-wicket stand of 98 alongside fast bowler Garth McKenzie (32).

The home team now needed 256 runs to win in a session and a half, and again they were cruising to victory. Ted Dexter (76) rode the pressure to play a carefree knock full of grace and panache, combining with a more watchful Raman Subba Row (49) to reach 150 for 1, with plenty of time left. Then Richie Benaud took over. Suffering from a sore shoulder, which limited his ability to spin the ball, he still managed to make it bite in the footmarks left by the fast bowlers. Statham and

Trueman may not have dismissed Australia, but their boot indentations played a part in England's rapid demise.

The popular Benaud, who had insisted that his squad play attractive, fair cricket with a smile on their faces, proved that good guys can come out on top. He out-foxed Dexter and Subba Row, and then bowled Peter May for a duck. Brian Close and John Murray followed for not many more, leaving Benaud with five for peanuts. The crowd was stunned and panic took over the English dressing-room. When Ken Barrington was trapped by Ken Mackay, the game was all but over. England had lost nine wickets for 51 runs. Benaud finished with figures of 6 for 70. The Ashes were retained.

Australia (6)

Chasing a target of 382 for victory in the fourth innings of the first Test against Pakistan at the MCG in 1979, Australia seemed to be making light work of it, reaching 305 for 3. Allan Border had batted for six hours to make a sublime 105, adding 177 with Kim Hughes (84). The visitors turned for inspiration to their opener Sarfraz Nawaz, who had already taken two wickets. And did he deliver! Bowling one of the greatest spells in Test history, Sarfraz induced an inside edge from Border from a nip-backer and then ran through the rest of the batsman like cheese wire through a soft Brie. His remarkable effort lasted 33 balls, with which he dismissed seven batsmen for just one run. In what was turning out to be a nigglesome series (*see* Chapter Nine **Umpiring Howlers**), the joy of the Pakistanis was unbridled, as the Australians formed a batting conga backwards and forwards between pitch and pavilion. Five batsmen made ducks, two of them golden. From the sweet taste of famous victory came the bitter tang of ignominious defeat. Border ensured he was not dismissed in the next run chase at Perth and the series was levelled.

Australia (7)

Richie Benaud's well known adage – captaincy is ninety per cent luck and ten per cent skill (but don't try it without that ten per cent) – was proved correct in the remarkable victory by England against Australia at Headingley in 1981, one of only three occasions when the side following on has won a Test match. Stellar all-rounder Ian Botham had been anything but, during his twelve Tests as skipper, failing to win a match as his form deserted him. After a loss at Trent Bridge and a draw at Lord's (where he made a pair, including a golden duck in the second innings), Botham resigned, to be replaced by the crafty tactician Mike Brearley. In hindsight, it was a selectorial masterstroke, given that England won the match, but Australia should never have let it happen. There was no doubt that relinquishing the captaincy released the pressure on Botham, who took a six-wicket haul in the first innings and then scored a fluent fifty. But England were still dismissed for just

174 and were forced to follow on. Then at 105 for 5, when Beefy strode to the middle, his team were still 122 runs away from avoiding an innings defeat. Bookmakers were reputed to have offered odds of 500-1, which a couple of the shrewder Australian players had allegedly accepted, claiming that no contest was that one-sided. Yet when ninth batsman Graham Dilley joined Botham, England were still 92 runs adrift. 'Let's have a bit of fun,' said Both, before flaying the ball to all parts of the ground. Dilley scored a fifty, while Chris Old and Bob Willis stuck around long enough for the inspired Botham to reach 149 not out. Even then, Australia should have knocked off the 130 runs needed for the win and they looked set to do so at 56 for 2, but Brearley wound up Willis and then released him down the slope, and the fast bowler grabbed eight wickets as panic set in. Botham and Willis received the plaudits, but so too did the lucky skipper.

India

A tournament final between Asian powerhouses India and Pakistan is the organiser's dream fixture; such is the passion of the rival fans. Rarely do the games match up to the hype, but the final of the Austral-Asia Cup in 1986, played at Sharjah, was certainly an exception. It ought to have been a routine victory for India, who had posted 248 in their 50 overs. Pakistan's wickets were falling with regularity, as no batsmen seemed able to stick around with linchpin Javed Miandad. With three overs to go and just three wickets in hand, 30 runs still needed, even Miandad thought a win impossible, later admitting that he was determined to lose with style. But a couple of fours and a six reduced the deficit to eleven off the last over, to be bowled by 20-year-old seamer Chetan Sharma. Miandad hit one four, but found himself at the wrong end with two balls to go and five still needed. Number eleven Tauseef Ahmed was quaking at the striker's end. The bunny could only bunt the ball into the covers, where India's best fielder, Mohammad Azharuddin, was waiting. But his shy missed the stumps, leaving Miandad on strike and Sharma facing his clash with destiny. The Pakistani maestro took an age to compose himself, making a short prayer to Allah and then counting all the fielders to compute the angles. All the while, Sharma contemplated the yorker that would stop Miandad scoring the requisite four runs. Eventually he ran in, but the ball slipped in his hand, squirting out as a leg-side full toss. Even before it had soared clean over the midwicket rope, Miandad had his arms aloft in celebration. The impossible had been achieved and India took several years to recover, struggling to contain Pakistan for the next decade.

Australia (8)

The crowd at the World Series ODI match between Australia and England at Sydney in 1987 had to wait until the last over for the contest to take off, but it was worth hanging about for. The home team should have won and looked set to do so, after

Dirk Wellham had scored 97 in their total of 234 runs and the visitors had been reduced to 186 for 5. David Gower and Ian Botham had played enterprising knocks, but when they fell, the onus lay on Allan Lamb in his pastel blue pyjamas, who seemed to be struggling with his timing. Indeed, with an over remaining and 18 runs still needed to win, he was yet to hit a boundary. A wild throw from Wellham on the cover boundary allowed two off the first ball from the tall, thin left-armer Bruce Reid, which was soon followed by a four through square leg. 'That makes it interesting,' said Bill Lawry on Channel Nine commentary. A towering six over midwicket next ball certainly did, bringing the runs needed down to six off three. England were favourites for the first time in the match. Lamb could only knock the fourth delivery out to Wellham at extra cover in the circle for a single, but the throw was needlessly strong, Reid fumbled and the batsmen ran through for an overthrow. Lamb was back on strike and took advantage to stroke the fifth ball past square leg for a win with a ball to spare. Australia had bossed 99 overs of the match, but left the stadium as the losing side.

England (5)

England, hosts on four occasions, are yet to win the World Cup, although they have come mighty close. So desperately close in 1987, in fact, that they must have wondered how it was that Australia took the trophy home from India instead of them. Having edged out the favourites, India, in the semi-final, Mike Gatting's team were tipped to defeat Allan Border's makeshift eleven that had passed under the radar to the final. Cheered on by 100,000 vengeful locals at Eden Gardens in Kolkata, David Boon top-scored with 75 runs to help post a target of 254 runs, aided by a cameo from Mike Veletta, who smashed 45 runs from just 31 balls. Opener Tim Robinson copped a first ball duck, but England still fancied their chances, especially with Gatting and Bill Athey moving serenely towards the total. Then Gatting suffered a brain fade that was roundly blamed for his team surrendering the match. Border brought himself on to bowl his slow left-armers, more in hope than expectation. The first delivery pitched on leg stump, whereupon Gatting played a premeditated reverse sweep, a stroke much less common than it is today. It was a shot he played well and therefore worth the risk, but when it goes wrong, you don't half look like a plonker. The ball top edged, bounced off his shoulder and looped into the gloves of Greg Dyer, who was almost too shocked to celebrate. The crowd found its voice though, cheering Gatting all the way back to the pavilion. His team eventually lost by seven runs. Like Jean van der Velde or Devon Loch, the final is remembered more for the manner of the loss than the victory.

Sri Lanka

Rarely can a team have played so well and yet found themselves on the losing side as a result of a single, desperate session. The first Test between Sri Lanka and Australia at Colombo in 1992 was dominated by the home team until tea on the fifth day. Profiting from the weather conditions, Sri Lanka gained a hefty lead of 291 runs after the first innings, as three of their batsmen scored hundreds. Australia did better second time around, but none of their own top order kicked on, relying on a wagging tail to set a target of 181 runs to win. Surely, it was never going to be enough? As Sri Lanka raced to 127 for 2, with Aravinda de Silva looking supremely assured, the journalists would have been filing copy. But confidence can quickly lead to over-confidence, especially when the opposition team is led by Allan Border, a skipper who wouldn't accept defeat until the last run was scored. De Silva attempted a loose stroke down the ground, which was superbly caught over his head by Border himself. Border then pouched an edge from Arjuna Ranatunga second ball, sending the portly captain back for a duck. The wheels dropped off. The last eight wickets fell for 37 runs, as Sri Lanka capitulated to 164 all out, still 17 runs short. Shane Warne, in just his third Test, had been walloped for 107 wicketless runs in the first innings. But he ran through the tail, taking 3 for 0, to complete the collapse. Not surprisingly, ten thousand spectators booed the Sri Lankans at the prize ceremony, as the scribblers hurriedly rewrote their reports.

South Africa

In their first match after readmission to the Test fold in 1992, South Africa looked on course to win a poignant one-off match in the Caribbean, a contest that could never have taken place under apartheid. The match was a new start in an entirely different sense for the West Indies too, given that legends such as Richards, Greenidge, Marshall and Dujon had recently retired. The visitors had dominated the first four days, taking a deserved first innings lead on the back of Andrew Hudson's fine 163. Allan Donald then announced his arrival on the Test scene with four wickets, allowing the Proteas to line up a fourth innings target of 201. The Bridgetown pitch was playing hard to get, but at 122 for 2 at the start of the fifth morning, it looked as though South Africa were taking up Test cricket where they had left off 22 years previously (*see* Chapter Thirteen **One-Sided Affairs**). By lunch, reality had bitten, in the shape of Courtney Walsh and Curtly Ambrose. Bowling a sublime line and length, at quick speeds on a bumpy track, they hunted as a pair, snaring all ten wickets in the innings. The batsmen were given no respite. Donald was last man out, first ball, to Ambrose. Eight wickets fell for 26 runs in a session. Welcome back to Test cricket!

Australia (9)

Whether Brian Lara's magical run chase in Bridgetown during the third Test against Australia in 1999 counts as a calamity is open to question, such was the quality of the knock. While the Aussies did drop a couple of half chances towards the end of

Lara's virtuoso effort, the West Indies won that Test, rather than the Australians losing it. At the same time, Australia having scored 490 in the first innings, captain Steve Waugh, who had scored 199 of them, must have been confident that his team would not lose. Indeed, with the West Indies faltering in reply at 98 for 6, they were in need of a saviour or two. They arrived in the form of Sherwin Campbell (105) and Ridley Jacobs (68), plus a wagging tail, which teased the total to 329. Yet the deficit would be telling, unless the bowlers could find inspiration. Courtney Walsh provided it, trapping Matthew Elliott for a duck with his second ball. He would take five wickets in total as the Aussies limped to just 146, although they were grateful for a quickfire 32 from Shane Warne down the order.

A target of 308 runs ought to have been enough on a fifth day pitch, with Warne and Glenn McGrath up to their usual tricks. Starting the last day on just two runs, with three wickets down and two more soon to follow, all eyes were on Lara. Fresh from a double hundred in Jamaica, only he had the genius to perform the unthinkable. A 133-run partnership with Jimmy Adams allowed the rocking Kensington Oval to dream, although McGrath did his best to shatter it during an inspired spell of fiery fast bowling, which snuffed out three quick wickets before tea, including Nehemiah Perry first ball. Only the bowlers, Ambrose and Walsh, were left to give Lara support, with 60 runs still needed. In a torrid last session, Ambrose resisted and Lara attacked, slowly bringing the target within reach. McGrath hit Lara on the helmet, causing the two gladiators to square up, adding to the spice. Then Ambrose was caught with six runs still required. The big man had to drag himself from the crease, where he was replaced by Walsh, who, after all, had made the run chase possible in the first place. Somehow, Walsh survived an over from McGrath, who did not deserve to be on the losing side, before Lara crashed a final boundary to release the crowd from its fetters: victory by one wicket in the final session of the match. No, maybe this wasn't a cricketing calamity, but it is fun to reminisce!

England (6)

The year 2003 was one of contrasts for England as far as major World Cups were concerned, in particular against Australia. The final of the rugby tournament was sealed through a collective belief that their team was better than Australia's and that this was its time to shine. The squad knew how to win tight matches. For the cricketers, who had enjoyed precious little joy against the old enemy for over a decade, such conviction was lacking. Yet England needed to beat Australia in the pool stages to progress in the World Cup. Lose and they were going home. (The shameful fiasco over Zimbabwe, whereby England captain Nasser Hussain was left to take a political decision about boycotting the Robert Mugabe puppet show, had contributed to this perilous predicament.) The match started well for the underdogs, as Marcus Trescothick and Nick Knight smacked Glenn McGrath about, he who was a regular tormentor of English openers. Another, Shane Warne, was cooling his heels after testing positive for banned substances, so the door was open for a big score. But this day was to belong to Queensland journeyman Andrew Bichel. His medium-fast seamers nipped out three of England's best in just seven deliveries, before returning to take another four, as he mopped up the middle order for good measure. England limped to 204 in their 50 overs, as Bichel ended on fantasy figures of 7 for 20. Yet all that seemed in vain, as Andrew Caddick ripped through the Aussie top four, leaving the remaining batsmen gasping at 48 for 4. At 135 for 8, the match was all but wrapped up. With a bit of belief, England could win with ease. Bichel joined Michael Bevan, the arch-finisher, in what seemed a hopeless search for 70 runs. But the pair did not panic. The Australians had won the last eleven matches on the bounce, so no challenge seemed insurmountable. Bevan trusted his partner, dabbing the ball for singles, while Bichel chanced his arm. With every scrambled run and bludgeoned boundary, the nightmare scenario for England became ever more realistic. One wicket would have brought McGrath to the crease and with him almost certain victory, but somehow the Aussies managed to reach the point where they needed only 14 from twelve deliveries. Hussain turned to his young swing bowler, Jimmy Anderson (0 for 54), instead of Caddick (4 for 35) on a gut feeling. Anderson had swung out the Pakistanis earlier in the tournament, but that was in muggy conditions. Now the ball arrowed straight into the middle of Bichel's bat and off to the boundary it sped for a six and a four. Bichel had enjoyed a near perfect day, while England were on the next plane home.

Australia (10)

One of the primary charms of cricket to the player or viewer is its knack of retaining intrigue after the result has been decided. The outcome of Australia's tour of the West Indies in 2003 had long since been settled by the visitors, who had won the first three Tests in the four-match series with relative ease. The West Indies batsmen had sizzled on occasion, but they could not match the consistent weight of runs from Ricky Ponting and his crew. Every Test represents a clean start, especially with an ignominious whitewash at home to avoid, but the Antigua Test seemed to be going the same way as the others. Despite matching first innings scores, the Caribbean bowlers were once more put to the sword by Justin Langer (111) and Matthew Hayden (177) who bashed 242 for the first wicket. Even though Australia wobbled thereafter to 418 all out, the result looked safe, as no side had ever chased so daunting a target in the fourth innings. The first three wickets contributed little and when Brian Lara, for whom nothing was impossible in Antigua, fell with the score on 164 for 4, the West Indies needed something a bit special. It came from Guyana, in the form of Ramnaresh Sarwan (105) and Shivnarine Chanderpaul (104), who were not ready to give up hope when all seemed lost. Sarwan tore into the bowlers, clashing verbally with Glenn McGrath as emotions ran high. Chanderpaul dug in, putting away the bad ball and retaining his usual poise. But when they both fell to Brett Lee, Australia were again overwhelming favourites. But Vasbert Drakes and Omari Banks coolly knocked off the remaining runs to claim a famous victory. Leg-spinner Stuart MacGill had taken the important scalp of Lara, but no others as his 35 overs were taken for 149 runs, while the ARG again became a wreck yard for bowlers. For the West Indies, it was one more reason to party, having the proved that magic still lingers in the islands.

Australia (11)

For an achiever like Steve Waugh, who had led his team through countless challenges during his captaincy, India represented the final frontier. He had toured the republic on three occasions, always returning empty-handed, including a mauling in 1998 (*see* Chapter Three **Battered Bowlers**). Australia had not won there since 1969. If he could conquer the Indians in India in 2001 his trophy cabinet would be full. They had all but done it, too. An easy win in Mumbai had given the tourists a 1-0 lead in the three-Test series, taking their total of consecutive Test wins to a record-setting 16. In the second Test at Kolkata, after Waugh had made a hundred, India were on the verge of throwing in the towel, following on with four wickets down and still needing 42 runs to make the visitors bat again. One more wicket would bring the keeper to the crease and expose a lengthy tail. Yet VVS Laxman (281 runs) was starting to make batting look easy on a turning pitch. Rahul Dravid (180), demoted to number six and with a point to prove, was never likely to give his wicket away. The pair proceeded to bat out the whole of the fourth day, earning a lead of 383 runs with a partnership of 376. Shane Warne suffered most (one wicket for 152 runs at 4.47 runs per over), as Waugh bowled everyone but himself and keeper Adam Gilchrist. In the final session of the fifth day, India took seven wickets to win the match. Off-spinner Harbhajan Singh ended up with 13 wickets in Kolkata and then another 15 in Chennai to clinch the series. Waugh would never win a series in India, but his charity work on the subcontinent since then has secured the love of its people.

Australia (12)

Ordinarily, a captain would be confident of victory, having racked up over 550 runs in the first innings and watched the opposition wobble at 85 for 4 in reply. In the second Test of the Border-Gavaskar series at the Adelaide Oval in 2003, Australia had taken complete control of the match, aided by Ricky Ponting's sublime double hundred and contributions down the card. Andrew Bichel had then snapped up three key Indian wickets, before a running mix-up sent Saurav Ganguly back to the pavilion with a face like a skelped bahookie. But for captain Steve Waugh, there could be no cause for complacency, as the two batsmen in the middle were none other than Rahul Dravid and VVS Laxman, who had performed such an unlikely turnaround in Kolkata two years earlier. One of that great Australian team's qualities was that it scored its runs so quickly – 400 had been amassed in the first day alone – leaving oodles of time to collect 20 wickets. Shane Warne and Glenn McGrath would usually get first pick on the carcass, but both were missing in Adelaide. Therefore, India had as much time as they wanted to draw level with the home team's daunting target and then force a result. Dravid (233) and Laxman (148) again added over 300 runs together, before Ajit Agarkar bowled the spell of his career to take six wickets and dismiss the Aussies for 196 in the second innings. In a tense finale, Rahul Dravid again dug deep enough to score a gritty unbeaten 72, which took his team home by three wickets. For sheer entertainment, the match remains one of the very best. Whether Steve Waugh would have seen it that way is unlikely, but without the enterprising nature of Australia's batsmen in the first innings, the match would doubtless have petered out into a draw.

Zimbabwe

The first Test between the West Indies and Zimbabwe in Trinidad in 2000 could have fallen into a number of different chapters in this book, given that the scorecard was studded with ducks, pairs, collapses and first-ballers. Umpires made mistakes, fielders dropped catches and a batsman was fined for smashing the stumps with his bat. Yet this all added up to high drama on the last day. West Indies opener Adrian Griffith set the tone, lbw for a duck in the first over, before his team were knocked over for 187. Zimbabwe's reply started as badly as possible, as they lost one of their mainstays, Neil Johnson, to the first ball of the innings. But after Andy Flower had been reprieved by the umpire after gloving a ball to the keeper on zero, he played the knock of the match, an unbeaten 113 to give his team a valuable 49-run lead. Griffith again fell for none, soon followed by debutant Chris Gayle to the first ball of his second innings. The West Indies were all out for 147 – none of their batsmen reached fifty in either innings. Zimbabwe needed 99 to win. The pitch was bowler friendly, but even against the old warhorses Walsh and Ambrose, Zimbabwe should have reached three figures between them. Indeed, until then, they had never failed to reach 100 in their history. But they did not even get close, skittled out for 63. Top-scorer Grant Flower (26 from 126 balls) edged the sole boundary of the whole innings, before smashing his stumps with his bat after Ambrose had castled him with a shooter. Nobody else made double figures. Just a few years earlier, it would have been unthinkable that Zimbabwe could have beaten the West Indies in a Caribbean Test match. In 2000, it was hard to understand how they had not.

Bangladesh

Discounting the team of teenagers and club players selected by the West Indies during its contractual disputes in 2009, Bangladesh is yet to win a match against a major Test-playing nation. The young country has come mighty close on a handful of occasions, none more so than against Pakistan in the third Test at Multan in 2003. Indeed, with a mite more composure, the maiden victory would have come with some ease. A first innings lead of 106 gave cause for hope, although the batsmen fluffed their lines in the second, slipping to 154 all out. But 261 would take some chasing, especially when Younis Khan was run out for a duck and the hosts lost their fifth wicket for under a hundred. All hope rested on the shoulders of Inzamam-ul-Haq, but given he dwarfed all of the Bangladeshis, there was no room for complacency until he was dismissed. Inzi never looked like getting out, so attention turned to the tailenders. With 56 runs still needed, the eighth wicket fell, bringing fast bowler Umar Gul to the wicket. Lean, fast and excitable, Gul was the complete opposite of his lumbering bear of a partner. A run out was always on the cards. And it duly presented itself. The wicketkeeper, Khaled Mashud, was ready for it and threw down the stumps at the bowler's end. Gul was short of his ground. But there was only one problem. In his haste, the bowler, Mohammad Rafique, had already knocked the bails off with his hands. Not out. Gul was eventually run out, but not until the score was 257. Number eleven Yasir Ali managed to negotiate enough deliveries to get Inzi back on strike and the big man was soon being showered in rose petals. For Bangladesh, the wait goes on.

England (7)

If the cricketing gods do have a compassionate side to their characters, then they showed it in the final of the ICC Champions' Trophy in England at the end of the 2004 summer. Against all odds, the West Indies won the title, dedicating it to their countrymen who were struggling against deadly hurricanes in the Caribbean. For the losers, England, however, there was little consolation, as it was a match they let slip through their grasp with both bat and ball. The West Indies were not expected to get anywhere near the final in the first place, but they eased past South Africa and Pakistan on the back of serene fifties by Ramnaresh Sarwan. England, who had whitewashed Brian Lara's men earlier in that summer's Test series, were also unlikely finalists, having made light work of Sri Lanka and achieved a notable victory over Australia.

Riding on the crest of a wave, Michael Vaughan was heavily tipped to lift the trophy, especially when Marcus Trescothick raced to a hundred. But it was a lone hand, England eventually being dismissed for 217. This fightback by the bowlers seemed to have been in vain, as Chris Gayle, Sarwan and Lara fell cheaply. When Shivnarine Chanderpaul, so often the hero for the West Indies, was caught by Vaughan, the score was 147 for 8 and the fairy story had been ripped up. The late September sunshine faded, leaving Barbadians Courtney Browne and Ian Bradshaw to mount an astonishing rearguard action in the gloom against Darren Gough, Steve Harmison and Andrew Flintoff.

Either wicket would have surely won it for the hosts, but the two islanders were used to batting together in pressure situations. In a triumph of will over adversity, the pair played themselves in and then set about chipping away at the target. They made it with an over to spare, Bradshaw hammering the ball through the covers and sinking to one knee in celebration. Neither he nor Browne seemed that surprised. Only the most hard-hearted of Englishmen could have begrudged them so uplifting a moment.

Pakistan

But for the heroics of Mike Hussey, Peter Siddle and Nathan Hauritz, this entry would have been a black mark on Australian captain Ricky Ponting's resumé. Having won the toss, he chose to bat in bowler-friendly conditions in Sydney in the second Test against Pakistan at the start of 2010. Opening bowlers Mohammad Sami and Mohammad Asif accepted the gift and ran through the hosts for 127 by the end of day one. Ponting was caught first ball. Tails up, the touring batsmen then took control, swiping their way to 333 and a lead of 206. Surely there was no way back, even for the Australians, as the pitch was still doing plenty. Indeed, at 257 for 8 – effectively 51 for 8 – the match was lost.

But where there's life, there's hope, and with a batsmen like Mike Hussey still at the crease, Ponting knew he still had a faint chance. He had ignored recent cries for Hussey's retirement, exactly for situations like this. What sets Hussey apart, even from his own countrymen who are all taught to drink from the same well, is his dedication to doing the simple things perfectly. His conditioned mind told him to keep doing the basics and not throw his wicket away with an ambitious heave. This was not the Sir Ian Botham 'have a bit of fun' approach of Headingley. Good fortune came in the form of Peter Siddle, who played the innings of his life, scoring 38 runs off 117 balls in a partnership worth 123. Last man Doug Bollinger, who had been waiting with his pads on for three and a half hours, was out first ball and Australia had a defendable lead of 175.

Hussey had steadfastly made 134 not out. Defensive field settings and a raft of dropped catches – four by wicketkeeper Kamran Akmal – had helped his cause, but his was still one of the great rearguard knocks. He had given his bowlers a chance, however slim. Pakistan then set about losing the game again, when winning seemed the far easier option. Spinner Hauritz, by now a regular name on the team sheet, took a five-for, including a brilliant catch to dismiss linchpin Mohammad Yousuf, and Australia had won the match by a comfortable 36 runs.

Ponting's decision to bat first had been comprehensively vindicated!

Chapter Eight
Team Collapses

Sudden collective panic can ruin the best laid plans of captains and coaches, surrendering the advantage to the opposition in a flurry of wickets. Close matches and even whole Test series can be decided in a single session of mayhem, as every edge flies to a fielder and the umpire's finger waggles. When order resumes, the dazed batsmen are left blinking in confusion.

England

Over-confidence, no matter the state of the pitch, leaves the possessor open to calamity and that was exactly the fate for England's best cricketers in the first Ashes Test of the 1888 summer at Lord's. Some of the young Antipodean squad were there to make up the numbers according to the pundits, as Australia had lost many of the side which had carried them to victory throughout the decade. England, on the other hand, were at full strength, bristling to teach the colonials a lesson. In reality, the opposite happened, although a mere club side might have bowled England out cheaply on the soggy wicket, panned by *Wisden* at the time as 'a mudheap'.

Having won the toss, Australia batted first and limped to 116, before taking three quick wickets of their own by stumps on the first day. WG Grace was not out, holding the hopes of the nation in his mighty beard. But he did not add another run to his overnight tally, as England subsided to 53 all out, losing eight of their batsmen for a mere 21 runs. Only some lusty lower order hitting from number ten Johnny Briggs, who scored 17, avoided the follow on. Australia fared little better, losing their opening batsman Alec Bannerman (brother of Charles, the first Test centurion) for a duck, his second of the match. The next six quickly followed, leaving the visitors marooned on 18 for 7. A last-ditch knock of 20 not out by JJ Ferris, his highest in Tests, saved Australia's blushes, although he ran out of partners with the score at 60. England therefore needed 124 to win, which must have seemed like 424 on that pitch. Only Grace could have taken them close, but when he fell to Ferris with the score at 34, having blazed 24 runs himself, the die was cast. With the ace removed, the house of cards collapsed, and the overwhelming favourites had lost by 61 runs. This was not the ignominy of The Oval in 1882, due to the state of the pitch, but it was a bloody nose that nobody had foretold.

The rest of the series confirmed England's superiority, as they won each of the remaining two matches by an innings, although the toss proved vital in the third at

Old Trafford. Australia were shot down for 81 and then 70 on a potato field. The tourists' highest innings total was 116 in the series, while Bannerman, one of their top batsmen, ended with three ducks in six innings, scoring just 19 runs.

South Africa

England blooded eight players in the first Test of their South African tour in 1895-96, a three-day match played on matted pitches in Port Elizabeth. One of the debutants was the irrepressible CB Fry, who top-scored with 43 runs in a modest total of 185. Of the England bowlers used in the match, only George Lohmann (who opened the batting too) had any experience of Test cricket, but given that that included 74 wickets in just 14 matches against Australia, perhaps it was inevitable that a greenhorn South Africa side would struggle against his nagging accuracy. In the first innings, Lohmann took seven wickets, as the hosts were dismissed for just 93. England then set a target of 319, but that was soon forgotten as Lohmann set about dismantling South Africa for what was the lowest innings total to date: all out for 30 inside 19 five-ball overs. Lohmann returned figures of 8 for 7, mopping up the tail with a hat-trick. He had taken 15 wickets in the match for just 45 runs.

South Africa (2)

But these were not the best match figures by an Englishman against South Africa, not by a long chalk. In March 1889, this time in Cape Town in the second Test, slow left-armer Johnny Briggs, the first man to 100 Test wickets, had terrorised the hosts, pocketing 15 wickets for just 28 runs. (The match was never billed as a Test match, but it was accorded Test status later.) England had managed 292 runs in their first innings at a good rate for the time (3.55 runs per six-ball over). South Africa quickly folded in reply, all out for 47, despite the obduracy of opener Bernard Tancred, who carried his bat for 26 runs, the first to achieve that feat in Tests. Briggs took 7 for 17 in 19.1 overs. Following on, the calamity continued as Tancred's fellow opener, Albert Rose-Innes, was run out without facing. Briggs again took control with 8 wickets, this time for just 11 runs. South Africa were eventually all out for 43, staging a minor recovery from 20 for 7. Apart from the run out, all the other batsmen were bowled. Sadly, neither Briggs (epilepsy) nor George Lohmann (tuberculosis) lived to see their fortieth birthdays.

South Africa (3)

The visiting South Africans had endured a torrid tour of Australia in 1931-32, due in no small measure to the brilliance of Sir Don Bradman, who scored a hundred in each of the first four Tests, including two doubles, as he amassed 806 runs in just five innings at an average of over 200. By the fifth Test in Melbourne, the South

Africans would have been delighted to see Bradman hobble off before having the opportunity to bat. But it was cold comfort, given they had just been skittled for 36 runs in 23 overs. Medium pacer Bert Ironmonger was wrecker-in-chief, taking five wickets for only six runs. The Australians hardly filled their boots either, though, managing just 153, having lost captain Bill Woodfull first ball of the innings. Ordinarily, the Victorian's series total of 421 at an average of 70 would have been impressive, but not when compared with Bradman's. Stan McCabe also fell first ball, but the lead of 128 was still useful. It proved more than enough, as once again Ironmonger ran through the guests, taking 6 for 18, and they were all out for 45. Leg spinner Clarrie Grimmett, who had already taken 33 wickets in the series, was not needed to bowl in the match. South African opener Jim Christy followed up Woodfull's diamond with one of his own, while Quintin McMillan added a duck to his earlier first-baller. Although by far the weaker side, fate had played South Africa an unfair hand. Heavy rain washed out the second day and the hot sunshine that replaced it on the third day made the pitch treacherous. In playing time, it remains the shortest Test ever, all over in 656 balls, inside six hours, with barely a contribution from Australia's four top performers in the series. The Springbok match total of 81 is still the lowest aggregate for any team in Test match history.

South Africa (4)

It is perhaps a trifle harsh to highlight any South African weaknesses in their formative years, as the republic did not have the same structure as England or Australia, often assembling elevens from whoever was available at the time. The touring side of 1924, for example, was even forced to scour local league sides prior to the match in a bid to find bowlers who had experience of English conditions. Yet the batsmen would still have been ashamed of their efforts in the first Test at Edgbaston, dismissed for just 30 inside 13 overs, by the new ball pairing of Arthur Gilligan (6 for 7) and Maurice Tate (4 for 12). Nobody reached double figures. If extras had not top scored with eleven, it could have been so much worse. In the second innings, however, the red-faced batsmen made some atonement, scoring 390, as Rhodesian Bob Catterall stroked a century. But it was not enough to avoid an innings defeat.

Australia

Australia's lowest innings score in Test history ultimately proved irrelevant. The first Ashes Test at Edgbaston in 1902 had started well for the visitors, despite the fact that they had lost the toss and been put out to field on a flat deck. CB Fry had perished for a duck, after which captain Archie MacLaren was run out in a mix up with the exceptional stroke-player Ranjitsinhji. MacLaren made it clear who he felt was at fault, making the honourable Indian prince sufficiently upset to have his castle rocked soon afterwards. England had duly lost their three best batsmen for just 35 runs. But a sequence of dropped chances allowed a fight-back, led by a hundred from Johnny Tyldesley and an unbroken ninth wicket stand of 80 runs between Bill Lockwood and Wilfred Rhodes. MacLaren declared, inviting the Australians to face his Yorkshire duo of Rhodes and George Hirst in poor light, who duly ran through them in an hour and a half for just 36 runs. Only Victor Trumper showed resilience, surviving 70 minutes to score half the total. Three of the Aussies were out first ball and nobody else made it past five. The next day, thousands flocked to the ground, hoping to see history repeat itself, but heavy rain had turned the wicket into a paddy field. Match drawn. Australia went on to win the series 2-1.

New Zealand

Although being all out for 26 is still the lowest total for an innings in Tests, it is not the worst *collapse* for New Zealand. That ignominy arrived in 1946 in Wellington, when the team was utterly outplayed by an Australian outfit that was blooding some its premier stars of the future, such as Keith Miller and Ray Lindwall. Strangely, this was the first time the trans-Tasman neighbours had met in the Test arena. Neither country had played much cricket during the war and the match was to be a mutual celebration of the important role played by ANZAC soldiers. It probably ought to have been cancelled due to poor weather, but such was the throng of spectators willing to watch that the captains agreed to make the best of it. Would that happen nowadays? Australia were missing Don Bradman through injury, but they were still a far stronger side. New Zealand's captain, Walter Hadlee, father of Richard, won the toss, which he immediately regretted. The decision to bat first backfired, as Bill 'Tiger' O'Reilly ripped New Zealand out for just 42 runs. Five wickets fell with the score on 37, as the last eight wickets cost only five runs. The Kiwi batsmen were back out in the middle by lunch on the second day, and in the pavilion by tea, 54 all out, as they crumbled once more like a wet biscuit. This time, the last seven wickets fell for 18 runs.

England (2)

English cricket was at a low ebb by the time of the fifth Test at The Oval in 1948. Don Bradman's Invincibles had already won back the Ashes in dramatic fashion in the fourth Test (*see* Chapter Four **Costly Drops**) and had humbled nearly every county on their astounding cavalcade through the provinces. Now back in the capital for the finale, England were desperate to send Australia home with something to think about. But confidence was low and Ray Lindwall needed no second invitation. After such a long tour, the Aussie fast bowler had one last effort in him and he did not waste it, combining with his fellow new-ball assassin, Keith Miller, to rock the hosts' top order before lunch on a soggy pitch. But it was Lindwall's spell after lunch that cooked England's scrawny goose. Eight overs, four maidens, eight runs and five wickets. The fielders clutched every half chance, as England wilted to a total of 52 runs. Thirty of those were scored by Len Hutton, the only batsman to show any semblance of timing, before he was last man out. The pitch made for uncomfortable batting, no doubt, but was it a 52-all-out track? The Australian openers, Sid Barnes and Arthur Morris, did not think so, sharing a stand of 117, as Morris went on to accumulate 196. Aside from Bradman's famous duck and Eric Hollies's five wickets, the home team had little to celebrate, losing by an innings and 149 runs in a little over three days. The rout was complete.

Australia (2)

In a tight Test series, filled with punch and counter-punch, the teams will cancel each other out for most of the contest. Sadly, if there is to be a winner, then the victory will most likely stem from a single horror session from the opposition batsmen. Good bowling, fine catches, uneven bounce and dodgy umpiring can all play their part in a collapse; but ultimately the burden of responsibility remains on the shoulders of the batsmen.

The relatively low-scoring Ashes series of 1954-55 was largely a triumph for ball over bat, with only four innings passing 300 in the six matches. England were always able to scrap to a competitive total on the back of a stand-out performer such as Colin Cowdrey, Peter May, Trevor Bailey or Len Hutton. But the rug was pulled from under the Aussies' feet at vital moments of the series. Their chief tormentor was Frank 'Typhoon' Tyson, who bowled at speeds rarely witnessed on a cricket pitch. Coupled with unpredictable bounce and the support of Brian Statham, any Australian failure was largely understandable. England had lost the first Test by an innings and 154 runs in Brisbane, with Tyson taking just one wicket for 160 and leaking more than four runs an over. But after some helpful advice from the gentlemanly Keith Miller, Tyson shortened his run up to increase his control, whilst losing none of his pace. Another influential moment for Tyson came as he was batting in the first innings of the second Test in Sydney: Aussie quick Ray Lindwall caught him with a bumper on the back of the head. The fired-up Englishman reacted by taking 10 wickets in that match and then a whirlwind 7 for 27 in the final innings of the third Test at the MCG, terrorising Australia on a demon pitch and reducing them to 111 all out.

Six more wickets followed for Tyson in the next Test in Adelaide, as Australia again slipped to a single Nelson in their second innings. On all three occasions, the home side had had a good chance of winning the match. Instead, England were 3-1 up and the urn was safely stowed in the hold. The visitors had won a series down under for the first time since Bodyline.

New Zealand (2)

The second Test match between New Zealand and England played in March 1955 at Eden Park in Auckland, looked destined to become a tense affair once Len Hutton's touring team had taken a slender lead of 46 runs after the first innings. The uncovered pitch was doing a bit, to say the least, but it was unthinkable that England would not have to bat again. Northamptonshire fast bowler Frank Tyson had just enjoyed a sublime tour of Australia, where he had unsettled batsmen who were better than those in the Kiwi line-up. Alongside fellow quick Brian Statham, the new ball proved too slippery on the uneven surface for the top order batters, three of whom were back in the shed with the score at 9 runs. Only the gifted left-hander Bert Sutcliffe was showing any form of stickability, reaching double figures. But Hutton soon turned to his spinner Johnny Wardle, who tempted Sutcliffe into an ill-judged slog with his slow left-arm chinaman. Quick off-spinner Bob Applegate then rattled through the rest of the card, twice getting batsmen on consecutive deliveries. He ended with figures of 4 for 7 from his six overs, including the wicket of wicketkeeper Ian Colquhoun for the second time in the match to complete a king pair for the gloveman. New Zealand were eventually all out for 26 runs in 27 overs, without a single boundary scored, which remains the lowest Test innings score on record.

India

India's batting nadir in 1974 was played out at the home of cricket in conditions that could not have been further removed from those of the sub-continent. Mike Denness's England had scored a glut of runs in the first innings, winning the toss and making the most of a friendly Lord's surface in the second Test of the three-match series. Dennis Amiss and John Edrich had taken the score to 334 for just the wicket of debutant David Lloyd (46 runs), who was keeping Geoff Boycott out of the side. Both set batsmen fell early the next morning, but Denness and Tony Greig soon added centuries of their own, contributing to a total of 629 all out. Indian spinner Bishan Singh Bedi conceded 224 runs in his 64 overs, although he was rewarded with six wickets. In reply, India were all out for 302, despite a fine 86 by Farokh Engineer, who had been keeping wicket for the last two days. Unfortunately for the visitors, the last wicket fell just before the close of play on the third day, allowing the English bowlers an evening's rest before enforcing the follow-on. As it happened, only two bowlers were needed. The morning was damp, cold and overcast – just perfect for swing exponents Geoff Arnold and Chris Old. The Indian batsmen pawed at thin air, occasionally nicking the odd delivery through to Alan Knott behind the stumps. Only Eknath Solkar left with his head held high, cracking an unbeaten 18 from just 17 balls, with two fours and a six. He had seen the writing on the wall. Soon, poor old Bedi was bowled first ball and India were all out for 42.

The Queen…almost

The organisers of the Centenary Test between Australia and England in March 1977 were nearly left with pink faces, as both teams collapsed to low totals on the first and second day. HM The Queen was due to arrive on the third day, but with wickets falling in clusters, there was a real risk of her turning up to find the game in its death throes. Hundreds of dignitaries, including all those who had ever played in Ashes series, were watching a damp squib at the MCG, as the Aussies had been bundled out for 138 and England capitulated for just 95 runs. Australia were already three down by the start of the third day, but happily Rod Marsh, ever the man for the big occasion, scored a breezy hundred, the first by any Australian wicketkeeper in Tests. David Hookes slapped Tony Greig for five fours in an over (*see* Chapter Three **Battered Bowlers**), before Derek Randall flew the flag for England, scoring a dazzling 174. Dennis Lillee finished with eleven wickets to help Australia win a royally exciting encounter.

Australia (3)

Ian Botham's heroics at Headingley in 1981 (*see* Chapter Seven **From the Jaws of Victory**) appeared to be sinking down the plughole, as Australia steamed towards victory in the fourth Test at Edgbaston. Terry Alderman and then Ray Bright had bowled the visitors into a position of strength, both taking five-fors. The pitch had confounded everyone, including England's insightful captain Mike Brearley, who chose to bat first. Australia struggled too in the first innings – indeed nobody made a fifty in the match – but they were fully expected to knock off the 151 runs needed to take a 2-1 lead in the series. But even with Australia cruising at 87 for 3, with two set batsmen at the crease, the home team had reason to believe. After all, Australia had crumbled from 56 for 1 to 111 all out in pursuit of 130 at Headingley. Bob Willis had been the destroyer that day, but on a dry pitch at Edgbaston, spin bowler John Emburey appeared the most likely hero. His rearguard 37 runs in the second innings had ensured the target would at least test the opposition. And it was Emburey who took the crucial wickets of Graham Yallop (30), and Allan Border (40) with a ripper, which opened the door for Botham to charge through. Brearley had been tempted to call on a second spinner, Peter Willey, but followed his hunch on Botham. The strong Somerset all-rounder was reluctant at first, but soon he was galloping in as the wickets tumbled. In a flash, Australia were all out for 121. Botham had taken 5 for 1, ending with figures of 5 for 11. The fifth Test at Old Trafford delivered Botham a golden duck, a hundred, four catches, five wickets and a win, as he took his third consecutive man of the match award, and England secured the series.

England (3)

England Test wins over Australia in the 1990s proved hard to come by, but on the

1990-91 tour down under, the mental disintegration had yet to take hold. The visitors were doing their best to undermine themselves on that tour, as internal rifts threatened to spill over into public spectacle. All the same, defeat on the pitch was not a pre-ordained certainty. The first Test at the 'Gabba had turned out to be a comfortable 10-wicket win for the hosts, although England had gained the upper hand after the first innings. Ashes specialist Terry Alderman soon put paid to any hopes of victory, taking six wickets as the visitors subsided to 114 all out. In the second Test at the MCG, Graham Gooch returned from injury and wild cat spinner Phil Tufnell was handed a debut. Again, England put themselves in a position to win the match, on the back of a David Gower hundred and two fifties by Wayne Larkin. Angus Fraser doggedly bowled his side into a lead and at 103 for 1 after tea on the fourth day, it seemed that only one team could win. But then the wings fell off the Tiger Moth. Rangy left-arm Bruce Reid was the destroyer, snapping up seven cheap England wickets as nine fell for 47 runs. Gower failed to score and the final 6 wickets cost all of 3 runs. Suddenly, Australia had over a day to score 197, which they reached with two wickets down. Tufnell finished his debut without a run, catch or wicket, although he had several stone-cold appeals turned down by Aussie umpire Peter McConnell. From 2-0 down in the series, England never recovered. The sequence of domination had been initiated.

West Indies

Reaching the final of the 1983 World Cup at Lord's was enough for most Indian fans, whose team was starting to show signs of the superpower India would become. At odds of 66-1 at the start of the tournament, few backed them to win. They had beaten the mighty West Indies in the first match of the tournament, the Caribbean players' first defeat in three cups, but that was surely an aberration. After all, the bowling attack of Garner, Holding, Roberts and Marshall, combined with the batting power of Richards, Greenidge, Haynes, Gomes and Lloyd, complete with Dujon behind the stumps, would be far too strong in the final. Even India's win over the hosts, England, in the semi-finals was deemed a one-off (ending in comedy as losing captain Bob Willis stacked all his fielders on one side of the wicket so that they could reach the pavilion before the pitch invasion). The final certainly started predictably, as the pace quartet, led by Roberts, bowled India out for 183. The total looked to be 50 runs short as Richards took control, but a match-winning catch by Kapil Dev over his shoulder at midwicket removed the Antiguan for 33. India's medium pacers then ran rings round the West Indies middle order, reducing them to 76 for 6. It was a telling blow of the axe – eventually the mighty oak was felled for just 140. All India went wild as Kapil Dev lifted the trophy and belief flooded through its many millions of cricketers. The touchpaper had been lit. Who knows how much longer the transformation would have taken if that catch had been dropped?

West Indies (2)

Calypso Collapso has been all too regular in the last decade, but in the 1980s, you could count the small totals on one hand. The formidable Caribbean team may have blasted the opposition away with its fast bowlers, but it was also unfortunate for the rest of world cricket that the only batting line-up who could have regularly stood up to those bowlers, just happened to be in the same team. When the bowlers you face in the nets are better than the ones you will face in the middle, it must give you an edge! However, they could not practise against the devilry of Abdul Qadir on a Faisalabad dust bowl.

In the first Test of the 1986 tour of Pakistan, the seamers had held sway for the first three days. Malcolm Marshall terrorised the home batsmen, claiming Rameez Raja for a first baller and breaking the arm of Saleem Malik. Only a rearguard fifty from Imran Khan avoided a score much lower than 159. The West Indies patiently gathered a first innings lead, despite the illness of captain Viv Richards and goldies for both Jeff Dujon and Patrick Patterson. The match seemed to be going the way of the visitors, who had lost only four matches in the last ten years, as their bowlers nipped out two quick wickets before stumps on the second day. But nightwatchman Saleem Yousuf, who was on a king pair, bravely dropped anchor with the middle order, scoring his first Test fifty. Wasim Akram, buoyed by his six wickets in the first innings, then hammered 66, adding a gritty 32 runs for the tenth wicket with Saleem Malik batting in an arm cast. The target of 240 would take some chasing, but it was quickly academic as Imran Khan removed Greenidge and Haynes, freeing Abdul Qadir to weave a magic spell over the middle order. Richards was caught second ball, before Dujon completed his pair, although he survived the first ball to avoid the dreaded 'king'. Pakistan's close fielders pounced on every opportunity, as Qadir's leggies and googlies earned him 6 for 16 in just nine overs. The best of the West had been humbled for 53 runs. Piqued, Viv's men cruised to an innings victory in the next Test in Lahore, ripping out the opposition for just 77 runs in the second innings.

England (4)

England's lowest total in Tests, 45 all out, made in Sydney in 1887, was at least in a winning cause, so perhaps it does not count as an utter calamity, although it must have felt like one at the time (*see* Chapter Seven **From the Jaws of Victory**). Their next worst, 46 all out against the West Indies in Trinidad in 1994, did not have the same happy ending. Blown away inside 20 overs by the rapid aggression of Curtly Ambrose and Courtney Walsh, any aspiration of winning the match quickly evaporated. Perhaps most galling for Michael Atherton's unfancied tourists was that it was a match that they ought to have won, having earned a lead of 76 runs after the first innings. The West Indies struggled to wipe out the deficit and could have been shot

Forgotten something?

out for far less than the 269 they managed on a spicy surface. Still, a total of 194 to win the match and square the series was not beyond England. Unfortunately, Ambrose stood in their way. The match was nearing the end of the fourth day, when he took the new ball. In the era of rest days, the tall Antiguan was fully refreshed and he flew at the English batsmen, knowing he could return the next morning after another break. Atherton, so often the first and strongest line of defence, faced the first ball. As it rocketed into his front pad, the whole crowd rose in appeal. The umpire obliged. That wicket sparked a furious spell of pace and aggression, cheered on by a knowledgeable crowd who sensed they were watching something special. Ambrose took six wickets as England were undone. A batting line-up far stronger than England's would have struggled to contain Ambrose that evening.

West Indies (3)

For any devotee of West Indian cricket, the 14th of March 2004 was a day of great sadness. There had been several clear indications that the glory era of Caribbean cricket had been consigned to the history books. Being bowled out for 47 by England in the first Test at Jamaica in just 25 overs not only highlighted the demise, but it confirmed that the glory days would be a long time coming back. The morning of the fourth day began with the home batsmen confident of building a telling lead on a pitch that certainly offered bounce, but was hardly a terror track. Both teams had fought hard to reach scores of over 300 and the draw looked the most likely result. On reflection, the West Indies would have been the more frustrated of the two, spilling several chances and leaking 60 extras, the highest amount when extras have top-scored in a Test innings. In just seven furious overs, the match, and ultimately the series, was decided. There was nothing fancy in it: Steve Harmison and Matthew Hoggard just kept putting the ball in the right place. Nicks flew to hand, decisions went their way and batsmen contributed to their own undoing. The home team's powerhouse middle order of Ramnaresh Sarwan (who bagged a pair in the match), Shivnarine Chanderpaul and Brian Lara added not a single run between them. At 21 for 5, the game was up. The sole intrigue was whether England could finish them off for less than the 46 run total of 1994. Harmison had a good run at it, taking 7 for 12, the best seven-for by any bowler in the modern era. But plucky wicketkeeper Ridley Jacobs and the tailenders edged the score to 47. The match was over by lunch.

West Indies (4)

The Jamaican collapse had fallen short of the West Indies' previous low mark, 51 all out, against Australia in the first Test at Port-of-Spain in 1999. In Steve Waugh's first match as Aussie skipper, he did well to win the toss and bat on a sticky pitch that demanded application. The total of 269, as it turned out, was a useful score, although the top order were bailed out by a tenth wicket partnership of 66 between fast bowlers Glenn McGrath and Jason Gillespie. The West Indies seemed to be making fair progress, as local Trinidadians Brian Lara and Dave Joseph on debut added 88 for the third wicket. But when Lara fell, brilliantly run out by Justin Langer at short leg, the sandcastle collapsed for a miserable 18 runs. Set a daunting 364 to win, the crowd expected their men to dig in, but they were sorely disappointed. McGrath and Gillespie bowled unchanged for 20 overs and the West Indies shipped their wickets in doleful succession. Again, it would have been much worse – perhaps eclipsing the New Zealand total of 26 – had Ridley Jacobs not cracked 19. Gillespie scooped four wickets, denied the chance of his own five-for when local favourite Merv Dillon was comically run out without facing. McGrath had taken his first ten-wicket haul in Tests, as the match raised eleven ducks. The West Indies lost their last 17 wickets for only 69 runs. The Trinidadian crowd called for Lara's head and he reacted with a run spree that soon had them dancing in the stands once more.

England (5)

Revenge is a dish best served with hot pepper sauce. In 2004, Harmison's Shaker-in-

Jamaica dismissed the home team for just 47 runs. Five years later, the West Indies spied a chance for revenge in the third innings of the first Test match against England, again at Sabina Park in Kingston. England reached 318 in the first innings, having won the toss. Kingpin Kevin Pietersen scored a carefree 97 before accepting the challenge to hit over the top and bring up his century in style. While other batsmen might have simply made three singles before going on to score a double hundred, KP went for the big yahoo and was caught. In reply, the West Indian batsmen had earned a useful lead of 74 runs. The next critical moment came just before lunch on the fourth day, when the draw still seemed the most likely outcome. Instead of blocking the last two balls before lunch, England number three Ian Bell wafted at a wide ball from the bean-pole spinner Sulieman Benn, edging through to the wicketkeeper. The Windies spied an opening. Whatever fast bowler Jerome Taylor had had for lunch, it fired him up. A fast out-swinger knocked Pietersen's off peg out of the ground; Strauss edged through to the keeper; Collingwood inside-edged and Prior missed a slower ball. Benn had Broad caught at short leg for a duck and just 15 overs after lunch, England were 26 for 7. Only an aggressive 24 from Andrew Flintoff saved his team from making a higher entry on the list. Harmison was the last man out, for a duck, as England subsided for 51. The ghost of 2004 had been exorcised.

India (2)

India had edged out Pakistan in a highly charged quarter-final in the 1996 World Cup and were strong favourites to lift the cup for the second time. However, defeating a plucky Sri Lanka side, filled with clean hitters and canny bowlers, was never likely to be a foregone conclusion. Therefore, Indian skipper Mohammad Azharuddin's decision to bowl first at Eden Gardens in Kolkota – where batting second under lights was a notoriously tricky proposition – indicated over-confidence. Sri Lanka recovered from a poor start to make 251, propelled by a dreamy knock from Aravinda de Silva, who stroked 66 runs from 47 balls. The Indian hero of the quarter-final had been seamer Venkatesh Prasad, who had taken three top order wickets when Pakistan were looking ominous. Against Sri Lanka, however, Prasad was milked for 50 runs off only eight overs, before part-timers finished his allocation. Sachin Tendulkar threatened to make easy work of the chase, cracking a breezy 65 of his own to reach 98 for 1. But when he was sensationally stumped, the wheels came off the Indian gurney. The captain followed for a duck, kick-starting a procession of wickets, which left the home team in tatters at 120 for 8. Their supporters vented their fury by setting fire to sections of the stadium and littering the field with bottles and fruit. Eventually the match was restarted, but another riot persuaded the match referee, Clive Lloyd, to award the match to Sri Lanka. Not out batsman Vinod Kambli was left in the middle, crying tears of sadness and shame, a spectacle that captured the sentiments of a nation.

West Indies (5)

While India were capitulating in Kolkata, the West Indies were busy butchering a simple chance of reaching the final. Right up until the final dramatic conclusion to the semi-final, the match was only going to end one way: a famous West Indies win. Australia had done well to reach 207 for 8 in their innings, having faltered to 15 for 4, losing the Waugh twins, Ricky Ponting and Mark Taylor in the process. But it never looked enough as Shivnarine Chanderpaul combined with first Brian Lara and then Richie Richardson to reach 165 for 2. Even when a cramping Shiv was out for 80 in the 41st over, a calm approach would have taken his side home. But the Windies hit the panic button. Their decision to send in two big hitters backfired, when their immediate demise only fed the butterflies of the incomers. Poor Keith Arthurton continued his shocking tournament with another duck (*see* Chapter Six **Duck Hunters**), as Shane Warne suddenly started to look unplayable. Richardson watched from the other end in horror as one batsman after another gifted his wicket. Yet, he still had destiny in his capable hands. Ten runs were needed off the last over, bowled by Damien Fleming, with two wickets left. Richardson hit the first ball for four, but then had a brain fade of his own. He risked a dicey single, which would have brought Curtly Ambrose onto strike, but his fellow Antiguan was run out inches short of his ground. Courtney Walsh missed a straight one first ball and it was all over. For Richardson, the match was a sad way to end a fabulous career. The West Indies had done everything but pass the winning post.

West Indies (6)

The path of the 2000 Test series between England and the West Indies appeared to be going the way of the previous twenty years. The tourists had won a comprehensive victory in the first match at Edgbaston, before securing a healthy first innings lead at Lord's, as England were shot out by Walsh and Ambrose for 134. The Windies were eyeing up a quick-fire 200 to put the game beyond reach of England, but instead their batsmen formed a disorderly queue between the pavilion and the pitch. Darren Gough started the collapse by taking a steepling catch at third man to dismiss Sherwin Campbell, who had made 82 in the first innings. If that had been spilled, the series could have ended so differently. But it stuck and the West Indies were soon out for a barely believable 54. England had an unexpected sniff of victory, although it needed a gutsy rearguard effort from Dominic Cork (33 not out) to reach the 191 target after Walsh and Ambrose had almost spared the blushes of the batsmen. The loss was telling, as it gave England a belief that had been missing for decades. The balance of power between the nations had shifted. At Headingley, in the fourth Test, the West Indies again collapsed, this time for 61 alout, as Andy Caddick took four wickets in an over. The match was decided inside two days.

Australia (4)

Before the start of the fourth Test at the MCG, the Ashes had already been retained by Australia on the 1998-99 tour down under, but Alec Stewart's Englishmen still had an opportunity to tie the series with a stirring comeback. Comfortable wins for the hosts in the previous two Tests hinted otherwise and England's first innings total of 270 looked light, despite a battling hundred from Stewart. Steve Waugh's unbeaten 122 guided Australia to a 70-run lead, before England again stuttered towards 244. Michael Atherton, so often the rock for his side, bagged a pair, as his chronic back disorder deprived him of any elasticity – hardly the best condition for facing his nemesis, Glenn McGrath, who dismissed him regularly enough anyway. The target of 175 ought not to have tested the home side too sternly and at 130 for 3, with both Waughs looking comfortable, the Barmy Army's trumpeter sounded a retreat. England fast bowler Dean Headley did not listen. Grandson of the late, great West Indian batsman George Headley and son of another Test player, Ron Headley, Dean was blue-blooded in cricketing terms. This MCG Test provided his finest hour, where he showed great heart, stamina and skill in taking six wickets, including a rash of four wickets for four runs. Even then, the indomitable Steve Waugh (30 not out) nearly took his side home, but Darren Gough yorked the tailenders to secure an unlikely win by twelve runs. Australia had lost seven wickets for 32 runs.

A second innings collapse by England in the fifth Test at Sydney snuffed out any hopes of drawing the series. Headley took another eight wickets in that match, but played only two more Tests for England, through a mixture of injury and selector myopia. He finished his career with a strike rate of 50.4, which compares favourably with the finest bowlers of all time.

Pakistan

Snookered by Pakistan in the first Test in Chennai, during the two-match series of 1999, India knew that anything less than victory in the second Test at Delhi would result in national disgrace. Having set their neighbours an unlikely 420 runs to win on a wearing pitch, butterflies were stirred by an aggressive opening partnership of 101 between the dangerous strokeplayers, Saeed Anwar and Shahid Afridi. Only once Anil Kumble had removed Afridi and then Ijaz Ahmed to the next ball, did local heart-rates start to dip. They had picked up again though once Kumble had seen off the first six batsmen, with the score at 128. Victory was assured, but could Kumble emulate Laker by snaring all 10? Eventually, it came down to a stare-off with Pakistani all-rounder Wasim Akram, who was proudly blocking off Kumble, so that number eleven Waqar Younis would not have to face. Pace bowler Javagal Srinath ensured that no wicket fell at his end, creating an exciting game within a game at the other. The result was beyond question, but would Kumble have the energy, having bowled straight through for almost two sessions, to pick up Wasim? Finally, a chance was offered to VVS Laxman and the job was done. Pakistan had lost 10 wickets for 106 runs to one man.

New Zealand (3)

New Zealand were at it again in 2001, although this time was all the more shocking, as the batsmen were expected to save the match and even threaten the target of 431 to win in the fourth innings. Yes, it would have set a new world record, but on a flat Auckland pitch, which had just yielded 240 runs in the match to Younis Khan, the batsmen ought to have felt confident. Without Wasim Akram and Shoaib Akhtar, Pakistan lacked spark on a slow drop-in paddock. The new ball came and went, and at the end of the fourth day, the score was 105 for 1, with the only wicket falling to a run out. Game on. But what happened next was not in the script. The short version of the story is that New Zealand were all out for 131. The long version is not much longer. Eight wickets fell for 10 runs. The last five batsmen all failed to score. Mohammad Sami on debut was chief mayhem maker, bowling a seven-over spell of 5 wickets for 6 runs.

Procession of wickets

Pakistan (2)

After the excitement of the semi-finals, the final of the 1999 World Cup in England was the dampest of squibs. For the victors Australia, whose fingernails were down to the quick after two humdingers against South Africa (*see* Chapter Fifteen **Nearly Men**), a stress-free conclusion was welcome. Pakistan, despite being at the top of their form coming into the match, did not stand a chance, such was the level of the opposition. Having won the toss, Wasim Akram chose to bat, but Mark Waugh in the slips soon set the tone for the match, leaping to pouch a half-chance from opener Wajahatullah Wasti. The other opener, Saeed Anwar, had stroked back-to-back hundreds to beat first Zimbabwe and then New Zealand in the semi-finals, so when he unluckily inside-edged a ball on to his stumps, the tide had already turned. Due to the Lord's ticketing policy, the ground was filled with suited corporates, rather than the horn-blowing, flag-waving fans, who were locked outside. The Pakistani batsmen were on their own, as Shane Warne spun his web, earning four wickets, while his fielders plucked the ball from the air. Inzamam-ul-Haq received a rough decision which didn't help, but few batting line-ups would have lived with Australia that morning. Adam Gilchrist, Mark Waugh and Ricky Ponting then tore into the crestfallen bowlers, knocking off the requisite 133 in just 20 overs. The match had lasted less than 60 overs, the first of three consecutive one-sided finals won by Australia.

Pakistan (3)

Played out at Sharjah in 2002, this match proved to be an unmitigated disaster for Pakistani Test cricket and set them back several years. In the second Test against Steve Waugh's Australian side at the peak of its powers, a loss by this young side would have been understandable, but the manner of the hiding crushed their faithful fans. The first Test in Colombo had been full of promise, as they fell just 41 runs short of a famous victory. Australia had endured a collapse of their own in the second innings at Colombo, where Shoaib Akhtar bowled three overs of late-swinging yorkers at speeds of near 100mph, removing Ricky Ponting and both Waughs in one over, before adding Gilchrist and Warne to his tally. But Australia had enough street-fighting snarl to win the match and they soon twisted the knife at Sharjah, ejecting both openers for ducks. Pakistan had chosen to bat first, an ill-judged decision it seemed, as the last wicket fell for only 59 runs, their lowest score in Tests. In reply, the Waugh twins again struggled, Mark making two and Steve falling first ball, but Matthew Hayden crafted a patient hundred in sweltering heat, as Pakistan were left to stare down the barrel of a 251-run deficit. They never came close, trumping even their earlier demise, to surrender for just 53 runs and losing the match inside two days. Hayden himself had scored more than their two innings combined.

Zimbabwe

In the early 2000s, the Sri Lankan bowlers were like canny pole-vaulters, breaking their own world records just a little at a time. In 2001, left-arm seamer Chaminda Vaas became the only bowler to take eight wickets in an ODI, trapping opener Dion Ebrahim for a diamond duck, as Zimbabwe were dismissed for 38 in Colombo. Sri Lanka's batsmen scored the winning runs in 26 balls, the fastest victory in an ODI. Vaas was in the wickets again in the 2003 World Cup, this time at Paarl against Canada, who were scattered for 35, as nobody made double figures. The chase lasted fully 28 balls this time. But the Zimbabweans were not to be outdone, crashing to 35 themselves inside 20 overs at Harare in 2004. Ebrahim top-scored this time, albeit with only seven runs. Skipper Tatenda Taibu fell first ball. Sri Lanka dallied to victory in 56 balls. In the three tonkings, Vaas scooped 15 wickets for only 45 runs.

Zimbabwe (2)

Even at full strength, Zimbabwe was always the slightly weaker brother of South Africa. After the team had been shorn of its better players by Robert Mugabe's meddling, the gulf widened beyond a fair contest. On 4 March 2005, Zimbabwe's young team suffered one of the most humiliating days in Test history, after choosing to bat first on a flat Newlands pitch in Cape Town. Not long after lunch, all 10 wickets had fallen for 54 runs, as only one batsman reached double figures. By the end of play that day, South Africa had bullied their way to 340 for 3, including the fastest ever fifty in Tests by Jacques Kallis: 24 balls with five sixes struck. All three wickets were gifted to teenager Graeme Cremer, although his nine overs disappeared for 86 runs. South Africa skipper Graeme Smith felt genuine pity for the Zimbabweans, declaring overnight, as the result had long been decided. The next Test was won by an innings too. The neighbours have not played a Test series since.

South Africa (5)

India remains the final frontier for touring captains to conquer, as the conditions are so much in favour of the home team. Turning pitches, howling crowds, the threat of sickness and the occasional one-eyed umpire have conspired to send many of the best Test teams away to lick their wounds. Modern tour parties are more prepared for the experience, especially with the increase in the number of tournaments on the sub-continent. However, any victory, especially in Tests, remains a commendable entry on a skipper's CV. South African leader Graeme Smith has achieved plenty for his country in his long stint in charge, proving wrong all those critics who believed he was given the job too young at 22 years old.

Smith therefore had grounds for optimism, as his country began a two-Test tour of India in 2009-10. The first Test in Nagpur was utterly one-sided, as the visitors piled on 558 runs on the back of Hashim Amla's unbeaten 253 and Jacques Kallis's 175, before Dale Steyn helped bowl out the Indians twice, taking 10 wickets. India had suffered an unlikely collapse in the first innings, slipping from 192 for 3 to 233 all out on a batsman's pitch.

In the second Test at the Eden Gardens in Kolkata, history appeared to be repeating itself. Amla reached another hundred, alongside debutant Alviro Petersen, bringing the total to 218 for 1 just before tea on the first day. If South Africa could bat for another three sessions, then the match and the series would be safe. But when the two centurions gifted their wickets, the rest of the line-up raised the white flag. JP Duminy bagged another golden duck (*see* Chapter One **Famous First Ballers**), lbw to an ecstatic Harbhajan Singh, mimicking the out-shot played by Ashwell Prince to the delivery before. AB de Villiers was wastefully run out by Steyn and soon the team were all out for 296: 9 wickets lost for 78 runs on a featherbed. India were in a less than charitable mood, as four of their vaunted top order made hundreds, leaving South Africa two days to save the match. Amla scored another brilliant unbeaten hundred, but the last wicket fell to Harbhajan with just seven deliveries left to bowl. The Gardens went nutty, leaving Smith to rue the collapse and the two recent Test series when England had survived twice for a draw with nine wickets down. (*See* Chapter Fifteen **Nearly Men**.)

India (3)

The nightmare scenario of playing your very worst cricket while your rivals deliver to their full potential can lead to a horror scorecard like the Coca Cola Champions Trophy ODI final in 2000. The tri-nation tournament at Sharjah had been dominated by Sri Lanka from the start, as they won all four of their preliminary matches against India and Zimbabwe to reach the final. India had duly beaten Zimbabwe to meet their neighbours in the shoot-out. This was no weakling Indian side either, boasting such talent as Sachin Tendulkar, Saurav Ganguly, Yuvraj Singh, Vinod Kambli and Zaheer Khan. But none of them brought their A-game. Sri Lankan skipper Sanath Jayasuriya, on the other hand, was at his best, murdering the Indian bowlers with a vicious 189, eventually stumped in the 48th over as he strived for the world record and a double hundred. Venkatesh Prasad was the most heavily mauled of the bowlers, disappearing for 73 from only seven torrid overs. (Somehow, amidst the mayhem, Tendulkar bowled 10 overs for only 28 runs!) Sri Lanka posted 299 and the crowd braced itself for India's reply on what seemed to be a batter's paradise. But the fireworks never came. Chaminda Vaas tore through the top order, dismissing Tendulkar, Ganguly, Yuvraj and Kambli before the score reached 20. Muttiah Muralitharan then nabbed three wickets of his own. A needless run out and a fifth Vaas victim (5 for 14) wrapped India up for 54 runs inside 27 overs. Sri Lanka had won by 245 runs, the largest deficit in ODI history at the time. (*See* Chapter Fourteen **Minnow Mayhem**)

West Indies (7)

On the 2010 tour of the West Indies, Zimbabwe arrived with more optimism than had been felt for several years. Notable ex-players had been signed up to help the beleaguered nation regain its cricketing dignity and Test status. But winning was always going to be a bonus, even against a below-strength West Indies side that knew all about defeat. The opening Twenty20 match on a dry Port-of-Spain pitch started as badly as possible for the batting visitors: three overs, three wickets, no runs. Gangly spinner Sulieman Benn then took his fourth wicket – the fourth duck – to leave Zimbabwe heads spinning at 11 for 4. Benn finished his four overs with crazy figures of 4 wickets for 6 runs and retired to the outfield with victory all-but assured.

Zimbabwe were grateful for an over of 22 runs taken off medium-fast Ravi Rampaul by Elton Chigumbura, which represented 20 percent of their overall total of 105 runs, yet it would surely never be enough. Would it? It turned out to be plenty. Zimbabwe's new brains trust had quickly learned that the pitch was a turner and all but the final two overs were sent down by spinners. The West Indians flailed at the ball, either missing altogether or sending it into the eager hands of fielders. The side ended 27 runs short, underlining how vital Chigumbura's earlier assault had been. The West Indies had sunk to a new low.

Chapter Nine
Umpiring Howlers

The standing cricket umpire's decision may be final, but it doesn't have to mean that it is always right. Mostly, mistakes even themselves out and the better side still wins. When a blooper decides a match, however, the man in the white coat reluctantly finds himself the centre of attention.

Bernard Bosanquet

Experienced cricketers will raise their eyebrows to the heavens when a novice cricketer appeals after a batsman is clean bowled. Somebody will then tactfully explain why he has acted like a prat and the novice can join the eyebrow-raisers next time it happens. On Lord Hawke's tour of New Zealand in 1902-03, an unofficial England XI were carving through Canterbury at Christchurch. One of the bowlers was Bernard Bosanquet, credited with inventing the googly or 'Bosie', which stunned the cricketing community like Dick Fosbury's flop was to do in athletics. Primarily a batsman, Bosanquet's innovation turned him into a deadly bowler, until the opposition worked out that his wrong 'un was being done on purpose. On this occasion, however, his orthodox leg-spin appeared to have bowled the batsman, Walter Pearce, round his legs and the English waited for Pearce to leave. However, umpire Charles Bannerman (the Aussie opener who had scored the first Test ton) had not seen the ball hit the stumps. The non-striking batsman, Canterbury captain Arthur Sims (*see* Chapter Ten **Chasing Leather**), told his partner to stay put until the umpires gave him out. In effect, a batsman was appealing to the umpires for a not out decision, a situation that has since been unheard of, until the modern system of referrals. The square-leg umpire had been ducking, so he was unsighted too. Eventually, Pearce was adjudged not out and the game continued. But the matter turned even more sour after the English close fielders began sledging Sims. Etonian Bosanquet was at least courteous about it all, calling Sims a 'nice cheat', although his team-mates were less circumspect. Eventually a written apology was needed to dowse the flames.

England

The colossus of pre- and post-Great War Australian cricket, Warwick Armstrong, developed a penchant for riling the establishment. To make matters worse for the administrators, the 'Big Ship' tended to be in the right. Armstrong was in the twilight of his career when the Ashes rivalry reignited after the First World War, but he had plenty left in the tank to overpower a beleaguered England touring side 5-0 in 1920-21, scoring three hundreds in the process. On the reciprocal tour, later in 1921, the humiliation continued for England, as Armstrong's men won the first three Tests, before drawing the final two. The 22-stone skipper, who enjoyed the adoration of his squad, was vehemently against draws, believing that every match should be played to its conclusion. No great surprise when you have the best players! He once taunted officialdom by taking a rare visit to the outfield, where he read a newspaper for the remainder of a 'bore draw'. His greatest coup, however, came in the rain-affected Old Trafford Test, when the England captain, Lionel Tennyson, declared forty minutes before stumps on the second day, hoping to give the Australian openers a sticky session. Under the laws of the day, he was an hour too late, although none of the England players or umpires picked up on it. Armstrong, who had been bowling his leg-spin when the declaration arrived, knew the law and took no little pleasure in pointing it out. This 'rather lamentable' blunder, according to Wisden, was resolved by the England batsmen resuming their innings. But, amid the confusion, Armstrong achieved the unique feat of bowling two consecutive overs from the same end, landing another dig in the umpires' ribs.

England (2)

The first Ashes series after the Second World War was supposed to have been a triumph of goodwill between friends, reuniting champions Don Bradman and Wally Hammond for one last showdown. It turned out to be a PR disaster. Firstly, both Bradman and Hammond were several years older and neither seemed in rude health or form. For Bradman especially, who was suffering from gastritis and had lost a lot of weight, a failure might have signalled an inglorious end to his career. Batting first at the 'Gabba, Arthur Morris fell early, bringing The Don to the crease, but he was visibly struggling to find that old spark. A full delivery outside the off-stump from Bill Voce induced a loose stroke from the maestro and the ball flew to second slip Jack Ikin, who caught it waist high. All of the England fielders celebrated, but they soon looked back in confusion to see Bradman loitering at the crease, waiting for the umpire's decision. The close fielders were not in any doubt that the catch had been clean, nor was the commentator, nor the next man in, Keith Miller, who had already left his seat. But the umpire, George Borwick, adjudged it a bump ball and Bradman was reprieved. The English disappointment was compounded as Bradman's second life gave him a second wind, and he rollicked his way to 187, putting on 276 with Lindsay Hassett (128). England soon lost by an innings and 332 runs, Ikin suffering a first baller in the process. The difference in talent between the two teams meant that Australia would more than likely have dominated the series anyway. But a different decision could have called time on Bradman. Instead, he scored 680 runs at an average of 97, as his side won the series 3-0. Hammond, on the other hand, did not manage a fifty in his eight innings and seethed at the 'Ikin affair' throughout the trip.

West Indies

The 1960-61 Test series between Australia and the West Indies was one of the most exciting on record. The first match had been famously tied (*see* Chapter Twelve **Expensive Run Outs**'); Australia had steamrollered the second; and then been flattened themselves in the third. In such tight affairs, the umpires are inevitably drawn into the intrigue and the first flash point had occurred in the second Test at the MCG when West Indian opener Joe Solomon had lost his cap whilst playing a delivery from spinner Richie Benaud. The errant cap fell on the stumps and dislodged a bail. Benaud appealed and the batsman was rightly given out, although the home crowd showed their dissatisfaction. For the first time ever, an Australian captain was being jeered by an Australian crowd whilst winning a match! In Adelaide for the fourth Test, the West Indies appeared to have momentum that would see them through to a maiden series win on Australian soil. Back-to-back centuries from Rohan Kanhai, a hat-trick by Lance Gibbs and an all-round performance from Frank Worrell had put the visitors in the driving seat. Their third innings target of 460 runs was never going to be chased down, but had Worrell left enough time to take 10 wickets? With just 7 wickets needed on the fifth day, the answer ought to have been 'yes'. But Norm O'Neill, Peter Burge, Benaud and Wally Grout all sold their wicket dearly, as did the gritty Queenslander Ken 'Slasher' Mackay. But when he was joined at the crease by last man Lindsay Kline with still an hour's play left, the game seemed to be lost. Indeed, the Windies thought it had been, when the feline Garry Sobers dived forward from silly mid-off to catch Mackay off the bowling of Worrell. All the fielders appealed confidently, but umpire Col Edgar – one of Australia's most experienced officials – said it was a bump ball. Mackay and Kline then dug in and repelled everything thrown at them to secure an invaluable draw. Mackay took the final delivery from fast bowler Wes Hall in the ribs, rather than risk edging it, to post an enduring symbol of Aussie defiance.

West Indies (2)

Edgar was again called to make a decision at the climax of the final match, with Australia needing four to win with three wickets in hand. A win to either side or another tie were all possible. Again Mackay was at the crease, but the controversy surrounded Wally Grout who cut Alf Valentine for two precious runs. However, the off stump bail had fallen off in the process, which was brought to the umpires' attention by keeper Gerry Alexander. After a discussion, the verdict was not out. The two runs stood. Photographs suggest that Grout had indeed dislodged a bail, most likely with his bat, but it had taken a split-second to fall. Grout then sportingly spooned a catch, bringing number ten Johnny Martin to the middle. He could only top edge towards Wes Hall, but the fast bowler failed to collect it and the batsmen scrambled a single. With the scores tied, Valentine spun a ball past Alexander's gloves and the series was lost. The umpiring controversies did little to dampen the mood of the losing side, which was cheered from the pitch as winners. As the West Indies set sail from Sydney, fifty thousand Australians gathered in the streets to see them off, in appreciation of the entertainment and excitement they had provided.

Sunil Gavaskar

No matter the rage boiling beneath the surface, when the dreaded finger rises, the batsman has to clear off. Some find it harder than others and regularly pay the financial penalty. In league and village cricket, dodgy decisions can occasionally make it into the local newspaper as emotions overflow into flying fists and bats, but happily this is a rarity. In the deciding Test of the three-match 1981 series in Melbourne, India needed a win to share the spoils. Captain Sunil Gavaskar was finally making runs and he was in the process of knocking off a hefty first-innings deficit with fellow opener Chetan Chauhan. Aussie favourite Dennis Lillee then struck Sunny on the pads, in front of middle stump, and the home umpire Rex Whitehead adjudged the batsman lbw for 70. Gavaskar stood his ground for a moment, convinced that he had inside-edged the ball. The tourists had been peeved by a number of Whitehead's earlier decisions in the series, so the opener was venting his frustration. Lillee was an equally expressive individual. He set about explaining to the batsman why he was out and where he should go to have a think about it. Just as Sunny was tearing himself from the crease, Lillee let go a parting shot, which severed Gavaskar's final guy rope. Grabbing Chauhan, he ordered a walk-off, which could have quickly led to India forfeiting the match. The Indian management intervened at the boundary edge, sending Chauhan back out to the middle and ushering the captain into the dark coolness of the pavilion. (In the event, Gavaskar was to have the last laugh: Australia collapsed to 83 all out, chasing just 143 for victory, due to a valiant effort by an injured Kapil Dev.)

West Indies (3)

On the steamship MCC tours, the New Zealand leg of the journey was a time to let the hair down and boost the averages after the rigours of touring Australia. In 1980, the West Indian outfit under Clive Lloyd, who had just dispatched the Aussies in a gripping series, adopted that same end-of-term attitude. Viv Richards, who had been at his best in Australia, had gone home with a back strain, but the line-up had plenty of others to fill the void. New Zealand took full advantage of the West Indies lack of focus, winning the only ODI and then putting up staunch resistance in the first Test at Dunedin. Richard Hadlee was at the height of his powers on a quick pitch, but the West Indians believed they were being pinged unfairly by the home umpires, Fred Goodall and John Hastie. Seven of Hadlee's 11 wickets in the match were lbws, a record for a bowler in Tests. Eventually, tempers spilled over when a delivery from Michael Holding hit the glove of John Parker, but was given not out by Hastie. Holding reacted by kicking the stumps down. Chasing 104 to win in the fourth innings, New Zealand crept home for a famous win with just one wicket left.

By the second Test, the tour was nearing a diplomatic tragedy, with the Windies threatening to go home. The match went ahead, Goodall again getting the nod, although Hastie was replaced. All went well enough until Goodall turned down an appeal for a catch behind. Everybody, including the batsman Geoff Howarth, knew that the ball had brushed the glove, but Goodall did not see it, so gave it not out. By tea, Howarth was on 99 and the visitors threatened to stay in the pavilion, demanding that Goodall be replaced. Eventually, they reappeared, but the final session became a farce, as the fielders chased the ball over the boundary and spilled catches. The lowest point came when Guyanan quick Colin Croft bundled into Goodall in his run-up, sending the umpire sprawling. Croft claimed it was an accident, as he often ran in close to the umpire. Goodall asked Lloyd to remove Croft from the attack, but the captain refused. Somehow, the Test and the final match were completed without blood being spilled.

Mike Gatting

Umpire Shakoor Rana's finger-wagging Faisalabad showdown with England captain Mike Gatting in 1987-88 would have graced an American talk show, but it remains another blight on cricket's shaky reputation as a sport in which players respect impartial officials. Rana had been in hot water before, when New Zealand captain Jeremy Coney had threatened to take his side off the field after a thick edge from Javed Miandad was turned down in 1984. But in that case, just as in the Gatting incident, the umpire's ruling was the straw that broke the camel's back. The Kiwis had been incensed by a string of such poor decisions – as they regarded them – by other umpires in the series and Rana's blooper was a step too far.

Likewise, England felt that they had been triggered out of the first Test in Lahore by local umpire Shakeel Khan. Chris Broad was infamously sawn off when the ball had missed the bat by a distance. It was hinted that the Pakistani officials were tit-for-tatting a string of dodgy decisions by home umpires in the preceding series in England. In the second Test, Broad had scored an excellent hundred, putting England in a strong position, especially as Pakistan were 106 for 5 at the end of the second day. Gatting was pushing for another over before stumps and brought on spinner Eddie Hemmings. With the batsman set and Hemmings approaching the wicket, the captain tinkered with his field. Rana saw Gatting's hand gesture to a fielder and called play to a stop. Such last-second manipulations by a captain are

OUT FOR A DUCK

neither rare nor off-putting to the batsman. An umpire's intervention is not grounds for abuse. But given the level of tension between players and officials, a tiny spark would be enough to light the fireworks. Gatting was already upset with Rana for wearing a Pakistani sweater and donning the cap of a Pakistani bowler. When Rana mumbled under his breath that the England captain was cheating, Gatting flipped. Soon the two were in each other's faces, trading insults with index fingers drawn. The controversy rumbled on throughout the next day, which was ideal for the home side fighting to save the match. Gatting was eventually forced to write an apology and he did so on a scrap of paper, a memento that Rana treasured for the rest of his life. Ultimately, it was the England management who backed down, hanging the captain out to dry. Gatting was far from blameless, but his reaction was understandable if not condonable.

South Africa

The 1998 Test series between England and South Africa could easily have gone the way of the visitors, had they enjoyed the rub of the green. Decisions do tend to even themselves out, but such was the significance of the more contentious moments and the dominance of the South Africans for most of the series that England were in need of this helping hand. A strong shout for lbw by fast bowler Allan Donald at the end of the third Test at Old Trafford was turned down, which allowed England's last wicket partnership to hang on for the draw. Had it been given, South Africa would have been 2-0 up, with two to play. Instead, the home side could win the final two matches to claim the rubber. The fourth Test at Trent Bridge came to the boil in the third session of the fourth day, with England chasing 247 to win. Indeed, the clash between Michael Atherton and Donald became the defining theme of the series. If Donald could knock down England's load-bearing wall, then the house might cave in. Bowling with extreme pace, he succeeded in pinning Atherton on the gloves with a throat ball and began a celebratory appeal after keeper Mark Boucher had pouched the catch. Everyone in the middle, including the batsman, knew that the ball had looped off the glove, but this fact had evaded the notice of the one man that mattered: New Zealand umpire Steve Dunne. The dreaded finger stayed down and Atherton went on to score an unbeaten 98 to win the match for England. For the neutral, Dunne's reprieve began a compelling duel that brought the best out of both players. The climax occurred when Boucher grassed a regulation catch off Nasser Hussain, which left Donald howling with rage. For the theatre alone, Dunne deserved a medal.

South Africa (2)

In the fifth Test of that series, at Headingley, there could be no such sympathy for the umpiring of Javed Akhtar, who seemed to lose the plot. On almost every

146

occasion that the ball thudded into the pads, the bowler would appeal and the Pakistani neutral umpire would waggle his index finger. Two of his dodgy decisions went against England, but eight proved costly for the visitors, who ultimately fell short by just 23 runs, so losing a series they had seemed destined to win. The South African chase on the fourth day was hampered by a string of disputable lbws to the top order, which restricted them to 27 for 5. Some you win, some you lose: but this was becoming a farce. Dr Ali Bacher, the top man on the South African board, was convinced that Akhtar was having more than just a bad day at the office, alleging that he had been paid to favour England. The umpire responded with a libel court summons, which Bacher ignored. Akhtar never stood as a neutral umpire again, retiring later that year.

Pakistan

The second Test between Australia and Pakistan in Hobart in 1999 offers a neat example of how umpiring errors will often even themselves out in a match, let alone a series. Having lost the first Test, the visitors were in need of a lift, but they had struggled to just 222 in their first innings. Opener Michael Slater gave his side a typically ebullient start, guiding the total to 191 for 1 before perishing to the spinner, Saqlain Mushtaq, for 97. (Slater was out in the nineties on nine occasions, on top of his 14 Test hundreds.) His wicket sparked a wicked collapse, as Saqlain ran through the line-up, Australia losing eight wickets for only 55 runs, butchering a regal opportunity to establish a match-winning lead. The man who might have stopped the rot was Justin Langer, who had reached fifty in adding a hundred partnership with Slater. With so much talent in the wings, the tough Western Australian was battling for his place in the team, so a hundred *in extremis* would be an emphatic statement to the selectors. But he was triggered for a bat-pad catch by home umpire Peter Parker on 59, although replays showed that the ball had not taken the edge. Indeed, Parker apologised the next day for getting it wrong.

Pakistan, meanwhile, had pushed into a dominant position, on the back of a brilliant Inzamam-ul-Haq ton, which set a daunting target of 369 to win. Australia faltered to 126 for 5, losing Mark Waugh first ball and Ricky Ponting for his second duck of the match (*see* Chapter Six **Duck Hunters**). Langer was joined in the middle by wicketkeeper and fellow Western Australian left-hander Adam Gilchrist, playing in only his second Test. Another wicket would expose Shane Warne and the tail to Wasim Akram, Waqar Younis and Shoaib Akhtar with a full day's play remaining. That wicket appeared to have arrived, early on the fifth day. Wasim drew a loose cut shot from Langer, which caught the edge of the bat and flew through to the keeper. The Pakistan players whooped and hollered, but Parker's finger stayed firmly by his side. Sadly for the stout official, the replay was repeatedly shown around the ground, including comprehensive evidence from 'Snicko' that Langer had indeed feathered it. Pakistan brooded for the rest of the day, as Langer (127) and Gilchrist

(149 not out) set about winning the match and establishing their reputations. For Wasim especially, who stormed off the pitch at the end, two wrongs did not make a right.

England (3)

The Elite Panel of ICC Umpires was set up in 2002 not only to improve the standard of officiating, but also to curb any insinuation of favouritism by home umpires, which has not been uncommon in cricket history. For England, an obvious candidate for membership of the panel was West Country-man David Shepherd, beloved of players and spectators alike for his eccentricities and superstitions, such as hopping from one foot to the other whilst the score was on a triple Nelson. If sport exists as a vehicle for uniting peoples of different lands and cultures, then Shep's jig was fuel for its engine, as it gladdened the heart of every cricket enthusiast. But the avuncular figure had nearly retired from the sport a year earlier, out of disappointment at his own performance in the second Test of the England-Pakistan series at Old Trafford.

Having won the first Test at Lord's by an innings, England's batsmen were showing good form and fancied their chances of chasing down 370 to win the match and seal the two-match series. At the very least, a draw ought to have been achievable. The target might have been less, had the bowlers not been bullied by Inzamam-ul-Haq for 114 and then 85, although he had been given a reprieve in the first innings when caught behind off a no-ball by Dominic Cork. In a breathless conclusion to the match, England first eschewed the win and then the draw, as Pakistan's bowlers tied them in knots. Amid the mayhem, however, four wickets fell to no-balls that were missed by the umpires, Shep and West Indian Eddie Nicholls. Left-hander Nick Knight, batting down at number seven, was sent off by Nicholls to a huge no-ball from Wasim Akram that would have also missed the stumps by some distance. Knight's golden duck was his last Test innings for England. Shep then failed to spot three more no-balls, as England stuttered to defeat, with just seven overs remaining. Disconsolate that he had failed to meet his own high standards, Shep contemplated hanging up his white coat. Happily, he continued for another four years before retirement, having stood in 92 Tests and 172 ODIs. Tributes flooded in from across the cricketing world when he died in 2009.

Dreaded finger

Sri Lanka

Few monikers can hurt a bowler more than 'chucker'. Once the tag is fixed, it is almost impossible to remove, no matter how much bio-mechanical reconstruction is undertaken. A dodgy action will usually be picked up at first-class level, before it is let loose in a Test or ODI, although some have slipped through the net. The great CB Fry was even banned for chucking. The 1950s and 1960s especially were plagued by throwing claims and counter-claims, with several careers being ruined as a result.

More recently, the superb off-spinner Muttiah Muralitharan's bent-arm action has been repeatedly questioned and tested, although the ICC has deemed it legal at every turn. Some umpires aired their own interpretation of it, no-balling him in prominent matches, including the forthright Darrell Hair seven times in the Boxing Day Test match against Australia at the MCG in 1995. Fellow Australian umpire Ross Emerson had done likewise in an ODI in 1996, so it was perhaps undiplomatic to let Ross officiate Sri Lanka again when they met England in a tri-nations series in Adelaide in 1999. The ICC had since given Murali a licence to bowl all his varieties, pending scientific investigation, so Emerson was acting unilaterally at square-leg when he called him for throwing during England's innings. Captain Arjuna Ranatunga took umbrage and walked his players from the pitch, eventually returning to avoid forfeiture. Murali was switched to the other end, so that Emerson could not see the bowler's action. As it happened, England's Graeme Hick (126 not out) was reading Murali like a book, so the Sri Lankan was taken out of the attack anyway.

In the end, Sri Lanka were indebted to Emerson, as he stubbornly chose to give Mahela Jayawardene not out, when a referral to the third umpire would have shown that the young batsman was run out by a yard. Jayawardene went on to score his maiden ODI hundred and win Sri Lanka the match. It proved to be Emerson's last international match, after the ACB found out that he was on sick leave from his day job, on account of stress.

Darrell Hair

Umpires need to be men of conviction, but they must also show tact when needed. Burly Australian umpire Darrell Hair certainly had the self-belief to stand up for what he believed to be right – a quality that made him popular with the players over the two decades that he stood. But he did not always don velvet gloves when it came to controversy, preferring to act first and explain later.

Asian countries especially found fault with the big man. In just his first Test match in Adelaide in 1992, India claimed that he was too harsh on their batsmen, which led in part to their loss by 38 runs. Sri Lanka rankled when he called Muttiah Muralitharan seven times for throwing in a Test match. Pakistan helped draw a line under his career, after forfeiting the fourth Test against England at The Oval in 2006, when Hair insisted the ball had been altered by the Pakistani fielders to aid reverse swing. The fielding side was docked five runs and the old ball was replaced, allowing the match to continue (Pakistan were well-placed to win it) but when the visiting fielders refused to leave their changing-room after tea in protest, the match was deemed the first Test forfeiture in history.

Perhaps more leeway or communication from both sides of the impasse would have avoided another shameful chapter in cricket's long book. Hair was quickly hounded out of the Elite Panel, only returning to handle a couple more Tests after 'rehabilitation', whatever that entailed. Were his actions pig-headed and inflammatory or courageous and correct? Either way, the ICC did not give Hair the benefit of the doubt. The Pakistanis were cleared of ball tampering and the result was later changed from an England win to a draw. But then it was changed back to a win again. Who knows where it will end up? The true losers were the capacity crowd, who were denied a gripping contest.

Ravi Bopara

Ravi Bopara's Test career for England to date has blown hot and cold. Or, rather, cold and then hot and then cold again. His debut series against Sri Lanka in 2007 included two golden ducks and a pair. Unsurprisingly, he lost his place, but the next time opportunity knocked – in the Caribbean in 2009 – fortune smiled on the Essex man. The pitch was flat and the catching slipshod, allowing Bopara to stroke a hundred with the class he had shown repeatedly on the English county circuit. The confidence now flowing, he held together his side's innings with 143 at Lord's, batting at three against the touring West Indies later that year, before adding the third consecutive ton at Chester-le-Street. The problem three spot for England seemed to have been filled. Glory against the Aussies surely beckoned in that summer series.

But Bopara is not the first promising England batsman to have been found wanting in the Ashes. Starts were brusquely ended by good deliveries or poor shots, as Bopara began to look out of his depth. By the fourth Test at Headingley, he needed a score to safeguard his place. Instead, he fended to gully with a single run to his name in the first innnings, as England were knocked over for a miserable 102 all out. Australia rattled along to 445, despite Stuart Broad's six wickets, leaving England a mountain to climb. Just when Bopara needed Lady Luck, she turned her back in a sulk. His first ball from Ben Hilfenhaus rapped him on the pads. Replays showed that the ball would have missed the off stump, but Asad Rauf's finger was long since raised to the skies. Would he have rescued his team and his career? We'll never know. England were mid-collapse (six wickets for 28), eventually surrendering by an innings and 80 runs. Bopara was axed for the last Test, bringing a neat symmetry to his batting graph: three hundreds and three golden ducks in just 15 innings.

Australia

Umpiring at the climax of a closely-fought village match can be nerve-racking enough. With nine wickets down and just a handful of runs needed for victory, only a masochist wants to be asked to adjudicate on a tight lbw, bat/pad or run out. It is much easier if the batsman smacks the ball into the car park or has his stumps flattened. What pressure must an umpire be under in a tight Test match? Of course, they are paid to have the best seat in the house, but surely there are occasions when they would rather be extras and not architects of the plot. In the second Test of the 2005 Ashes at Edgbaston, the Aussie batsmen Brett Lee and Michael Kasprowicz dragged the total forward to its sticky conclusion: three runs to win, with one wicket left. Australia had lost from a similar position before in recent memory. Against the West Indies in 1993, Craig McDermott had fended a short delivery from Courtney Walsh through to the keeper Junior Murray. Australia had lost by just one run, having added 40 for the last wicket. Instead of winning the series, they then lost the final match too and with it the rubber 2-1. On that occasion, the local umpire, Darrell Hair, had given the catch behind, although opinion is still divided on whether the ball actually touched the glove. Back in Edgbaston, Steve Harmison played the role of Walsh, while Kasprowicz was burdened with McDermott's yoke. The bouncer certainly hit Kasper's glove, no doubt about it, and Geraint Jones completed the tumbling catch. Whether the hand was on the bat or not became academic as Billy Bowden raised his crooked finger. After many replays, the decision was probably wrong, but the unlucky batsman admitted that he would have been annoyed if he had not been given it as the bowler. Would referrals have improved these scenes of sporting drama?

England (4)

No chapter on umpiring blunders would be complete without mention of Australian Daryl Harper who, rightly or wrongly, has emerged as a living, breathing, button-pushing argument against decision referrals. When the ICC brought in the referral system, it asked for time for any teething problems to settle. In theory, the system ought to reduce the number of howlers – inside edges for lbws, no edges for caught behinds – that sort of obvious blunder. Indeed, it has exonerated and condemned various batsmen, to the betterment of the contest. Captains have quickly learned how to play the system, but again the ICC will have to find a way of stopping such cynicism.

Yet the Umpire Decision Review System (UDRS) has not entirely eliminated human error. For example, Shivnarine Chanderpaul, playing for the West Indies against England at Barbados in 2009, was adjudged lbw when everyone else watching the replays could tell the ball was passing over the stumps. Daryl Harper thought otherwise and the decision stood. England, who have consistently voted against referrals, were the unlucky recipients of a Harper boob in the fourth Test of the South Africa series of 2009-10 in Johannesburg, when they appealed for a catch behind off Graeme Smith who was on 15 not out at the time. The nick was clearly audible from the stump microphone, but Harper did not hear it, as his volume was reputedly set too low. Smith marched on to score a vital hundred.

Chapter Ten
Chasing Leather

One batsman making hay is bad enough for the fielding side, but when his mate joins in the run harvest, the bowlers are in for a pasting. From a position of relative strength, the match can be taken away with a stirring partnership, which leaves the opposition bewildered and exhausted. Defeat usually follows.

Derbyshire

In the final decade of the nineteenth century, the Yorkshire clothing partners Marks and Spencer were fast making a name for themselves. But they had nothing on the pairing of Brown and Tunnicliffe, opening batsmen for the White Rose and regular tormentors of county attacks during the golden age. On their own, both enjoyed stand-out careers. John Brown scored a brilliant 140 to decide the 1894-95 Ashes series down under (his first fifty scored in only 28 minutes, the hundred achieved in 95), while John Tunnicliffe scored over 20,000 runs for his county in 498 matches. Together, they were dynamite. In total, the pair compiled 19 century partnerships for Yorkshire, the best of all reserved for the hapless bowlers of Derbyshire in 1898, who shipped 503 runs on the first day alone. Brown ended on 300, Tunnicliffe on 243, as the partnership reached 554, which stood as the world record for any wicket for the next 34 years. Tunnicliffe lived to see it broken, but tragically Brown died of heart failure in 1904 at just 35 years old, with plenty more runs left unscored.

Essex

The bowlers of Essex had a torrid three days in 1932, when they failed to take a single wicket for 787 runs. On the first day, Surrey's Jack Hobbs and Robert Gregory enjoyed an unbeaten partnership of 232 for the second wicket, to win at The Oval in blazing sunshine. Essex's weary fielders then had to travel to Leyton, their home ground at the time, to take on mighty Yorkshire. The weather was cooler, but the pitch was equally flat and a collective groan gurgled up from their throats as the visitors won the toss and chose to bat. The openers were the Yorkshire stalwarts Herbert Sutcliffe and Percy Holmes, who had been instrumental in their county's dominance of the last decade. Sutcliffe was 37 years old, but still churning out the runs. Holmes was fully 44 years old and suffering from backache, but he soon warmed up his aching joints. By the end of the first day's play, the pair had reached

423 for 0. Had they been a few wickets down, thoughts of declaration would have been raised, but with the chance of breaking the record of Brown and Tunnicliffe, the captain gave his openers until one o'clock to reach 555 or more. A large crowd turned out to cheer them on and they duly obliged, Sutcliffe reaching 313 and Holmes 224. Sutcliffe then gave his wicket away, but quickly regretted it, as a scorebook error ticked the tally back to 554. As a riot brewed outside the scorers' hut, another run was 'found' and the record reinstated. Essex then collapsed twice, to lose by an innings and 313 runs. 'My word,' said Holmes apparently, 'if it hadn't been for my lumbago we'd have brayed 'em.'

EW Swanton

As an aside, this partnership had an indirect influence on the infamous Bodyline tour the following year. The celebrated cricket journalist EW (Jim) Swanton had been sent by the London *Evening Standard* to cover the match, but such was the competition for the sole telephone at the ground that he could not file his copy in time. The editor consequently decided not to send him on the Ashes tour, saying 'if you can't file from Essex, what chance have you got from Australia?'. Swanton, who was vocally anti-Bodyline, believed he would have given a more robust version of events. Instead, the MCC hierarchy was fed all's-well reports from the legendary batsman Jack Hobbs, who was a friend of the players, so they never really knew what was going on in Australia, until the arrival of a telegram after the Adelaide Test accusing the England team of unsportsmanlike behaviour. (*See* Chapter Eleven **Insult to Injury**).

Quetta

The first wicket partnership record of 555 was eventually overhauled by the Karachi Whites openers in 1977 in a first-class match in Pakistan, as the Quetta bowlers bled 561 runs before breaking through. Waheed Mirza (324) and Mansoor Akhtar (224 not out) combined to break the record. For Mirza especially, it was his moment in the sun, as he opened infrequently and only scored one more first-class hundred in his career.

Warwickshire

The visiting Warwickshire team were eyeing up the train timetable at lunch on the last day of their county match against Derbyshire at Blackwell in 1910, having reduced the opposition to eight down, with 111 runs still needed to avoid an innings defeat. The three o'clock express could have them back in Birmingham for a few pints in the pub before an early night with the missus. Neither of the batsmen at the crease had much of a pedigree. Arnold Warren had bowled well against Australia five years earlier in his only Test, taking seven wickets, including Trumper twice. He liked to slog, but he was no batsman. John Chapman was more capable, but in only his second season as a county player, he was yet to flower. The Warwickshire bowlers never did make their train, as the pair smashed 283 in less than three hours to save the match. Chapman hit 165 while Warren tonked 123. Their record still stands for the ninth wicket partnership in first-class cricket. Chapman managed only one more hundred in his career. It was the one and only for Warren. How unfortunate for the bowlers that these rarities arrived at the same time…

Canterbury

The world record for the eighth wicket in first-class cricket was set in Christchurch in 1914, just months before the Commonwealth set down its bats and balls for the First World War. Long before the notion of an ICC-backed trans-Tasman series, foreign tours to New Zealand relied on patronage from benefactors and philanthropists like Arthur Sims, an Englishman who had played alongside WG Grace and then emigrated to Canterbury. A colourful character, who was eventually knighted for services to commerce, Sims had attracted notoriety a decade after accusations of cheating by a touring English side, whilst playing for Canterbury, although an apology was later accepted (*see* Chapter Nine **Umpiring Howlers**). In this instance he had gathered together a team of Aussies for an exhibition tour, including the irrepressible Victor Trumper, the most celebrated batsman of the age. Having dismissed Canterbury cheaply on the Friday, Sims's Australian XI took to the crease. Trumper usually opened, but his captain kept him back, so that the Saturday crowd of five thousand spectators could see him bat. The maestro eventually had his turn with the score at 209 for 7. Like a man possessed, he hammered the Cantabrians round the park for a little over three hours, scoring 44 fours and 3 sixes to fall just 7 runs short of a triple hundred. Sims, who had been on 80 not out when Trumper joined him, reached 184 not out, sensibly dealing in singles to get the great man back on strike. In total, the pair added 433 for the eighth wicket, a world record for first-class cricket. Albeit that the stand came in extraordinary circumstances, no other pair since has come within a hundred of matching it. Sadly, it was Trumper's last first-class ton before his death from liver disease the following year.

Victoria

Kippax and Hooker may sound like the title of a low-budget 1970s cop show, but in 1928 they were a pair of batsmen performing a jail-break for New South Wales at the MCG. Skipper Alan Kippax batted number four that day, called to the crease early as his team struggled in response to Victoria's 376 all out. He was powerless to intervene, as his fellow batsmen collapsed just before stumps on the second day, 5 wickets being lost for 4 runs, including Don Bradman for just a single. Kippax was

1 not out at the start of the third day, Christmas Day, with the score at 58 for 7. Worse was soon to follow, as two more wickets fell, leaving the visitors on the ropes at 113 for 9. The remaining batsman was Hal Hooker, a genuine cottontail bunny, who would have batted at twelve if it were possible. At one end, Kippax took the bowlers to task, knowing full well that every ball Hooker faced could be their last. Hooker played blocker, defying the close fielders to survive at the other end when needed. Between lunch and tea, the number eleven scored just 4 runs, but the scoreboard kept leaping up as Kippax delighted the festive supporters who had left their homes as word spread. Hooker opened up a little after tea, reaching his maiden fifty just before stumps. Kippax was 220 not out. The next morning, when Hooker was finally out for 62, he had batted for more than five hours, helping to add 307 for the last wicket. Kippax, not out on 260, had made 240 of them.

England

The 1934 Ashes series in England seemed to be heading towards the home team's advantage. Despite losing the first Test at Trent Bridge, they had easily won at Lord's in the second and enjoyed the best of the third at Old Trafford, scoring 627 runs in the first innings. Throat infections and suspected diphtheria had weakened the Aussie camp, forcing Don Bradman to bat down the order. By his own standards, his had been a modest series to date, as England's leg spinners had succeeded in both containing and removing him. Ashes fever had gripped the nation and although England were dismissed for only 200 in the first innings of the fourth Test at Headingley, Australia were reeling at 39 for 3 at stumps on the first day. Opener Bill Ponsford was 22 not out, but fast bowler Bill Bowes had removed Bill Brown and Bill Woodfull (common name back then was Bill), as well as nightwatchman Bert Oldfield. What happened the next morning is the stuff of dreams or nightmares, depending on your persuasion. Batting at the ground where he had scored 300 in a day in 1930, Bradman again tore into England, flaying 304, while Ponsford was eventually out for 181. The pair had added 388. The four-day match ended in a draw, but there would be no such luxury at The Oval in the fifth Test, designated as a timeless, winner-take-all decider. With all eyes on Bradman, the magician delivered a special 244, combining with Ponsford again to fashion 451 runs for the second wicket. Australia went on to regain the Ashes comfortably. Bradman's demolition act stole the headlines, but all the best performers need a straight guy, so great credit to Bill Ponsford too. Why would you get out when you had the best 'seat' in the ground to watch Bradman in full flow?

Trinidad

In 1944, Frank Worrell gorged himself on Trinidadian bowlers, sharing a partnership of 502 with fellow Barbadian John Goddard in Bridgetown. Two seasons later, he piled more misery on the island's bowling attack, this time in Port-of-Spain, amassing an unbeaten 574 runs with Clyde Walcott. Modest to a fault, Worrell was unimpressed by his accomplishments, according to *Wisden*, despite contributing to the two highest fourth wicket first-class partnerships at the time. 'The conditions were loaded in our favour,' he said. 'I wasn't all that delighted about it.' Neither were the Trini bowlers!

West Indies

England seemed to be dead and buried in the first Test against the touring West Indians at Edgbaston in 1957, having been shot out by off-spinner Sonny Ramadhin for just 186 on a flat track. The visitors replied with an imposing 474, built around a free-flowing 161 from Collie Smith. Ramadhin then nipped in with two quick wickets, leaving England two down and still facing a deficit of 223 runs to make the West Indies bat again. Doughty Yorkshireman Brian Close survived two and a half hours with an injured hand. When he perished, early on the third morning, England needed another saviour. Captain Peter May stepped forward, ably assisted by Colin Cowdrey, who hit his maiden Test hundred. The pair stayed together for more than eight hours, frustrating Ramadhin, who failed to take another wicket in the match. Cowdrey was eventually out for 154, having put on 411 with his skipper. May, who batted from Saturday afternoon until Tuesday afternoon (including a rest day), raised 285 not out, having guided the score from 65 for 2 to 583 for 4. He then declared, releasing his own spinners, Jim Laker and Tony Lock, who nearly dismissed the exhausted West Indies to claim a famous win. England never looked back in the series, surging to a 3-0 triumph.

Australia

In the fourth Test against the Australians at the Kensington Oval in Bridgetown, Barbados, the West Indies were staring down the barrel by tea on the third day. The visitors had racked up 668 runs, with hundreds scored by Keith Miller and Ray Lindwall, a pairing more likely to blow you away with the new ball than with the bat. The total of 668 loomed larger once the top order – including Sobers, Worrell, Walcott and Weekes – had crumbled to 147 for 6. All that stood in the way of Lindwall, Miller and Richie Benaud were local players Denis Atkinson and keeper Clairmonte Depeiaza, in just his second Test.

Atkinson, who was white, was under pressure as captain, as his critics believed that he did not merit his place in the team on talent alone. Worrell was the more popular choice. Atkinson had also bowled 48 overs in the first innings, so must have been feeling the pinch, but he and Depeiaza survived until stumps. They batted the whole of the next day too. By the time that Depeiaza was out for 122 (his only first-class ton) in the first over of the fifth day, the pair had put on 347 runs for the seventh wicket. They had taken their team to safety. Atkinson edged the total past 500 and eventually fell for 219 runs. Being a six-day Test, Australia still had time to bat again. Atkinson remarkably bowled another 36 overs and took 5 for 56, before being required to bat out the last hour of the match to achieve the draw.

New Zealand

The fifth Test of the series between New Zealand and India in 1956 was one of the most lopsided between the two in their history, as the home team lost only three wickets in the match, while the visitors lost all 20. Vinoo Mankad (231) and Pankaj Roy (173) were not separated until after lunch on the second day, with the score on 413, breaking the then record for an opening stand in Tests. It was Mankad's second double hundred of the series. India declared on 537 and then spun the dizzied New Zealanders out twice to win by an innings.

West Indies (2)

During the drawn series of 1972 between New Zealand and Garry Sobers' West Indies in the Caribbean, the local bowlers became well used to the opposing batsmen dropping anchor. Kiwi opener Glenn Turner had no desire to score quickly, but given that he was protecting a fledgling line-up, there was no compunction to do so. He followed up a nine-and–a-half hour double century at Kingston in the first Test with an eleven-and-three-quarter-hour effort in the fourth Test at Bourda, which netted him 259 runs, at a strike rate of 34.12. Alongside him, Terry Jarvis chugged along even slower, reaching 182 in 555 balls at 32.79 runs per hundred balls. Between them, they frustrated the West Indian bowlers for 387 runs. Inspired, number three batsman Bev Congdon then scored an unbeaten 61 from 215 deliveries, at a strike rate of 23.37. The 543 for 3 total took 268 overs. Fantastic for the batsmen's averages – lousy for the spectators.

England (2)

After a decade of relative ascendancy over the old enemy, England had already surrendered the 1989 Ashes to Allan Border's team by the fifth Test at Nottingham. First caps were doled out to batsman Michael Atherton and fast bowler Devon Malcolm. Hopes were high of salvaging pride, indeed the nation demanded it, but those hopes and demands were soon stamped into a flat Trent Bridge pitch, as the Aussies won the toss and chose to bat. By stumps on the first day, their openers Mark Taylor and Geoff Marsh were still choosing to bat, having survived all three sessions; they had scored 301 between them, in the days when 300 runs in a Test day was still a rarity. The stand was eventually broken by spinner Nick Cook with the tally at 329. Taylor went on to make a double hundred, as Australia declared on

602 for 6. Despite a belligerent Robin Smith 101, England wilted twice and lost by an innings and 180 runs, their largest defeat to Australia on home ground.

India

At Colombo in 1997, India failed to take a wicket for two full days. Sri Lankan second wicket pairing Sanath Jayasuriya (340) and Roshan Mahanama (225) came together at the very start of the third day and were still together on the morning of the fifth, adding 576 runs in between. India had already batted out the first two days, so with no chance of a victory, the Sri Lankans carried on going to set the Test record for a single innings: 952 runs.

South Africa

South Africa's bowlers had their tails up early in Sri Lanka's first innings of the opening Test at Colombo in 2006, having reduced the hosts to 14 for 2, including the dangerous Sanath Jayasuriya. Premier fast bowler Dale Steyn had taken both wickets and was looking good for another big haul, with early figures of 2 for 3. South Africa's total of 169 all out batting first had seemed on the light side, but perhaps the match was destined to become a low-scoring shoot-out. Far from it. Mahela Jayawardene (374) and Kumar Sangakkara (287) destroyed the partnership record for any first-class wicket, stroking 624 runs together. Steyn did not take another wicket until the score was 751 and his own figures were 26 overs for 129 runs. Jayawardene could have been run out attempting the first run of the partnership, but the shy at the stumps missed.

Western Australia

Facing one of the Waugh twins is worrying enough for the opposing bowlers, but all too often there would be a second to make the task twice as difficult. In 1991, the Western Australia bowlers suffered from double vision, as the New South Wales brothers piled on 464 unbeaten runs for the fifth wicket at Perth. Mark took them for 229 while Steve clobbered 216. At the time, it was the highest fifth wicket partnership in first-class cricket and it remains the highest by brothers. And spare a thought for the poor scorer who had to keep up!

Pakistan

The Waughs famously made a stand of 231 on a lightning fast pitch that turned the deciding Test against the West Indies at Kingston in 1995. The Chappell brothers likewise combined with 201 against England in the deciding Test at The Oval in 1972. But arguably the most important brotherly partnership bloomed at the Harare

Sports Club in Zimbabwe in the first Test of the series against Pakistan in 1995. The Flowers, Grant and Andy, rescued their team from 42 for 3 to 311 for 4, when Andy was out on 156: a stand of 269. Zimbabwe declared on 544 and did not need to bat again, as a powerful Pakistani batting line-up were dismissed twice. Zimbabwe had won the first Test in their history, although Pakistan came roaring back to win the three match series.

Bangladesh

The highest opening partnership in Tests was made at the expense of Bangladesh's bowlers in 2008 in Chittagong in the second match of the series. South African skipper Graeme Smith and Neil McKenzie plundered 415 runs in just over a day, before Smith fell on 232. McKenzie was not out until the team total was 514, having made 226 of them. The last time that South Africa had played a Test in Chittagong, albeit at a different ground, Jacques Rudolph and Boeta Dippenaar had batted through a whole day together to put on an unbroken 429-run partnership for the third wicket. At one point, therefore, South Africa had scored 844 runs in Chittagong without losing a wicket. The unfortunate Mashrafe Mortaza bowled in both innings, taking just one wicket for 200 runs.

Derbyshire

Nottinghamshire had scored over 500 runs in the first innings of their county match at neighbouring Derbyshire in the 2001 season, thanks largely to a fine 170 by John Morris. The veteran had never quite made it at Test level, more famous for his fly-by in a Tiger Moth in 1991 than his five Test innings. All the same, he made over 50 first-class hundreds in a lengthy career. By the fourth morning, Derbyshire would have been harbouring thoughts of an unlikely victory, having snatched a 50-run lead and reduced the visitors to 185 for 5 before lunch. Firebrand skipper Dominic Cork had earlier scored a hundred and he urged his bowlers to have one last push against Morris and a young South African called Kevin Pietersen, who had made a duck in the first innings. The attacking fields soon spread. Morris carried on from where he left off, helping himself to another 136 runs and a match aggregate of 306. Pietersen watchfully reached his hundred off 144 balls. His next 118 runs came off 105 deliveries, including eight sixes. In a madcap afternoon, the master and apprentice thrashed an unbeaten 372 runs for the sixth wicket. Over 1,600 runs had been scored in four frenetic days, but more importantly for England, a star had been born.

India (2)

Sri Lankan batsman Mahela Jayawardene truly knows how to make a nuisance of himself. To the Test record of 624 against South Africa he added the Test record for

Timeless test

the fourth wicket, 437 runs made alongside Thilan Samaraweera in 2009 in Karachi against Pakistan. He then played his part in the Test record for the sixth wicket, this time with his namesake Prasanna Jayawardene at Ahmedabad, also in 2009. Replying to India's sub-par 426, Sri Lanka were 50 runs shy and five wickets down when the keeper Prasanna came out to join Mahela, who had 86 runs to his name. At lunch on the third day, a result was still possible, especially as one more wicket would allow India access to a lengthy tail. By lunch on the fourth, the Jayawardenes were still at it. Mahela finally fell for 275, while Prasanna carried on to reach 154 not out. The pair had added 351, almost doubling the score, to leave India with no hope of a win.

Zimbabwe

The highest eighth wicket partnership in a Test match will still haunt the Zimbabwean bowlers who felt the force of it. Again, it was dominated by one batsman, with the other providing measured support to keep the barrage coming. The contest was the first Test staged at Sheikhupura, a historic city near Lahore in north-east Pakistan. The visitors started impressively, reaching a total of 375 before reducing the home team to 183 for 6. All of the top order batsmen were back in the hutch, leaving just the wicketkeeper and bowlers. When the keeper, Moin Khan, fell for 18, the door was wide open. But when you have a hitter like Wasim Akram in your ranks, anything is possible. Usually, it was Wasim's fast swinging deliveries that caused the opposition to fear for their lives, but on that day it was the speed the ball left the bat which threatened to remove the fielders' heads. In total, 22 fours and twelve sixes were struck, to the delight of the crowd, as Wasim batted for more than a day to reach 257 not out. His foil at the other end was the spinner Saqlain Mushtaq, who achieved his first fifty in Tests, finally out for 79 off 359 deliveries, with a strike rate of 22. He faced only four less deliveries than Wasim (strike rate of 70), proving that opposites do attract. As is often the case, the new batsman Waqar Younis was out first ball, having waited over three sessions for his turn.

South Africa (2)

When a part-time bowler removes the opposition captain on the last ball of a day's play in a Test match, it is usually time for celebration. For South Africa in the second Test at Cape Town against the New Zealanders in 2006, the sensation was more relief than unbridled joy. Stephen Fleming had batted for the best part of two whole days in his superb knock of 262, before inside edging a ball from Ashwell Prince at the end of the second day. The day had started at 265 for 6, so South Africa were confident of restricting New Zealand to 300 and then building a substantial lead, which would have justified the decision to bowl first in the wintry conditions. A quick wicket in the morning brought number nine James Franklin to the middle, a batsman who had hitherto failed to meet his potential in Test cricket. Three and a half sessions later, that potential had been fulfilled, as he scored his maiden hundred, sharing an eighth wicket partnership of 256.

Hampshire

On the second morning of the county match between Warwickshire and Hampshire at Edgbaston in 2002, not out batsman Alan Richardson would have been thinking about his bowling rather than any batting heroics. The number eleven batsman had avoided a duck the evening before, but with the groundsmen hovering and his colleagues already warming up to bowl, the confidence in a weighty partnership was low. At the other end, however, remained opening batsman Nick Knight, who had resolutely crafted 151 throughout the first day, a heavy percentage of his team's 274. Any extra runs would be a bonus. As it happened, the next wicket did not fall until well after tea. Richardson hung about, before cutting loose when his eye was in, reaching his solitary first-class fifty and eventually being stumped in the nineties. Knight, meanwhile, had gratefully continued to 255 from 493 balls, carrying his bat. The pair had added 214 runs. Although the shell-shocked Hampshire team were then forced to follow on, they did recover enough composure to secure the draw.

South Africa (3)

What a difference a day makes! After two days' play at Kingsmead in Durban in

2004-05, South Africa were well on top. The dependable Jacques Kallis had scored more than all the England side put together, crafting a fine 162 runs to steer his side towards a valuable lead of 193. The England openers were in the middle of very different runs of form. Andrew Strauss (136) was in golden touch, having already scored 126 and 94 not out in the first Test at Newlands. Marcus Trescothick (132), on the other hand, had endured his second career diamond duck, against South Africa at Cape Town, and was looking for a score. By the end of the day, not only had the deficit had been wiped out but the openers had forged a partnership of 273. Trescothick was caught behind just before stumps, effectively making the match situation 88 for 1, with two days left to play. Graham Thorpe twisted the knife in the South African bowlers' drooping shoulders, nudging a hundred of his own. From a position of complete control, the home team were suddenly struggling to avoid defeat. A mixture of rearguard grit and bad light retrieved a draw. England ultimately claimed the series 2-1.

England (3)

In 2006, England were staring down the barrel of another home ODI whitewash, this time at the hands of a talented Sri Lanka side. In the first four matches, the visitors had doled out a lesson in 'going on', as each of their batting cards included a century, while England had managed not one. At Headingley in the final match, opener Marcus Trescothick proved he had been watching by biffing 121 runs to set up a target of 322. The spectators settled back in anticipation of a close contest, but instead they were treated to an exhibition of aggressive batting by Sri Lanka's openers, Sanath Jayasuriya (155 from 99 balls) and Upul Tharanga (109 runs from 102). The pair added 286 runs in just over 30 overs, as the English bowlers were bullied at a shade under nine runs an over. The makeshift new ball pairing of Kabir Ali and Tim Bresnan leaked over 50 runs in the first four overs alone. At the rate the Sri Lankans were batting, England would have needed another hundred runs to test them.

Chapter Eleven
Insult to Injury

'You don't need to be fit to play cricket,' says the ignorant bystander. 'Nothing ever happens.' The number of joint and back injuries suffered by bowlers go some way towards dispelling that myth; not to mention the perils of facing a speeding, swinging, bouncing rock on a bumpy surface…

Willie Bates

Billy Bates was one of Yorkshire and England's leading players in the 1880s, capable of stroking a hundred or bowling out the opposition with his off-spin. His crowning moment as a bowler came in the first Ashes series of that name, when Ivo Bligh's party returned with the original urn in 1883. During the second Test in Melbourne, Bates had taken 14 wickets to set up victory by an innings. He enjoyed the touring experience and returned to Australia with the 1887-88 side, but it was on that trip that tragedy struck him, quite literally, between the eyes. During a net session in Melbourne, he was hit in the face by a rising ball and his eyesight was irrevocably damaged. He never played first-class cricket again, ending with an exceptional Test bowling average of 16. The accident ruined his life, even leading him to attempt suicide. Depressed, he died at the age of 45.

Bates was by no means the only cricketer to have his career affected by an eye injury, though not necessarily one inflicted on the field of play. The Indian Prince Ranji, claimed by some to be the most gifted batsman of all time, ended his playing days with only one eye, having irrevocably damaged the other on a hunting safari. The Nawab of Pataudi, India's celebrated captain during the 1960s and 1970s, scored a double hundred despite being partially blind in his right eye after a car crash.

Bill Woodfull

The image of Bill Woodfull clutching his chest during the Melbourne Test of the 1932-33 Bodyline Ashes series is often used to illustrate the battering that the hosts received from Harold Larwood and Bill Voce, under the direction of Douglas Jardine. In fact, it was a delivery by Larwood in the third Test in Adelaide that ignited the controversy, as Woodfull was again struck just beneath the heart. The field had been positioned conventionally at the time, but Jardine turned to his 'leg theory' ring of men positioned from leg slip to short leg, once Woodfull had recovered from the blow. It was a ruthless gesture, which the Adelaide crowd deemed as overkill, fearing for the safety of the batsmen. Later in the pavilion Woodfull famously rebuked the England manager, Pelham Warner, with the words: 'I do not want to see you, Mr Warner. There are two teams out there. One is playing cricket and the other is not.' Woodfull did not score many runs in the series (by his own high standards), although he took his fair share of the blows, facing more deliveries than any other Australian batsman. As captain, he should also be credited for resisting the urge to return fire with fire, as there were bowlers at his disposal who could have dispensed Bodyline with the same potency.

Bert Oldfield

Plenty of Australians were hit during the Bodyline series, but wicketkeeper Bert Oldfield's injury became the most notorious, after he was knocked unconscious by a Larwood bouncer in that same third Test in Adelaide. Oldfield was part of the Australian furniture by then, having played for over a decade, and he was a great favourite of the spectators. The South Australian crowd were already boiling in response to England's tactics, which had been developed to negate their hero Bradman, so when Oldfield was struck, the touchpaper was lit. Some of the ugliest scenes ever seen in Test cricket followed and the authorities were fearful of a full-scale riot breaking out on to the pitch. England captain Douglas Jardine did not relent, ordering his quicks to continue the barrage and often positioning himself in the outfield to receive the worst of the verbals.

In terms of winning the match, the tactics were a success, but the tour was nearly abandoned amid a developing crisis that threatened to sever diplomatic links between England and Australia. The phlegmatic Oldfield, whose skull had been cracked, blamed himself for playing the delivery badly. After they had both retired, Oldfield and Larwood became close friends.

Harold Larwood

While it is right to portray Australia's batsmen as the victims of the Bodyline intimidation, Harold Larwood suffered too. His raw pace had been identified by Jardine and his co-conspirators as the tool with the potential to blunt the threat of Bradman, in an era when the amateur captain's word was gospel. What was the lad from the Nottinghamshire coalmines supposed to do: refuse to bowl short to a leg-side field, even though the laws did not forbid it? If he had, Jardine would have found someone else. Bowling consistently fast at speeds of 90 mph on rock hard Australian pitches took its toll on Larwood, as he suffered a stress fracture of his foot. Even when bowling became too painful in the fifth Test at Sydney, Jardine insisted that he stay on the field until Bradman was dismissed, just so that his threat lingered. His 33 wickets (Bradman four times) at 19.51 almost certainly proved the difference in the series, but he did not return to England as a hero. There was no bus ride through

London. Instead, Larwood was hung out to dry by the MCC, who tried to force him to apologise for his actions. He refused to sign the mock confession and never played for England again, despite topping the county averages for the rest of the mid-thirties. After the war, he emigrated to Australia where he was surprised to receive a warm and enduring welcome.

Terry Jenner/John Snow

The next time short-pitched bowling by an Englishman incited an Australian crowd to riot was at the Sydney Cricket Ground in 1971, when seamer John Snow bumped tailender Terry Jenner on the head, causing him to leave the field injured. Snow and straight-talking umpire Lou Rowan had been at loggerheads throughout the series, disagreeing over what constituted intimidatory short-pitched bowling. The Aussie policeman had also refused every shout for lbw by the English in the previous five matches of the series. Rowan cautioned Snow for the Terry delivery, which duly pepped up the crowd and they began chucking beer cans and pies on to the pitch at third man, where Snow was fielding. A couple of spectators shook Snow by the hand, but a drunk grabbed him and had to be pulled back by the crowd before attempting to do Snow an injury. Captain Raymond Illingworth marched his team off the pitch, against the wishes of the umpires, the first time such a gesture had ever taken place. Rowan warned that the match would be deemed forfeit if England did not retake the field, which they did after it had been cleared of rubbish. Bob Willis was sent to field at third man instead of Snow. England eventually won the match and regained the Ashes, although Snow had to join the celebrations later, as he had smashed a forefinger on a boundary railing, attempting to catch a steepler, and was taken to hospital for surgery.

Sir Donald Bradman

The best batsman, bar none, was blessed with astonishing reserves of energy and concentration, which allowed him to score so many big hundreds, albeit that he could usually score the same amount in one day for which a lesser batsman would need two. The strain on his body and mind did tell on occasion, as he was prone to moments of anxiety and stress. The pressure of living in the public eye and carrying the hopes of a nation through the troublesome 1930s, led to bouts of ill-health and fatigue, including chronic fibrositis, which threatened to end his career prematurely. The onset of peritonitis, following an emergency appendectomy at the end of the 1934 tour of England, ought to have killed him, but instead he made a speedy recovery. The newspapers charted his progress, jockeying for news, while Buckingham Palace insisted on regular updates. Australia had plenty of world-class performers during the late 1920s, 1930s and 1940s, so they were not wholly reliant on Bradman, but when you lose a man who averages 100, you're going to feel the pinch.

In each of the 1934, 1936-37 and 1945-46 Ashes series, Bradman entered the contest looking shaky, but then found the strength to inspire Australia to victory. In the final Test of the 1938 series at The Oval, however, there was no comeback after breaking his ankle whilst bowling his third over. Len Hutton was en route to amassing 365 in England's monster total of 903. The Don was the only one who could have matched Hutton, but he was forced to watch from the sidelines as the remaining batsmen were bowled out for 201 and 123 to lose by an innings and a staggering 579 runs, the heaviest defeat by an innings in Test history.

Denis Compton

Most of us can only dream of representing our country. Denis Compton had the envy of those masses, but was also envied by his peers during a glittering career. Not only was he among his country's finest at both cricket and football, but he enjoyed the looks and charm to be damnedly popular with the ladies too. His swash-buckling innings captured the nation's heart after the Second World War, when Britain was in need of a lift, just as Bradman had done for Australia in the Depression. But, as is the way for all cricketers, he did not have it his own way all the time. By playing top-grade sport in the summer and winter, his body eventually began to complain. Sure, he could fight through the pain barrier, as demonstrated by his valiant 145 not out in 1948 after Ray Lindwall had pinned him above the eye. But a chronic knee injury, picked up whilst playing for Arsenal FC, slowed him down towards the end of his career. Such was his popularity and importance to the nation, Compton's knee was monitored on both the front and back pages of the newspapers, especially during the 1950-51 Ashes series down under, where Australia eased to a 4-1 victory. For Compton, it was a horror show: he scored 53 runs in eight innings at an average of 7.57, hampered by his swollen knee and the excellence of his great mucker, Keith Miller. Compton would get the last laugh, however, scoring the winning runs in 1953, as England regained the Ashes for the first time in almost nineteen years.

Nari Contractor

The tenacious left-hander was one of the leading pioneers of Indian cricket, demon-strating the mental toughness to succeed at Test cricket. His quiet determination helped to eliminate the batting collapses that were too often a feature of India's performances in the 1950s. As captain, he also led his nation to its first series win over England, in 1961-62 in India. But Lady Luck was not always a close friend. At Lord's in 1959, he showed courage in reaching 81 in over four hours – half his team's runs – with two broken ribs. Later that year, having made a vital 74 at Kanpur in India's first Test win over the Aussies, he was denied a possible hundred when he smacked a ball from Alan Davidson that lodged between the legs of Neil Harvey, as

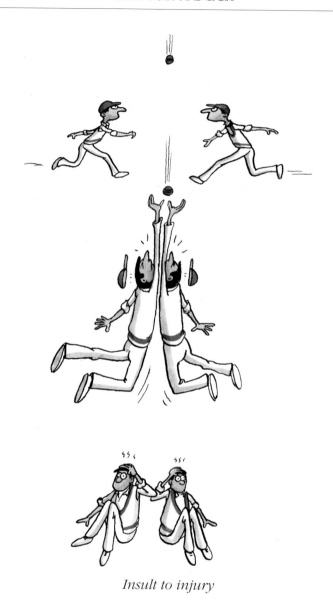

Insult to injury

the short-leg took evasive action. But his greatest moment of misfortune could have been so much worse. In a tour match against Barbados in 1962, batting in his prime, Contractor ducked into a bouncer from Charlie Griffith, one of the island's quickest. The ball crowned him on the back of the head and the batsman was out cold for six days. The injury would have killed him, had local surgeons not intervened, using several pints of blood donated by players from both sides. So perhaps Lady Luck was on hand when he needed her most. Sadly for Contractor, he never played for his beloved India again.

India

A side will normally need to take 20 wickets to win a Test match, but in the fourth Test against India at Sabina Park in 1975-76, the West Indies cantered home with just 11. A hazardous pitch, combined with fast, hostile bowling and a lack of protection and technique, all conspired to leave India battered and blue. In the first innings, Gundappa Viswanath gloved the ball to short-leg, dislocating and fracturing a finger in the process. Opener Anshuman Gaekwad, renowned for his courage against pace, retired hurt after scoring 81 runs, spending the next two days in hospital after being struck on the ear by a ball that reared off a length. Brijesh Patel edged a ball into his mouth and also retired hurt. Captain Bishan Singh Bedi declared with six wickets down, rather than risk more injuries to anyone else, and in particular to his spinners' fingers. Unfortunately, that happened anyway, as both he and BS Chandrasekhar later hurt their hands trying to take return catches. In the second innings, five batsmen declared themselves unfit to bat and therefore absent hurt.

Andy Lloyd

Warwickshire's opening batsman Andy Lloyd was picked by England for the first match of the home series against the West Indies in 1984 on the back of sound county form and a decent showing in the preceding ODI series, in which he had been obdurate against Garner, Holding, Marshall and Baptiste. Batting first at his home ground at Edgbaston, he made a confident start, despite the loss of Graeme Fowler and Derek Randall for ducks at the other end. Having reached 10 runs and scored his first boundary, the upright left-hander ducked into a rearing bouncer from Malcolm Marshall. The ball bludgeoned him right between the eyes and he was led from the ground all the way to hospital, where he stayed for the rest of the match with double vision. His season was over, as was his England career, although he did carry on playing first-class cricket until 1992. He remains the only opener who was never dismissed in Tests, although he might have preferred it if Marshall had knocked his middle peg and not his noggin.

Paul Terry

Another English batsman for whom the 1984 series against the West Indies will bring back painful memories was Paul Terry. The tall right-hander was enjoying a fairytale season for Hampshire, scoring five championship hundreds to gain selection for the third Test at Headingley in July. England were already two down in the five-match series. Fairytale could have become fantasy, if Terry could inspire a comeback not seen since Australia won the 1936-37 Ashes series. But Terry was no Bradman. The West Indian quicks kept him feeling for the ball outside his off-stump, before knocking him over for 8 and then 1, as the series was wrapped up. He kept his place for Old Trafford later that month, but it would prove to be his last. Lloyd's chief aggressor, Malcolm Marshall, was injured, but his replacement, Winston Davis, was just as fiery, breaking Terry's left arm with a short-pitched delivery. But the injured player's match was not over, as he bravely returned to the middle, with Allan Lamb needing two runs to make his third consecutive hundred. England also needed 23 runs to avoid the follow-on. Sadly for Terry, this last target had not been communicated to Lamb, who duly reached three figures, running two off the last ball of the over, so leaving the invalid to face the music. With one arm in a sling, Terry was forced to front up to Joel Garner, a task he had failed to master with two good arms. Needless to say, England were soon following on.

Mike Gatting

The West Indies already held a psychological edge over the English batsmen going into the 1986 series in the Caribbean, but that became a hoodoo after Malcolm Marshall flattened Mike Gatting's nose in the first ODI in Kingston before the Tests. Whether he would have batted on was made irrelevant as the ball ricocheted on to his stumps. Marshall is believed to have removed shards of Gatting's nose from the seam. Sadly for England, the gritty Middlesex man was in top form and could have made the contest less one-sided on unevenpitches where England's batsmen were relieved to lose only their wickets.

West Indies

While the injuries to the English during the 1980s tended to result in the player being permanently sidelined, the opposite seemed to happen when the West Indies players were hurt. Whether it was Michael Holding taking wickets with a stress fracture in 1984 or Gordon Greenidge thrashing a double hundred with a limp at Lord's, the Windies seemed to manage to play through the pain. The realisation that if you stepped down for a match, you might not get your place back, helped concentrate the mind. Perhaps most galling was the feat of England's chief destroyer Malcolm Marshall, who batted one-handed at Headingley in 1984 after a double fracture to his left thumb, sustained whilst fielding. Not only did Marshall help Larry Gomes to his hundred, but he also scored a boundary of his own. In the second innings, he ensured he would not have to bat again, grabbing 7 for 53 from 26 overs, bowling with his left hand in a cast. The Windies could certainly take what they dished out.

Syd Lawrence

The great sadness for David 'Syd' Lawrence was that the injury which effectively ended his cricketing career arrived just as he was maturing into a quality fast bowler in 1992. Given England's woes in that department for the rest of the decade, his loss was keenly felt. Genuinely fast, but often erratic, the genial Gloucestershire bowler was built like a boxer. His enthusiasm was winning him a following, especially after he had out-blasted the West Indies with seven wickets to help draw the series at home in the previous summer. On tour in New Zealand, Lawrence was brought in to play the third Test after a last-minute injury. The match was destined to be a draw, but England declared their second innings to give themselves 30 overs in which to steal an unlikely win. Lawrence ran in to bowl his third over and went over his left leg with a bloodcurdling yell, as his kneecap snapped in two. The screams and noise of the break, like a firecracker, stunned the crowd and sickened the players. A scuffle broke out as the manager, Micky Stewart, tried to stop a cameraman from taking indecent shots of Syd's agony. Lawrence's Test career was over.

Phil Simmons

Usually, the West Indian fast bowlers were the ones injuring England's batsmen, but the roles were reversed shockingly in 1988 during a tour match against Gloucestershire. At the end of a day's play, with the light failing, Phil Simmons, a belligerent 25-year-old from Trinidad, was hit on the side of his helmetless head by Syd Lawrence, bowling at full pace. Simmons was extremely lucky to survive, especially after his heart stopped en route to emergency brain surgery in Bristol. He made a remarkable recovery, returning to tour England again in 1991.

Chris Lewis

Compared with a jail sentence for drug smuggling, any cricketing crimes that Chris Lewis may have committed in his career are piffling. But posterity can be cruel and the talented all-rounder may be longer remembered for an act of naivety whilst on tour of the Caribbean in 1994, than for all his fine performances with bat, ball and in the field. Although hugely talented and athletic, Lewis's career was studded with disappointments, none more frustrating for his captain than his bout of sunstroke in a warm-up match. Having shaved his head bald, Lewis then exposed his bare skin to the midday sun, so inviting nausea for the next few days. 'The Prat Without a Hat' was the *Sun's* headline, an epithet which stayed with the all-rounder for the rest of his career. Before being sentenced in May 2009 to 13 years in prison for attempting to traffic £140,000 worth of liquid cocaine in fruit cans, Lewis had had one last bash at county cricket the year before, when he bowled in a one-day match for Surrey. His six overs were dispatched for 51 wicketless runs.

Steve Waugh/Jason Gillespie

In terms of slapstick, the notion of two fielders running for the same catch and colliding is top drawer. In reality, the results are less amusing. When Sri Lankan middle order batsman Mahela Jayawardene launched the ball in the air during the first Test of the 1999-2000 series against Australia in Kandy, both Steve Waugh and Jason Gillespie backed themselves to catch it. But neither made his intentions clear enough to the other. Waugh ended up diving nose-first into the leg of the onrushing Gillespie, breaking his own schnozzle and cracking the tibia in the seamer's right leg. The ball, incidentally, was not caught. In a tight match, the visitors had just lost a captain, a reliable batsman and a fast bowler in one sickening collision. The next day, they lost the match too and would lose the series 1-0.

Simon Jones

Built like a rugby player, Simon Jones was capable of sending the ball through at express pace in short spells, with an ability to extract late reverse swing from an old ball. He was every bit as important in England's regaining of the Ashes in 2005 as the other members of the bowling attack. However, it looks likely that injury will curtail his Test career to its current tally of 18 Tests. His debut against India in 2002 resulted in both runs and wickets, earning him the opportunity of a streak in the team during the Ashes series down under later that year. On a dismal morning for England in the opening Test at Brisbane, where Australia were inserted (*see* Chapter Five **Captaincy Woes**), only to score 125 for 1 by lunch, the Welshman had offered the only bright light, defeating Justin Langer. But that was his sole contribution for the next year and a half: as he slid to field a ball on the boundary he ruptured the cruciate ligament in his knee. As he was stretchered off, a larrikin in the crowd threw a Coke can at him and called him 'a weak Pommie bastard'. If ever he needed motivation to rehabilitate and come back stronger than ever, then that redneck had provided ample reason.

Glenn McGrath

It was the twist that turned the 2005 Ashes. Even the most diehard of England fans will surely admit that Australia were dealt an unlucky hand during that famous summer and no quirk of fate was more telling than the injury sustained by premier fast bowler Glenn McGrath just moments before the start of the second Test at Edgbaston. Warming up with a game of touch rugby, McGrath stepped on a wayward cricket ball and hit the turf with a yelp. For the Aussies, it was like having a limb removed, while for the English batsmen, who had just been skittled by McGrath at Lord's, hope flowed anew round the dressing-room. Ageing seamers Jason

Business Reply Plus
Licence Number
RRKS-LAYJ-UAAZ

Quiller Publishing Ltd
Wykey House
Wykey
Ruyton XI Towns
SHREWSBURY
SY4 1JA

Thank you for buying this book. If you would like to be kept informed about our forthcoming publications please fill in this card, or email us at admin@quillerbooks.com.

Name: --- Email Address: -----------------------------

Address: -- Postcode: -----------------------------

1. In order to assist our editors in determining the type of books our readers require please tick your areas of interest in the spaces below:

    ☐ Dogs & Gundogs   ☐ Deer   ☐ Equestrian   ☐ Falconry   ☐ Food & Drink
    ☐ Guns & Shooting ☐ Fishing   ☐ Field Sports ☐ Humour   ☐ Wildlife Art

    Are you interested in any subject area not covered above? Please specify - - - - - - - - - - - - - - - - - -

2. In which book did you find this card? Please specify title - - - - - - - - - - - - - - - - - -

3. How did this book come to your notice?

    ☐ Magazine advertisement. Which magazine? - - - - - - - - - - - - - - - - - -
    ☐ Book review. Which publication? - - - - - - - - - - - - - - - - - -
    ☐ In a bookshop. Which bookshop? - - - - - - - - - - - - - - - - - -
    ☐ Our www.countrybooksdirect.com website.
    ☐ Other internet site. Which site? - - - - - - - - - - - - - - - - - -

QUILLER PUBLISHING LTD

Visit our website at www.countrybooksdirect.com or our equestrian website at www.kenilworthpress.co.uk

Telephone: 01939 261616 • Fax: 01939 261606 • Email: admin@quillerbooks.com

Gillespie and Michael Kasprowicz did not carry the same threat and England smashed 400 on that first day, after being inserted by Ricky Ponting (*see* Chapter Five **Captaincy Woes**). Australia lost both games which McGrath sat out. Funny that…

Justin Langer

While some batsmen or bowlers will gladly take a turn in the pavilion if a niggle starts to become a twinge, others will need to be dragged off the pitch by the team doctor, even if the injury is to their own long-term detriment. Black belt Justin Langer was no shrinking violet, but even he could do little when cracked on the bonce by fast bowler Makhaya Ntini in the third Test of the series against South Africa in 2006. The bruising to his head and subsequent concussion meant he played no more part in the match. Tragically for Langer, this was his hundredth Test for Australia and the damage was done by the first ball of the match.

Chapter Twelve
Expensive Run Outs

Yes, yes…no…no… oh sorry, mate' is a regular call on village greens on a Sunday afternoon. The unfortunate batsman trudges back to the pavilion and puts a drink on the culprit's bar tab. These cock-ups happen regularly enough in the international arena too, often with calamitous results.

Australia

Dead rubbers can produce the most exciting contests. Way back in the Ashes series of 1928-29, the visiting England team, led by the popular Percy Chapman, had rushed into an unassailable three-nil lead in the five-match series, as Wally Hammond not only filled his boots, but his gloves, hat and suitcase with runs. Adelaide was the venue for the fourth Test and the home crowd welcomed the young sensation, Don Bradman, who had smacked his maiden Test ton in the third Test. But after three days, Bradman was not the talk of the taverns. He had been eclipsed first by Hammond (who had followed up consecutive double hundreds with an unbeaten 119), but more poignantly by an Australian youngster called Archie Jackson, who had crafted a gorgeous 164 on debut. Those that witnessed it purred at the purity of his strokeplay, drawing comparisons with Victor Trumper. Many are convinced that native Scotsman Jackson would have rivalled The Don as the greatest of all time, had he not tragically succumbed to tuberculosis just four years later. His efforts had earned a useful first innings lead and despite another 177 from the irrepressible Hammond (905 runs at 113 in the series) and a stubborn 98 from Douglas Jardine, Australia fancied their chances of chasing down 349 on a true pitch. At 320 for 7, the spotlight had finally fallen on Bradman, who had reached 58 and looked to be steering his side home, alongside the dependable Bert Oldfield. With just 29 needed to win, Oldfield knocked the ball to point for a quick single. Bradman set off immediately, but Jack Hobbs was quicker, swooping to arrow the ball to keeper George Duckworth, who completed the run out. All was not lost, as next man in Clarrie Grimmett could bat a bit and he painstakingly added 16 runs for the ninth wicket with Oldfield. Yet England had their own sting in the tail. Slow left-armer Jack White took eight wickets in the innings, but he owed the final two to brilliant catches by the two fast bowlers: Maurice Tate at short leg and then Harold Larwood on the boundary. Three sublime bits of fielding had pinched victory, when defeat looked to be inevitable.

England

With the improvement of technology – Snicko, Hawk-Eye, Hot Spot and fixed cameras – the ability of the umpires to find the right decision is *usually* enhanced. These handy gadgets have also improved the armchair fan's television viewing experience. But for some, this undermining of authority is regrettable, robbing the sport of the fundamental principle that the on-field umpire's decision is always final. In the deciding Test of the 2009 Ashes series, as Australia were chasing a mammoth 546 for victory, English palms were becoming sweaty as Ricky Ponting and Mike Hussey piled on a third-wicket partnership. The bowlers were flagging on a flat pitch until Ponting was run out by a bullet throw from Andrew Flintoff. In-form Michael Clarke fell for a duck, again run out, this time by Andrew Strauss. Moments later, Marcus North, who had also enjoyed a bonanza series with the bat, was neatly stumped by Matt Prior. Without technology, all three batsmen might have been given the benefit of the doubt.

Way back in 1929, in the fifth Ashes Test at Melbourne, Australia were again batting last, although this time they needed 286 to avoid a 5-0 whitewash. Their hopes lay with 40-year-old captain Jack Ryder and twenty-year-old whippet Don Bradman, who was desperate to make amends for his costly run out in the preceding Test. With every run a prize, the close-in fielders were on edge to stop quick singles. Taking one risk too many, Ryder found himself racing against a throw by mid-off Maurice Leyland. The ball hit the stumps, with Ryder several feet short. The umpire was not certain, so adjudged it not out, 'to the obvious surprise and chagrin of the Englishmen', according to *Wisden*. Almost certainly, a referral would have found him short. Instead, both batsmen survived unbeaten to pass the winning post. Who knows what would have happened, had Ryder been given out? England might have gone on to win. Bradman or a tailender might have scored the runs instead. Either way, it does not make Jack Ryder's battling 57 runs, in his last innings for Australia, any the less impressive.

Bill Brown

Nowadays, the non-striking batsman can set off from his crease long before the bowler has entered his delivery stride, giving yet another advantage to the batsman. In the days when a batsman out of his crease was still fair game, the bowler was expected to warn the batsman that he was pushing his luck, before running him out, although it still left a bad taste in the mouth. The man who gave his name to this type of dismissal was India's Vinoo Mankad, who infamously ran out Australian opener Bill Brown in the second Test in Sydney in the 1947-48 series. Mankad had previous, having done the same in a state match, and he gladly sent Brown on his way for 18. Brown was hardly delighted, but had to go. Next man in, Don Bradman, was apparently very supportive of Mankad.

The ill feeling that can be engendered by such things between the two nations bubbled back to the surface in the petulant series of 1979, when Pakistan were the tourists in Australia. Pakistani last man Sikander Bakht was 'Mankaded' by Alan Hurst, leading to the tit-for-tat dismissal of Andrew Hilditch, who was given out handled the ball, when helpfully tossing it back to the bowler Sarfraz Nawaz.* A line was drawn under the disagreeable practice after a bust-up between Kapil Dev and Peter Kirsten in an ODI in 1992. Kapil had repeatedly warned the veteran batsman, who did not take kindly to the decision to dismiss him. Kirsten made his feelings plain, before eventually trudging off. Famously, Courtney Walsh's decision *not* to Mankad the Pakistani Saleem Jaffar in the World Cup of 1997, probably cost his team the chance of lifting the trophy.

* Hilditch is the only non-striking batsman to have been dismissed in this fashion. Only nine batsmen have ever been out handled the ball in international cricket and they would make an impressive batting line-up, including Mohsin Khan, Mohinder Amarnath, Desmond Haynes, Graham Gooch, Steve Waugh, Michael Vaughan and Daryll Cullinan.

England (2)

The 1950 series between England and the West Indies culminated in the decisive fourth Test at The Oval. The home side needed to win to avoid losing a series to the Caribbean visitors for the first time, but such was the gulf in class between the two sides, anything other than a triumph for them would have been a travesty. The batting of Allan Rae, Jeffrey Stollmeyer and the three Ws – Worrell, Weekes and Walcott – had provided plenty of runs for spin twins Alf Valentine and Sonny Ramadhin to take 59 wickets between them in four Tests. They had never let the English batsmen cut loose all series. At The Oval, in front of a crowd packed with West Indian supporters, they ran rings round England again, as the batsmen amassed 503.

England still had a chance, however, if they could pass the follow-on target of 353. With rain and then sunshine forecast, the Windies might have to bat on a dodgy pitch in their second innings. If that pitch then flattened out, England would have a chaseable target on a featherbed. The onus on passing the follow-on lay with Len Hutton and Denis Compton – two of England's finest. So different in character off the pitch, they could complement each other in the middle and they added a hundred to the total. But no matter how brilliant the batsman, the basics still need to be obeyed. Closing in on his half century, Compton attempted a tight run and fell short after a mix-up. England were now struggling. Hutton continued on valiantly, but he eventually ran out of partners just nine runs short of the target needed to avoid the follow-on, having made 202 not out from 344. Almost inevitably, starting again on zero, Hutton fell quickly for just two and the rest of the batsmen followed for just 103. Valentine took 10 wickets in the match, his second ten-for of the series, as the West Indies sealed the series with an innings victory.

Australia (2)

The first tied Test in history in Brisbane in 1960 was not an outright calamity, given that both sides had played to win from the start and the match was completed in a sporting manner. All the same, the Australians really ought to have beaten the West Indies, needing just a handful of runs with four wickets in hand. The momentum had swung back and forth during the contest, as it would do throughout that famous series.

Garry Sobers and Norm O'Neill had scored vital hundreds. All-rounder Alan Davidson had enjoyed a wonder match, cracking a total of 124 runs in his two innings and taking 11 wickets. His 134-run partnership with Richie Benaud appeared to have swung the honours to his side, recovering from 92 for 6 to within seven runs of the 233 runs needed for victory. The pair had timed their chase to perfection, until Benaud called Davidson through for an impossible single in the penultimate over of the match. Joe Solomon at midwicket had time to set himself and throw down the stumps. New man in Wally Grout pinched a single off the last ball of the over: six runs to win off the final eight-ball over to be bowled by fiery speedster Wes Hall. The Barbadian had been immense in both innings, combining pace and stamina to blast out eight wickets.

The Aussies scrambled leg-bye off the first ball, before Benaud became Hall's ninth scalp, top edging a hook shot to the keeper Gerry Alexander. Number ten Ian Meckiff failed to score off the third, missed the fourth, and should have been run out attempting a bye. Hall made a hash of the throw, as the tension rose. Four needed off four balls. Hall grassed a return catch from Grout, when square leg Rohan Kanhai was better placed to take it. Three off three. Meckiff, back on strike, hoofed the ball down to cow corner and the batsmen ran two quickly, to bring the scores level. They attempted the third, taking on the arm of Conrad Hunte, but his flat throw to Alexander was too strong and Grout fell short.

Last man Lindsay Kline strode to the middle, needing a single to win the match from two balls. The fielders crowded the bat. Kline squeezed his first ball down to square leg, where Solomon swooped and threw down the stumps at the striker's end, with just one pole to aim at. All over. Australia had suffered three run outs in nine balls, amid some of the greatest drama to unfold in Test cricket.

Tony Greig

There are those who believe that the cricketer is within his rights to attempt anything on the field of play that will gain his team an advantage, as long as it is upheld by the umpires. For them, England captain Tony Greig's run-out of Alvin Kallicharran at the end of the second day's play during the first Test at Port-of-Spain in the 1974 series was smart thinking. For most others, it was a shocker. As the stumps were being pulled at the other end, Greig threw down the non-striker wicket when the little Guyanan centurion (142 not out) wandered back to the pavilion. Technically, as time had not been called, the local umpire Douglas Sang Hue had no choice but to raise his finger. It goes without saying that all hell broke loose. Crowd disruption and heated arguments followed until eventually the decision was overturned, with Greig admitting that he had pushed the boundaries of sportsmanlike behaviour. The appeal was withdrawn. That night, he was driven home by Garry Sobers for his own protection. The statement from the authorities the next day exonerated Sang Hue from any wrongdoing, but said that Kallicharran was reinstated in the interests of cricket. For once, common sense had prevailed!

Sammy Jones

Greig was not the first, nor would he be the last, to affect a sneaky run out. WG Grace, no sportsman at the best of times, caused controversy by running out the Australian Sammy Jones in the 'death of English cricket' match at The Oval in 1882. The ball was thrown in to Grace, as Jones completed a run safely. However, the bearded codger waited for Jones to pat down a bump on the pitch, before whipping off the bails and appealing. The umpire had no option but to give the batsman out. Some versions of the story accuse Grace of telling the youngster to leave his crease, promising that he wouldn't stump him. Either way, the ruse backfired on England, as Fred Spofforth vowed to make Grace pay for his skulduggery. True to his word, the Demon took seven wickets as England failed to chase down 85 runs, so leading to the creation (or cremation) of the Ashes.

Pakistan

When the runs are coming smoothly, a team rarely has to worry about run outs. But when confidence is slim and the scoreboard is proving hard to keep moving, the close fielders circle like wolves round a camp-fire. Run outs can become a contagious disease with terminal consequences. For the Pakistan side at the MCG in 1972-73, the second Test had revealed their own prowess in the field, as they had achieved three run-outs in Australia's two innings. Chasing a target of 293, the Pakistani batsmen had a good chance on a batting pitch that had yielded six hundreds already. But this was a team that was not used to winning big matches, especially not on tour. A series of ill-thought out strokes, as well as three mindless run outs, including two of their big-gun batsmen, contributed to their downfall. Zaheer Abbas, who had bullied both Lillee and Thomson in his first knock of 51, was run out in both innings in a match Pakistan ought to have won.

Sachin Tendulkar

Sometimes cricket can be just plain unfair. An unintentional collision between batsman and fielder, for example, which results in the batsman being caught short of his ground, is just tough luck. Not that the crowd have to like it. When Sachin Tendulkar clipped one off his legs during the first match of the Asian Test Championships in 1999 to the deep midwicket boundary, three runs was immediately the call to his partner Rahul Dravid. India were chasing 279 for victory in front of a hundred thousand impassioned fans in the Eden Gardens of Kolkata and at 145 for 2, they were in the box seat. The bowler was Shoaib Akhtar, the Rawalpindi Express, who had dismissed Dravid and then Sachin for a golden duck in the first innings with searing yorkers. Tendulkar turned for the third run, calmly watching the throw-in from the boundary. Shoaib was also watching the ball from behind the stumps. The two men collided and Tendulkar's bat was inches short of the line as the throw hit the stumps, by sheer good luck or misfortune, depending on your affiliation. When the red light shone to give the Little Master out, the crowd started a riot, believing that Shoaib had blocked Sachin on purpose. An hour later, after Tendulkar had appealed for calm, play resumed. Pakistan eventually won, after another three-hour break for rioting. A match that had been filled with brilliant batting and bowling was remembered for all the wrong reasons.

Sherwin Campbell

A similar incident fuelled a riot at the Kensington Oval in Bridgetown in 1999, when Barbadian opener Sherwin Campbell was run out after a collision with tall Australian fast bowler Brendon Julian. The clash marred an exciting climax to the seven-match ODI series, which the home team needed to win to share the spoils three apiece. Campbell appeared to be striking his team towards the target, when the accident occurred, allowing Michael Bevan to nip in and remove the bails. The local crowd, usually so refined, reacted angrily to the decision by throwing bottles on to the pitch. Aussie skipper Steve Waugh took his team off, narrowly avoiding a glass bottle aimed at his head. Eventually, Campbell was reinstated and went on to top score in the successful run chase. Waugh claimed that he had been told to continue the match, otherwise his team's safety on the way back to the hotel could not be guaranteed by the police. This veiled threat was vehemently denied by the police. Earlier in the series, the Guyanan crowd had rushed on to the pitch, obstructing the Australian batsmen – Waugh and Shane Warne – from attempting a third run that would have earned a tie. Their enthusiasm probably denied their team a victory, as the match referee declared the match a tie anyway.

Jackie McGlew

In the third Test of the one-sided series between England and South Africa in 1960, the visitors' skipper, Jackie McGlew, was undone by a direct hit after being floored by the bowler Alan Moss. McGlew's partner, Sid O'Linn, nudged the ball to extra cover and called for the single. Moss accidentally ran sideways into McGlew, knocking him over. Brian Statham swooped in and threw down the stumps. Tragically for McGlew, this was his first good knock on tour when his side needed a lengthy partnership to save the match. England captain Colin Cowdrey tried to call McGlew back, especially when the crowd started booing, but the umpires would not shift their stance.

Derek Randall

Geoffrey 'Fiery' Boycott had a reputation for being a selfish cricketer, who batted for himself rather than the team, but that was not a fair summation. You couldn't become the record Test run-scorer (at the time) and accumulate 151 first-class hundreds by being a total stick-in-the-mud. The infamous run out of local hero Derek Randall in his first Trent Bridge Test against Australia in 1977 was more poor judgement than selfishness. The Yorkshire opener, who was in a comeback Test after three years of self-imposed exile, was battling his way towards a hundred when the Nottinghamshire man came to the crease. Fresh from a brilliant 174 in the Centenary Test at the MCG, the Trent Bridge crowd was expecting a lengthy knock. Two boundaries indicated that Randall was in good nick, but he was to get no further. Boycott called an impossible single, which left Randall stranded. In the end, the local boy accepted his fate and sacrificed himself for the team's cause. As he walked off, steaming, Boycott sorrowfully covered his head with his hands. The run out proved to be about the only blip in a complete performance by England. Debutant Ian Botham took a five-for in his first innings. The slip catching was exemplary. Alan Knott scored a dazzling hundred. But the man of the match, if there had been one, was Boycott, who followed up his first innings hundred with a determined 80 not out to seal the victory. Randall was at the other end and scored the winning runs. Remarkably, Boycott had batted on all five days of the Test.

Geoffrey Boycott

Batting against eleven men hell-bent on getting you out is hard enough in itself: but you are also dependent on your partner at the other end for support. When he wants to see the back of you too, your chances of survival are practically zero. For Geoff Boycott, the England tour of New Zealand in 1978 was proving to be a nightmare. Promoted to captain after an injury to Mike Brearley, Boycs' crew were in mutinous mood, especially after the first Test in Wellington had been lost from a position of strength. The Yorkshireman's own form had deserted him too, so he could not prop up his decisions with weight of runs. Hardly a Virender Sehwag-style opener when in top form, Boycott was at pains to find the middle of the bat during the second innings of the second Test at Christchurch, at a time when England needed quick runs to set a target. Derek Randall was Mankaded by Ewen Chatfield (without warning) and young Turk Ian Botham was next man in. Boycott was threatening to bat the Kiwis back into the match and as Botham left the pavilion, vice-captain Bob Willis gave the instruction 'go and run the bugger out'. Botham dutifully did as he was told, calling his captain for a quick single he could never complete. Willis took responsibility, backing up his decision with four quick wickets as New Zealand crumbled to 105 all out the following morning.

Australia (3)

The West Indies in their pomp could out-bat and out-bowl the opposition, but if that didn't work, then they could out-field them too. The 1975 World Cup final against Australia at a packed Lord's was won through a fielding masterclass by the men from the Caribbean, as no fewer than five Australians were run out. Admittedly, the Windies would not have come close to winning without a scintillating hundred from their captain, Clive Lloyd, who counter-attacked against Dennis Lillee and Jeff Thomson, while Rohan Kanhai expertly held up the other end. On the Longest Day, in bright sunshine, the Aussies had a decent chance of chasing down the 291 in 60 overs, despite losing opener Rick McCosker to a diving slip catch by the astonishing Alvin Kallicharran. Alan Turner and Ian Chappell then threatened to steal the match away, but a deadly throw from backward square leg by a young Viv Richards sent Turner on his way. Richards, who had failed with the bat, swooped on another half-chance soon afterwards, seizing upon a moment of fraternal hesitation between Ian and Greg Chappell. Again, he achieved a direct hit and Australia's premier batsman was dismissed.

Having seen two of his partners run out, captain Ian Chappell was determined to make up for their loss, stroking an excellent 62 to put the chase back on track. At 162 for 3, with more than 20 overs left, Australia looked like favourites. But then Chappell forgot the old rule of never running on a misfield. Richards was now at midwicket where he parried a firm shot from the batsman. Belatedly,Chappell called for the run, but was found short of the crease as the lithe Antiguan regained the ball and flicked it like a thunderbolt to Lloyd, who removed the bails. Australia never quite recovered, losing two more wickets to run outs as the pressure intensified.

Coaches ask their fielders to provide two 'bonus' wickets a match through brilliant catching or throwing. On that day, the West Indies took six bonus wickets, yet won the match by only 17 runs.

Mike Atherton

For photographers wondering how best to capture England's woeful performance against Australia in the second Test of the 1993 Ashes series at Lord's, Mike Atherton provided the opportunity. Scrambling on all fours to reach his crease, having been sent back by Mike Gatting, the opener was in the process of being cruelly run out for 99. That Atherton should have been the symbol of the humiliation was unfair, given that he had given the stoutest riposte to the visitors' 632 for 4, in which the top three batsmen made centuries. Had Mark Waugh not perished for 99 himself, then the innings would have been the first in history where the top four had all tonned up. Having made 80 in the first innings, Atherton again mastered the Aussie bowlers and with Gatting alongside he seemed to be guiding his side to a draw as England followed on. On 97, Athers clipped a ball off his legs to deep midwicket and ran the first two hard. While the batsmen contemplated the third, Merv Hughes picked up the ball and hurled it like a missile to Ian Healy behind the stumps. Gatting was not interested, so Atherton retreated, but then slipped and was left scrambling in the dirt as Healy gleefully whipped off the bails. The snappers had a field day. Atherton never did make a Test hundred at Lord's.

Steve Waugh

When a batsman is injured during a match, the opposition skipper is usually content to grant him a runner. Apart from anything else, he may need one himself another time, while there is plenty of potential for a comedy run out. (Captains may decide that a batsman with cramp does not deserve a runner, as controversially happened in the 2009 Champions Trophy, when England's Andrew Strauss denied South Africa's Graeme Smith.) At the WACA, in the final Test of the 1994-95 Ashes series down under, fast bowler Craig McDermott was suffering from a back strain and was duly accorded a runner by England skipper Graham Gooch, who was playing in his last Test. The number eleven batsman, McDermott had come to the crease as a result of two consecutive run outs, involving the not out batsman Steve Waugh, who was approaching a typically tenacious hundred. The decision to choose Steve's twin brother Mark as runner seemed a sound one, given the pair had enjoyed many fine partnerships growing up. With Steve on 99, Mark called him through for a squeaky single and was run out by a smart piece of fielding by Gooch. Steve was left stranded one short of his ton. This is perhaps a case of 'what goes around, comes around', as Steve was involved in more run outs than any other international batsman. In the 27 run-outs during his Test career, he was the victim only four times. In ODIs, he was caught short 27 times out of 78. Given his worth to the team, this was undoubtedly the right way round. Interestingly, India's Kapil Dev played 131 Test innings for his country and was never once run out.

John Commins

The middle order batsman may not have enjoyed a long stint in Test cricket, playing only three matches for South Africa in the 1994-95 summer, but he did stick around

Ball watching

long enough to provide entertainment for the more sadistic of cricketing fans. The only Test against Pakistan yielded him just 13 in the first innings, batting at three. But, having pulled his groin muscle whilst fielding, Commins dropped down the order to six and limped to the middle with a runner. He bunted his first ball into the covers and instinctively set off for a quick single, forgetting that he did not need to run. In a scene of chaos, so often a feature when runners are involved, Commins eventually realised his error, turned and attempted to dive back into his crease. He did not make it and was run out first ball. The groin was damaged further, incapacitating him for the rest of the season. He never played Test cricket again.

Nick Knight

A grinding Test match at Bulawayo in 1996 between England and Zimbabwe, the first proper confrontation since independence, eventually came to the boil, when the visitors fell just short of chasing down the target of 205 on the final afternoon. The slow pitch had rewarded grafting batsmen – Andy Flower, Nasser

Hussain and John Crawley had all scored watchful hundreds – so the quick 73 runs by Alec Stewart in the fourth innings were a relief. At the other end, opener Nick Knight was also in one-day mode and the chase appeared to be on course. A middle-order collapse amid negative tactics by the Zimbabwean bowlers, which the umpires were loath to sanction, put the wobble on the scoring rate. Knight was left needing to score three runs from the last ball of the match to win, having smashed Heath Streak for six in the final over. Nine men were lined round the boundary ropes. The ball found the middle of his bat, but it slowed up in the outfield and was speared back into the grateful hands of Andy Flower, who completed the run out. Knight was dismissed for 96 and he never scored another hundred for England. The match ended as a draw, with the scores level, the first such occasion in Test history.

England's coach David Lloyd was apoplectic at Zimbabwe's delaying tactics in the post-match press conference, famously declaring that 'we flippin' murdered 'em': a statement that looked even odder after England had lost the ODI series 3-0 (*see* Chapter Fourteen **Minnow Mayhem**). The tour had been a triumph for the home team, but a PR disaster for England, who gave the impression they would rather have been somewhere else entirely.

England (3)

Even the best of friends can struggle to communicate under pressure. Nasser Hussain and Graham Thorpe, who enjoyed many stirring partnerships for England, appeared to be salvaging a draw from the debris of the sixth Test in Antigua in 1998. It was a match that the visitors needed to win to draw the series. However, the team was skittled for 127 in the first innings and then assisted the West Indies to 500 with dropped catches, missed run outs and wayward bowling. Dreams of victory were long forgotten. A face-saving draw would still represent a fine return and a 168-run fourth wicket partnership seemed to be the tonic. With rain in the air, approaching tea on the fifth day, just another hour of Hussain and Thorpe would have been enough for the draw. But then disaster struck. Thorpe called the centurion Hussain through for a quick single. Hussain hesitated, before eventually taking off, but too late to beat the throw from Carl Hooper. Just 26 runs later, the match was over, as the remaining batsmen were gutted by Courtney Walsh. Thorpe was left unbeaten on 84, denied an almost certain hundred. That evening, England captain Mike Atherton stepped down.

Andrew Strauss

Given his fondness for a run out, it was perhaps apt that Nasser Hussain's cricketing career should have signed off with one. For the victim, Andrew Strauss, who sacrificed his wicket having been shanghaied by his partner, it was a bitter blow, as he was on course for a second hundred in his debut match. Worse still, he was playing at Lord's, his home track, and batting his country towards a win over New Zealand in the first Test of the 2004 summer. Hussain accepted he had 'done a Boycott', but just like Boycott, he made amends by reaching his hundred. There could be no bitterness shown towards Hussain, who later announced his retirement as a professional cricketer. A stalwart of England throughout some of her darker days, he bowed out in bright sunshine, playing his favourite cover drive, with his buddy Thorpe at the other end, to reach a hundred. The team he helped create would go on to enjoy the success he had craved. Strauss quickly recovered, scoring another four hundreds in his first calendar year.

Taufeeq Umar

The Pakistani changing room must have been a mess of flying bats and long faces during the second Test at Sharjah against Steve Waugh's Australians at the peak of their powers in 2002. The batters managed just 112 runs in two innings, as local contractors tendered to provide a new revolving door for the pavilion. Most grumpy of all had to be the left-handed opener Taufeeq Umar, who faced two balls in the match and collected two ducks. A king pair? Not quite. Brett Lee needed two deliveries to dismiss him in the first innings. In the second innings, he fell victim to the familiar call of 'yes, yes, no, no! Go back… sorry' by his fellow opener Imran Nazir. Having been conscripted to keep wicket for three sessions instead of his injured captain Rashid Latif, Taufeeq was too stiff to turn quickly and was beaten by Ricky Ponting's throw. Out without facing a ball.

Eoin Morgan

The Irish left-hander is one of a clutch of naturalised batsmen to have bolstered England's ranks in recent years. His imaginative strokeplay, in particular the reverse sweep adapted from his hurling days back home, has made him a dangerous customer in the limited-over format, where he is reaping the rewards with Middlesex, England and the Royal Challengers Bangalore in the IPL.

The stage for his first ODI, however, was far removed from the razzmatazz of Lord's or the M. Chinnaswamy Stadium. The Cambusdoon New Ground in the town of Ayr on the south-west coast of Scotland has held five ODIs in its history, three of which were abandoned for rain. Crowds double if the players bring their wives. In its inaugural international match in 2006, Morgan's Ireland played its old foe Scotland in the European Cricket Championships. This was the teenager's debut and he walked to the wicket with his side in trouble at 7 for 1, which soon became 19 for 2, as fellow debutant William Porterfield left for 11. Yet another debutant, Niall O'Brien, then combined with Morgan to add 80 runs, as Ireland took control of the match. Morgan compiled a restrained knock, by his own modern standards, of 99 from 134 balls, before being run out, attempting to get his hundred. As such, he is the only man to have been out for 99 on his ODI debut. He left with a torrent of foul language, aimed at himself, which earned him a ticking off from the match referee. A fine or ban was suspended, for extenuating circumstances.

Ricky Ponting

If everyone has their fifteen minutes of fame, then Gary Pratt's arrived in the fourth Test of the 2005 Ashes series at Trent Bridge. When the Durham supersub swooped to run out Ricky Ponting, England were in the ascendancy, having made the Australians follow on for the first time since 1988. Ponting, who had earlier griped about England's prolific use of substitute fielders to rest their bowlers, was nearing a half century and looking in ominous form on a flat deck. If he kicked on against tiring bowlers, then Australia would soon take control of the match. Damien Martyn called his skipper through for a tight single, inviting Pratt to pick up and throw down the stumps in one fluent motion. The sub was on for injured quick Simon Jones, who would not bowl again in the series, so it was all above board. But Ponting did not see it that way, mouthing off at the camera and England's coach Duncan Fletcher to earn himself a financial penalty. Fellow batsman Simon Katich was also docked half his match fee for venting his frustrations at a poor lbw decision, just as he was finding his feet in the series. Given the slim margin of victory for England (3 wickets), these moments were pivotal. For Pratt, there was cricketing immortality and a ride on a London bus.

England (4)

A run out can often spark a collapse, which had seemed unlikely at the time. For England in the second Test of the ill-fated 2006-07 whitewash down under (*see* Chapter Thirteen **One-Sided Affairs**), defeat at Adelaide seemed scarcely plausible throughout the first four days. Paul Collingwood (206) and Kevin Pietersen (158) had helped to put the visitors in the pound seats with 551 for 6 declared. Harsh critics might have a dig at Pietersen for running himself out carelessly, attempting a quick single against dead-eye Ricky Ponting, but he did not expect to lose the match from there. Ponting scored a big ton of his own, as did Michael Clarke, to guarantee a draw for the home side. All England had to do was survive until an hour after lunch on the last day and the match would be dead. Instead, the team froze. The catalyst was the needless run out of Ian Bell, who failed to react to a call for a quick single from Paul Collingwood. The will to survive, rather than score runs, became typified by Collingwood, who carried his bat, but managed only 22 from 119 balls. Shane Warne was up to his usual tricks from the other end, taking four wickets, but England put their necks in the garrotte and asked to be strangled. Caught in the vortex, the team was eventually spat out as the shadows lengthened, to find they had lost a Test from a near impossible position.

Salman Butt

The Pakistani left-hander Salman Butt's hundred at Hobart against Australia in the third Test of the 2009-10 series was marred by his slapdash running between the wickets, which accounted for two of his team-mates in quick succession. First of all, he ran out his team's best batsman and captain Mohammad Yousuf, by turning down an easy third. Then he refused a simple single touted by Umar Akmal, the second best batsman, when he could have jogged through. In a six over spell, Butt had done what it could have taken the Aussie bowlers a whole day to achieve. Usually understated, Yousuf was pushed to vent his frustrations. 'We are not playing for self, we are playing for the country. I am thirty-five years old: if I get three runs, he is twenty-five years old, why can he not run? He is a little lazy runner, everybody knows that.' Butt was less worried: 'We've played enough cricket not to think about these small things.' Pakistan duly lost, by a bundle.

Chapter Thirteen
One-Sided Affairs

Nobody likes a sporting mismatch, unless the victims just happen to be an age-old rival whose nose is being rubbed in the mud. In that case, no victory can be too emphatic. For the beleaguered losers, on the receiving end of a thrashing, the experience can be a harrowing one.

England

The first post-war Ashes series was held in Australia in 1920-21 and the motherland came back from the colonies with a bloodied nose when it lost all five Tests. On paper, the batting of the two sides were comparable, but the England bowlers were vastly inferior, allowing the Aussie strokeplayers to gorge themselves. The closest match was won by Australia with a margin of eight wickets. Recently, English captains especially have implored their batsmen to go on and score a big hundred. For the determined Australian skipper, Warwick 'Big Ship' Armstrong, this was not an issue, as his men out-tonned the opposition ten to four. Leg-spinner Arthur Mailey had a ball for the home team, taking 36 wickets, the record for an Ashes series at the time, while his nine wickets in the second innings of the fourth Test at Melbourne were the best figures in an Ashes innings until Jim Laker's match. For England, the closest to him was Cecil Parkin with only 16 wickets. The great Jack Hobbs left with his colours still flying, scoring two hundreds at an average of 50 runs, but for the rest, it was a long journey home. Perhaps the tour came too soon after the Great War for England, but the squad had fallen short of its own expectations. In the return fixture, Armstrong's men won the first three Tests, making it eight on the bounce, before drawing the final two matches of another one-sided rubber.

South Africa

South Africa would have struggled to beat the Australian side of 1931-32 even if Don Bradman had not played, given the overall gulf in class between the teams. Bill Woodfull, Keith Rigg and Stan McCabe would have made enough runs between them to allow Clarrie Grimmett (33 wickets at 16.87) and Bert Ironmonger (31 at 9.54) to wrap up the series. But when the astonishing feats of Bradman are thrown in – 806 runs in five innings with four hundreds (two doubles) at an average of over 200 – then the gap between the teams leans towards the unfair. Only in the third

Test did South Africa rattle the Aussies, dismissing both Bradman and Woodfull cheaply and forging a first innings lead of 160 runs. But then Bradman and Woodfull hit big hundreds in the second innings and the demoralised visitors fell 169 runs short. Even when Bradman limped out of the last Test, conditions went against South Africa and they were shot out twice by Ironmonger, scoring just 81 runs in the match. Ironmonger finished with match figures of 11 for 24.

England (2)

Don Bradman's tour of England in 1948 ranks as the most complete tour of an overseas country on record, given that the tour party outplayed not only the host nation in Tests, but also all four corners of the country throughout a hot summer of Australian dominance. Few English players, Test or county, did not suffer at the hands of the Invincibles. The five-Test series was lost comprehensively 4-0. Of the 31 first-class matches played, Australia drew only eight, including the third Test at Old Trafford, where the Manchester rain intervened to halt a match in the balance. All the others were won convincingly; indeed 15 of them by an innings. Arthur Morris led the Test aggregates and averages with 696 runs at 87, but he was by no means a lone hand. The Don, Sid Barnes, Lindsey Hassett, Sam Loxton, Bill Brown, Neil Harvey and Keith Miller all scored at over 45 runs on tour, amassing 45 hundreds between them. Ray Lindwall took 86 wickets at 15.68 in first-class matches, while Bill Johnston claimed 102 at 16.42. The eight front-line bowlers all returned averages under 22! For the English, perhaps only Denis Compton and Alec Bedser would have pushed for selection in a combined team, such was the one-way traffic. It is little wonder that the Australian cricket fan gets misty-eyed at the mention of the Invincibles.

India

The Indian touring party, led by Nari Contractor, arrived in the West Indies in early 1962 for the five-Test series full of hope, having recently beaten England at home. Their weakness was expected to be in the bowling department, as they had no genuinely quick bowlers, but it was with the bat that they were found wanting, although Wes Hall (27 wickets), Lance Gibbs (24) and Garry Sobers (23) would have tested most line-ups. The West Indies batsmen excelled too: Rohan Kanhai, Sobers and captain Frank Worrell all averaged over 70 runs in the series. Inopportune collapses hurt the Indian side, particularly to Gibbs (8 for 38) in the second innings of the third Test at Bridgetown, where the last 8 wickets fell for 29 runs when a draw seemed inevitable. The squad was tired from a hard season of domestic cricket and became disheartened after their popular captain was so nearly killed in a shocking accident (*see* Chapter Eleven **Insult to Injury**). However, the 5-0 scoreline was unexpected.

England (3)

During the 1950s and 1960s, India suffered comprehensive series defeats on English soil, losing eleven matches out of the twelve played. On two occasions, the visitors were whitewashed, including a painful 5-0 reverse in 1959. Their batsmen failed to cope with the moving ball in often cold, overcast conditions, allowing bowlers such as Fred Trueman, Brian Statham, Alec Bedser, Jim Laker, John Snow and Ray Illingworth to fill their coffers. India would have to wait until 1993 to inflict a white-wash of their own on England, but it was no less sweet for the hosts' supporters when it arrived. Inevitably dubbed a 'Brownwash', the Indian team under Mohammad Azharuddin cruised to victory against a competent and experienced touring side, led by Graham Gooch.

Neither team were world-beaters at the time, so the contest was supposed to be close, yet India won each of the last two matches by an innings, having chased down England with 8 wickets to spare in the first. The home batsmen scored runs for fun, especially Sachin Tendulkar, Vinod Kambli and the captain. Their spinners left the visitors playing at shadows. Graeme Hick, for England, scored a big hundred in defiance, while Chris Lewis, enjoying happier days, hit his only Test ton. But it was more revealing that Hick's part-time off-spin also topped the bowling records with 8 wickets, while Anil Kumble took 21 for India.

No doubt, England's tour was hampered by security concerns and ill-health – the dreaded Delhi Belly – while the skipper Gooch endured a terrible run of bad form, averaging under 12. But the truth is that they were outplayed in every department and failed to adapt to the local conditions. India's struggles in England had been put into perspective.

Australia

By 1966-67, South Africa had taken giant steps forward as a cricketing nation, defeating Bobby Simpson's touring Australians 3-0 in a gripping five-Test series. South Africa had never previously won a single Test match against Australia on home turf, so the celebrations were heartfelt. Young talent in the form of dashing batsman Graeme Pollock and keeper/batsman Douglas Lindsay, with the fielding brilliance of Colin Bland and the all-round skills of Eddie Barlow, Trevor Goddard, Mike Proctor and Peter Pollock, conspired to make South Africa a team to be feared. By 1969-70, the team had matured under the thoughtful captaincy of Ali Bacher and it had also added the sumptuous strokeplay of big-haired tyro Barry Richards. The disgruntled Australian tourists, under Bill Lawry, were simply outclassed. Their strike bowler, Garth McKenzie, went for a miserable 333 runs in the series, taking just one wicket, gifted by Bacher when he stood on his stumps in the second innings of the final Test. Proctor, Barlow and Peter Pollock bowled with pace and guile, while Graeme Pollock and Richards gave a teaser of what the cricketing world would be

Pommie bashing

denied. In the second Test at Durban, Richards (140) was a triumph of free hitting, while Pollock (274) unfurled one of the great exhibitions of concentration and technique. Australia were trounced 4-0. And then it was all over. South Africa were excluded from Test cricket for the next two decades and a contender for the best team of all time was sacrificed in the name of apartheid.

West Indies

Given the quality of the players in the West Indian squad on its tour of Australia in 1975-76, the pre-series hype was justifiably loud. Clive Lloyd's young side had just beaten Australia in the inaugural World Cup final at Lord's (*see* Chapter Twelve **Expensive Run Outs**) and were brimming with talent that would test the best of the Australians in a six-match tussle.

By the end of the second Test at Perth, won by an innings by the tourists, the score was 1-1, but the Windies owned the momentum. Andy Roberts and Michael Holding were proving a match for Jeff Thomson and Dennis Lillee, while the Caribbean batsmen had powered to a total of 585 at the WACA, as Roy Fredericks hammered 169 from 145 balls. But then a malaise set in. Complacency mixed with injury, the odd dodgy decision and renewed Australian mettle, turned the series on its head. The hosts bowled with accuracy and venom, while their batsmen, with captain Greg Chappell to the fore (702 runs at 117 with three hundreds and three fifties), cashed in. No mercy was shown in the rout. Lloyd struggled to lift his troops, who slumped to a 5-1 hiding, losing four matches on the bounce, each by a margin.

The flight home could not have come soon enough. But the experience toughened the younger players for the challenges that lay ahead.

England (3)

The Test series dominated by the West Indies in England during the pleasant 1984 summer could have been played several times over and the hosts would still have struggled to draw a match, let alone win one. This is no great slight on the England players – it was simply that Clive Lloyd's team were at the zenith of their powers, capable of adapting their batting or bowling to any conditions. Their quartet of rapid, hostile bowlers, with no limit on the number of bouncers per over, helped turn even the most placid pitches into a trampoline. Joel Garner and Malcolm Marshall were at their ferocious best, ably supported by Michael Holding, Eldine Baptiste and the spin of Roger Harper. Their batsmen took it in turns to excel, although Gordon Greenidge and Larry Gomes enjoyed wonder series, while Viv Richards dominated the ODI matches.

Skipper Clive Lloyd, batting at five, rarely needed to break sweat. Whenever it looked as if England might gain the upper hand, one of his troops stepped forward to regain the initiative, whether with bat, ball or in the field. By losing the second ODI match, the West Indians did not achieve the immortality of the Australian Invincibles of 1948, but they did manage the first five-match Test whitewash by a touring side, which was quickly nicknamed the 'Blackwash'.

For England, it was a torrid experience, as two players were lost to bouncer-related injuries (*see* Chapter Eleven **Insult to Injury**). Captain David Gower endured a miserable series, scoring just one fifty and averaging 19. Ian Botham scored runs and took wickets, while his meat counter buddy Allan Lamb scored three hundreds, confirming his delectation for fast bowling. Other than that, this was one-way traffic.

England (4)

Two years later, England were to feel the lash of the Caribbean whip again, as the tour lurched from one island-beating to another. Whereas their efforts in 1984 had brought the best from the West Indies, the 1986 English side, again led by David Gower, did not test the hosts too keenly. The margins of defeat were wide and the collapses all too frequent. Clive Lloyd had retired, but Viv Richards moved seamlessly into the breach, raising the bar still higher. His demolition job of the English bowlers in the final Test in Antigua, hammering the fastest ever hundred in Tests from 53 balls (*see* Chapter Three **Battered Bowlers**), underlined the gulf in class. Desmond

Haynes and Richie Richardson scored runs, while Marshall and Garner again shared the wickets on uneven pitches that too often led to uneven contests. With Patrick Patterson bowling like a blindfolded knife thrower and Michael Holding employing every trick in his repertoire, the batsmen had little respite. Gower showed his class by scoring 370 runs, while Graham Gooch made four fifties. Mike Gatting, potentially the most likely to hamper the hosts' dominance, was sidelined in the ODI series by a Malcolm Marshall bumper that flattened his nose (*see* Chapter Eleven **Insult to Injury**). The 5-0 drubbing brought the tally to ten consecutive wins over England, which could have been extended to fifteen, had the first Test of the 1988 series (won 4-0 by the West Indies) back in England not been hampered by rain.

West Indies (2)

Throughout the two decades of Test match dominance by the West Indies, opposing batsmen were peppered with a barrage of fast bowling not seen since the Bodyline Series. Unsurprisingly, modern cricketers were quick to repay the favour as soon as West Indies cricket showed signs of decline. West Indies touring sides were still accorded five-Test tours, organised when their bowlers and batsmen would draw in crowds. But these extended series left the tourists open to the threat of ignominious whitewashes. The first to twist the knife were the South Africans in 1998-99, whose discipline in all facets of the game showed up a sloppy West Indian side under Brian Lara that was plagued by contractual disputes. Allan Donald and Shaun Pollock matched Courtney Walsh and Curtly Ambrose, while the three big batting guns – Lara, Carl Hooper and Shiv Chanderpaul – failed to fire. Jonty Rhodes excelled with both bat and in the field, while modern lights Jacques Kallis and Mark Boucher grew their reputations. Rainbow Wash, as it became known, was a mess for the visitors.

West Indies (3)

The barometer of West Indies success was dipping alarmingly with Brian Lara at the helm, as the squad arrived on the shores of New Zealand in 1999-2000. The season had started brightly enough with a 2-2 series against Australia, but the brilliance of Lara's batting had been papering over the cracks. Since then, the squad had been on an international merry-go-round, visiting Singapore, Toronto, Dhaka and Sharjah, before finally jetting off to New Zealand.

Oddly, the tourists started the two-match Test series in the best possible manner, by utterly dominating the first day. Having won the toss and chosen to bat, openers Adrian Griffith (103 not out) and Sherwin Cambell (170) had constructed a serene partnership, to leave the New Zealanders gasping at 282 for 1. Surely they could not lose from there? The only blight had been Campbell's sloppy dismissal just before stumps and it soon came back to haunt the side. Chris Cairns and Daniel Vettori found a second wind and ran through the remaining nine wickets for 89 runs. By knuckling down and stringing together partnerships – indicative of the contrast in the mindsets of the two teams – the hosts duly snatched a first innings lead, before slicing through the Windies for a measly 97 runs on a placid pitch. The New Zealanders triumphed by a barely believable nine wickets. Having scored 276 for the first wicket, the West Indies added just 180 runs for their next 19 wickets in the match.

The wheels came off for the rest of the series, as they lost the next Test by an innings and then all five ODIs. New Zealand played gritty, efficient cricket, but they were by no means a team of world-beaters. Lara ended the tour with an average of 35 with no hundreds, almost inconceivable at that time in his career. Jimmy Adams and Shiv Chanderpaul could only scrape into the twenties. Courtney Walsh returned with a bowling average of 75 with five wickets to his name. New Zealand had once more proved a burial ground for vaunted reputations.

West Indies (4)

The whitewash at the hands of the Aussies in 2000-01 was less of a surprise than the South African debacle, as the gulf between the sides was plain to see. Having opened the series at the 'Gabba with a capitulation to 82 runs, a landslide to a home win was inevitable. Glenn McGrath all but decided the second Test at Perth with a hat-trick on the first morning, including the best West Indies batsmen Brian Lara and Jimmy Adams, each first ball. A big Lara hundred in the third Test in Adelaide kept the Aussies honest, but a second innings collapse surrendered the momentum again. The Boxing Day and New Year Tests continued the party, all at a proud nation's expense.

West Indies (5)

The final nail in the coffin was hammered in by England, the team to suffer more than most in the 1980s. By 2004, the fortunes of the two sides were on different arcs. The West Indies were forced to pick bowlers who would have struggled to make their island teams in the 1980s – they even failed to defend 292 against Ireland in an ODI – while England were developing a line-up that would beat South Africa in South Africa and then win back the Ashes. England won the series 4-0, ending the summer with an even seven from seven, having earlier dispatched the Kiwis. Shiv Chanderpaul batted for hours in a vain attempt to rally his side, while Chris Gayle, Dwayne Bravo and Ramnaresh Sarwan gave hope for the future. Lara showed glimpses of his former prowess, but nothing more, despite the crowds willing him to entertain. Only fast bowler Fidel Edwards provided food for thought, as the English batsmen swelled their averages.

Bangladesh

When the ICC admitted Bangladesh as the tenth Test playing nation in 2000, it no doubt expected some teething troubles. In the last decade, there have been plenty, although popularity for the sport is growing in the country and more competent players are emerging. Surely it is only a matter of time before they claim a really big scalp? But in 2007, those elusive signs of improvement were not evident in Sri Lanka during the three Test series. Bangladesh were obliterated in all three matches. In the first at Colombo, having been inserted, they were spun out by Muttiah Muralitharan for 87, before the hosts' batsmen creamed four centuries, including a maiden Test ton for bowler Chaminda Vaas. An innings defeat quickly followed. In the second Test, again in Colombo, Bangladesh were all out for 62, their lowest total in Tests. Kumar Sangakkara, who had missed out in the first Test, hit an unbeaten double hundred, which again set up an innings win. The visitors did manage three figures in the first innings of the last Test in Kandy, albeit 131 was never going to be enough. Sangakkara added another 222 unbeaten runs to his tally (giving him an average of 428 for the series!), sharing a 300-run partnership with his old friend Mahela Jayawardene. Another innings defeat was the result. Muralitharan took 26 wickets in the series, while the most a Bangladeshi bowler managed was four.

England (4)

Andrew Flintoff had been the talisman for England in their triumphant regaining of the Ashes in 2005 after a painful wait of sixteen years. For the selectors, there was no other candidate to lead the team on the 2006-07 tour down under in a bid to retain them. Whether the job should have been given to him or to someone else who wasn't the mainstay of the bowling attack and also a vital cog in the batting wheel is largely irrelevant now, as the result – a 5-0 whitewash – stands. Besides, could any captain have stood in the way of Ricky Ponting's troops, who were hurting badly and bent on revenge? Bootcamps, bonding sessions and fifteen months of brooding guaranteed England a determined opposition.

The contest could not have started better for Ponting, releasing his frustration on the England bowlers with a violent 196 as Australia reached 346 for 3 by stumps on the first day at the 'Gabba. The horror of 2005 had been forgotten, as the home team wrapped up victory by 277 runs. Adelaide proved to be England's Waterloo, as they collapsed in the second innings to give Australia a sniff of victory that ought to have been beyond them (*see* Chapter Twelve **Expensive Run Outs**). Again Ponting was man of the match for his brilliant batting.

Adam Gilchrist scored a blistering hundred off just 59 balls to set up the win at Perth, wresting back the urn with the minimum of fuss. After that, the agenda was to make Glenn McGrath's prediction of a whitewash a reality. (Did he not foretell that before every Ashes series?) The Boxing Day Test at Melbourne was a festive party for the hosts: they cruised to an innings win as Matthew Hayden and his fishing buddy, Andrew Symonds, cut loose before Shane Warne filleted the English batsmen. Sadly for the crowd, it was all over by the end of the third day.

Another collapse in the second innings of the fifth test in Sydney allowed the rampant Aussies to canter to the whitewash finishing line by 10 wickets, a fitting farewell to McGrath, Warne, Langer and Martyn. The demolition job was catharsis for the Australians. These 'forgotten Ashes', wedged between the home victories of 2005 and 2009, are often glossed over by England supporters.

South Africa (2)

Long tours containing five or more Tests are confined to Ashes series nowadays, although the Australians and South Africans have managed to engineer six-match series in recent years by consecutively playing three at home and then three away. The first such double-header came in the 2005-06 season and was touted as a showdown between the two strongest teams in the world. Australia were deemed vulnerable, having just lost the Ashes in England, while South Africa's ambitious captain Graeme Smith had assembled a team with all the requisite parts to kick a wallaby when it was down.

A humiliating defeat on home soil could have cooked Ricky Ponting's goose, but he reacted in typical fashion, hammering three hundreds with Bradmanesque speed and regularity. Shane Warne, Brett Lee and Glenn McGrath did the rest, as Australia left for South African soil with a 2-0 advantage.

The word games had boiled over, prompting South African keeper Mark Boucher to encourage his home supporters to seek revenge for the sledging and barracking down under. The rallying cry fell on deaf ears. Even without Glenn McGrath, Australia's bowlers proved too strong, while the runs kept pouring off Ponting's bat. Poignantly, Smith did not manage a fifty in the first five Tests, before being sidelined with a finger injury. In the battle of the skippers, Ponting had buried him. Unofficially, Australia won the 'series' 5-0. Crisis, what crisis?

Chapter Fourteen
Minnow Mayhem

On most occasions when an established Test-playing nation takes on a minnow in a limited-overs match, the expected result is quickly delivered. Just occasionally, the little fish grow sharp teeth and bite a big chunk of pride out of the superpower's reputation.

India

Nowadays, it is barely a surprise to see the talented Sri Lankan cricket team beating top nations in the Test, ODI or Twenty20 arena. After their emphatic win in the 1996 World Cup, where their batsmen lit up the Indian pitches with attacking strokeplay, the islanders have enjoyed top table status. But in the 1979 World Cup, as a lowly ICC Associate Member, Sri Lanka were yet to earn their stripes against a Test nation. The batsmen had shown their potential four years earlier, amassing 276 for 4 against Australia in their 60 overs, which was a decent total in those days. But the bowlers had already conceded 328 runs. To beat India in the last match of their pool stages in Manchester in 1979, Sri Lanka needed her bowlers to fire too, especially against the household names of Gavaskar, Vengsarkar, Viswanath, Kapil Dev, Amarnath, Venkataraghavan and Bedi. Both teams had already been knocked out of the Cup, but there was no doubting the desire on either side. Like two brothers competing in the back garden, the elder dare not lose face, while the younger will do anything to win. The Sri Lankans' innings started steadily, but then took off in an entertaining and carefree partnership between Duleep Mendis and Sudath Pasqual, the youngest player in the tournament at just seventeen years old. Mendis struck three mighty sixes in his 64 off 57 balls, as his side posted 238 for 5. The Indian reply was delayed for a day with rain, but the pitch was unaffected, allowing the batsmen to start brightly: they reached 119 for 2, with plenty of time left. But when kingpin Gundappa Viswanath ran himself out for 22, the door creaked open. Leg spinner Somachandra De Silva put his foot in the gap with three middle order wickets, before opener Tony Opatha returned to knock it off its hinges by mopping up India's tail. The party in Sri Lanka lasted several weeks and culminated in admission to the Test family. If 1996 was the cherry on the cake, then 1979 was when they lit the oven fires.

Australia

Zimbabwe cricket was plunged into a state of ill-repair by Robert Mugabe's oppressive regime, yet there was a time when the ODI team especially was making waves in the international cricketing community. The minnows beat both India and South Africa to progress in the 1999 World Cup and then they qualified for the second phase of the 2003 tournament too. Led by talents such as Andy and Grant Flower, Murray Goodwin, Neil Johnson, Tatenda Taibu and Heath Streak, the developing side routinely gave the bigger nations a bloody nose, especially England. But perhaps the biggest win in their history came back in 1983 in their first ever ODI match. The novice Zimbabweans faced down the might of the Australians (476 caps combined) at Trent Bridge in the World Cup of that year. At 86 for 5, with Dave Houghton departing for a first ball duck, the match seemed to be following the script. Enter Duncan Fletcher. The all-rounder combined with Kevin Curran and Iain Butchart to drag the total to a respectable 239, scoring 69 not out in the process. However, with 60 overs to knock them off, Australia were still red hot favourites. But that would be to deny Fletcher his day in the sun. Coming on second change, he again shifted the momentum of the innings, taking the first four wickets. Once Kepler Wessels was run out and Curran had removed Allan Border, the game was up. Zimbabwe had won by 13 runs, raising a cheer amongst underdogs everywhere.

England

If you were to choose an all-star team of cricketers who had tormented England's hapless ODI team in the last twenty years, then there would be no shortage of candidates. The opening bowler, however, might not be an Ambrose, McGrath, Pollock or Akram, but rather a lesser known chicken farmer from Zimbabwe. Eddo Brandes – jovial, rugged, old-school and fond of a biscuit – had plenty of talent, but rarely put cricket's demands above those of his family farm or his desire to enjoy life. When he did put his mind to it, particularly against England, he could be a potent swing bowler and a destructive batsmen until his batteries ran out or the sun was over the yard-arm.

In the 1992 World Cup, Zimbabwe looked set to receive another lesson from the big boys, as they were bowled out for 134 at Albury on a bowler friendly track. England had a team packed with talent, but they suffered a dreadful start as Brandes trapped Graham Gooch lbw with the first ball of the innings. In a blistering opening spell, Brandes then dismissed England's Southern African trio of Allan Lamb, Robin Smith and his old school chum Graeme Hick. The chicken farmer finished with figures of 4 for 21 in 10 overs, as England lost by 9 runs. His next ODIs against England came in the 1997 series, which Zimbabwe won 3-0. By the final match, England were in tatters. Brandes twisted the knife, taking a sensational hat-trick containing Nick Knight, John Crawley and Nasser Hussain, to leave the chase reeling at 13 for 3. In total, Brandes played and won four ODIs against England. He took 11 wickets at a cost of 9 runs apiece, with a strike rate of one wicket every three overs. With those figures, he'd be the first name on the team sheet!

West Indies

The match that would become one of the most embarrassing in a proud nation's history (and one of the most celebrated in that of another) did not start out too badly for the West Indies. On a bowler-friendly pitch in the Nehru Stadium in Pune, skipper Richie Richardson won the toss during the pool match in the 1996 World Cup and duly inserted the amateur Kenya XI. It proved to be the right decision, as Courtney Walsh helped dismantle the top order, leaving the Kenyans gasping for air at 81 for 6. Given that batting was the underdogs' stronger suit, the writing was on the wall. But seventeen-year-old Thomas Odoyo chose not to read it, grinding out 24 runs and coaxing the target to 166 in just under the full 50 overs. If it was sloppy that the West Indians allowed the innings to last that long, what followed next was downright careless. Each batsman passed responsibility on to the next man, falling cheaply as though confident that someone else would eventually do enough. Star performer Brian Lara's loose dismissal, famously caught behind by the stout Tariq Iqbal (complete with glasses, blue headband and gloves like a sea lion's flippers), made the impossible seem almost inevitable. The West Indies were left sprawling on the canvas, all out for 93 runs, as the Kenyans went loopy.

Pakistan

Such was the surprise at Bangladesh beating Pakistan in the group stages of the 1999 World Cup, played at Northampton in England, allegations of match-fixing soon emerged. Evidence was never forthcoming to prove that the Pakistan team had thrown the contest, having already qualified for the Super Sixes stage of the tournament, although the selection of certain players and the decision to field first had aroused suspicion. The Bangladeshis certainly did not react as if they had won a rigged fight, calling a national holiday back home and celebrating like billy-o in every expat community worldwide. As it happened, the victory came with ease. Batting first, the Tigers had amassed 223 for 9 in their 50 overs, despite Saqlain Mushtaq's 5 wickets. The Pakistani quicks struggled to control the white ball in the early English season conditions, sending down 28 wides to make extras the second top score. Their batters never came close, crashing to 42 for 5, even with a vastly experienced line-up. Three were even run out by the keeper Khaled Mashud, while the opening bowler Khaled Mahmud scooped the man of the match for his three top order wickets. Pakistan capitulated for 161. Nobody in the match had reached fifty. The team selection, extras and the run-outs still don't look clever, but Bangladesh deserve more credit than that. Their supporters had no doubt that the team had earned their victory, pouring on to the pitch in wild celebration. Admission to the Test arena quickly followed for Bangladesh.

Australia (2)

Nobody expected Bangladesh to beat Australia in the 2005 tri-nation ODI series in England, least of all Aussie all-rounder Andrew Symonds, who warmed up in the boozers of downtown Cardiff the evening (and morning) before the match. There was a time when the management chose to ignore the late night antics of cricketers, but those days have passed and Symonds was told to carry the drinks for his team-mates. Not that it ought to have mattered to the World Cup winners, who were playing a team that had won only nine ODI matches from the 107 in its history. The game started badly for Australia, as they lost Adam Gilchrist for a second ball duck (lbw, but probably too high) and then Ricky Ponting for just one. On their day, both could have outscored the Bangladeshis by themselves. But their team had other riches and while 249 runs in the 50 overs was just about par, it would surely prove to be enough. Step forward Mohammad Ashraful. At just twenty years old and barely five feet tall, he looked like a child next to the hulking figures of Matthew Hayden and Glenn McGrath. The youngest player ever to score a Test hundred (on debut against Muttiah Muralitharan's Sri Lanka no less), Ashraful needed a stage to show-case his talent and Sophia Gardens provided it. Pacing his innings to perfection and picking off boundaries from McGrath when it suited him, the pint-sized destroyer reached 100 from the same number of balls. The coup de grâce was delivered by the equally short Aftab Ahmed, who lofted Jason Gillespie for six in the last over. Would Symonds have made a difference? Quite possibly. Bangladesh couldn't have cared less – they had still supplied one of the greatest shocks the game had seen.

Pakistan (2)

Pakistan captain Inzamam-ul-Haq would have raised his bushy eyebrows when inspecting the Sabina Park pitch in Jamaica on the morning of his team's group match against Ireland in the 2007 World Cup. It was tinged with grass as green as the shirts of his opponents, which risked turning the match into an even contest. Ranked number four in the world and with genuine prospects of lifting the cup, Pakistan ought to have blown Ireland aside, even if it was St Patrick's Day. But the coin fell against Inzi, allowing the Irish seamers first taste of what proved to be a juicy pie. Early edges flew to fielders who clung on and soon the match had descended into a dogfight. All 10 wickets fell to catches, including several in the slips, as Pakistan stumbled to 132. Far from being a stroll for the Irish, however, Inzi released his own seamers, who revelled in the conditions. But for an inspired knock of 72 runs by keeper Niall O'Brien, the only player all day to find his feet, this could have been a 'what if' moment for the minnows. His brother Kevin helped get the team over the line, to start the celebrations. Sadly, the mood soon changed, with the news of the untimely death of Pakistan's manager, Bob Woolmer. Pakistan's ejection from the Cup quickly became an afterthought.

Australia (3)

Aussie skipper Ricky Ponting has always been fairly dismissive of Twenty20, despite hammering an unbeaten 98 from 55 balls in his first attempt against New Zealand. His next knock, in England in 2005, yielded a duck in a match that the hosts won comfortably to stir up national expectation. 'Just a bit of fun,' said Ricky. 'Hit and giggle.' At the inaugural Twenty20 World Cup in 2007 in South Africa, the Australians were stung into taking the format a bit more seriously. A team of heavyweight batsmen – Hayden, Gilchrist, Ponting, Symonds, Hussey and Hodge – struggled to 138 in their 20 overs against a team of young Zimbabweans who were expecting a trouncing. The bookies had Australia at 50-1 on at the start of the evening. Even so, this modest total ought to have been defendable by experienced campaigners such as Lee, Bracken, Johnson and Clark. But they had nothing in their locker to rein in the bravado of Brendan Taylor, who held his nerve amid the rain delays to score 60 from 45 balls, including two vital sixes in the same over off Brad Hodge. Nobody in green and gold was giggling now. They duly tried a bit harder and thrashed England in the next match.

England (2)

Only a diehard Netherlands fan would have bet on his team causing an upset in the first round of the Twenty20 World Cup during June 2009. Their opposition, England, were officially the away team at Lord's that evening, but the Dutch squatters rights were expected to be brief, especially after the host nation's openers put on a hundred in the first 11 overs. The middle order lost its way amid the gloomy conditions, yet a total of 162 should have been enough. As the rain fell, the Orangemen appeared to gather in confidence. Amateur Tom de Grooth fearlessly smeared the bowling of the experienced English bowlers, cracking six fours and a massive six in his 49 runs off 30 balls. When he fell, the Netherlands were in sight of a famous victory and were grateful that their most experienced professional, Essex's Ryan ten Doeschate, was next to walk out. Even then, it almost turned sour. With two runs needed from the last ball, the facing batsman Edgar Schiferli could do no more than bunt the ball back to the bowler Stuart Broad. Instinctively, Broad threw the ball at the stumps for the win. He missed, the Dutch ran overthrows and then ran round the pitch in celebration. For the rest of that evening, St John's Wood became Holland Park.

Canada

However...whilst tournaments like the ICC Champions Trophy and the World Cup give lesser nations a chance to shine and improve, they also provide a stage for some woefully one-sided contests that prove counter-productive for the victim.

Minnow mayhem

Canada were never likely to upset the hosts in the group stages of the 1979 World Cup in England, but all slim hopes were extinguished when the skipper Bryan Mauricette opted to bat first on a soaking Old Trafford wicket. His batsmen had no answer to Willis, Old, Botham and Hendricks, eventually falling for 45 all out after a tortuous 40 overs. Only Franklyn Dennis reached double figures with a shame-saving 21 off 99 balls. England did lose two wickets, including a duck for skipper Mike Brearley, lbw to John Valentine, but Boycott and Gooch took them home within 14 overs. As it was a 60-over match, the 277 balls remaining in the innings amounts to the largest margin of victory over a team chasing.

Netherlands

Pakistan, given their ability to blow Saharan hot and Arctic cold, often dangle a juicy worm in front of a minnow, but they are also capable of skewering them without pity. In the 2002 Champions Trophy, the Netherlands came up against a side that had just been humiliated in the opening match by hosts Sri Lanka. There would be no mercy shown to the amateur outfit. Having been made to chase leather in comprehensive defeat to Sri Lanka, the Netherlands wisely opted to bat first, if only to reduce the loss margin. All out for 136, a routine run-chase was unfolding, until the Dutch snagged their first wicket with the score at 85, midway through the twelfth over, with 52 runs still required. Big mistake! Twenty-nine balls later, the match was over, as Shahid Afridi, who had failed against Sri Lanka, belted 55 runs from 18 balls, with four fours and six sixes. His strike rate of 305.55 remains a world record for scores of 25 and above in ODIs. Dutch off-spinner Adeel Raja took the brunt of Afridi's fury, as his 14-ball spell was belted for 31 runs. Those figures may not sound too painful, until you consider that his first six balls had been dots...

Netherlands (2)

The highest score in an ODI innings to date was made in 2006 against the Netherlands by Sri Lanka in Amstelveen. The Dutch were unfortunate that the visitors arrived after whitewashing England in a five-match series. Moreover, the Sri Lankans were peeved that the matches had been organised in the first place and they took their displeasure with their own board out on the hapless part-time bowlers. After Sanath Jayasuriya had given them a blistering start, smashing 157 off 104 balls, the middle order made a dash for the world record of 438 runs achieved by South Africa in their epic run chase against Australia the year before. Tillakaratne Dilshan, heir to Jayasuriya's throne at the top of the order, took up the baton, crashing 117 from 78 balls to guide the total to 443. Such was the Sri Lankan's disinterest in the one-sided match, the sparse crowd had the pleasure of watching a team that was batting first, chase down a target.

Bermuda

In the group stages of the 2007 World Cup in the Caribbean, lowly Bermuda were pitted against the might of India. In terms of experience, talent, finance, resources, population – you name it – this was a mismatch of ugly proportions. Bermuda could line up a hundred times against India and not win once. But if you play cricket with heart and passion, sometimes it will reward you with glory: and there was something truly glorious about policeman Dwayne Leverock launching his eighteen-stone frame to his right at second slip to pluck an edge from opening bat Robin Uthappa in the second over. The bowler, Malachi Jones, ran about the pitch as if his jockstrap was on fire. Leverock set off on a lap of honour, stopping only to perform a jig and blow kisses to the crowd, before being bundled over by his team-mates. Tears of happiness wet their cheeks. India were 3 for 1, with Bermuda well on top. Unfortunately, they did not take another wicket until the score was 205. Leverock's

10 overs leaked 96 runs (the tenth worst in history), as India streaked to 413 for 5 (the sixth largest total in history). Bermuda were all out for 156, to lose by 257 runs, the second highest deficit on record. India had routinely flexed its muscles, yet Bermuda had taken the award for Champagne Moment.

Ireland

The lads from the Emerald Isle have enjoyed some stirring victories over the big names in their history, but they have also been put back in their box on occasion. No time more so than in 2008, after a confident touring New Zealand had just dispatched England in an ODI series. The tri-nations tournament with hosts Scotland was always likely to result in victory for the Test-playing nation, but the organisers were hoping for a closer contest. An opening stand of 274 runs by James Marshall (161) and Brendon McCullum (166) put paid to that (Ireland had won the toss too), as New Zealand passed the 400-run mark. Ireland then dissolved for only 112 runs, gifting victory by 290 runs, the biggest margin ever in ODI history.

Chapter Fifteen
Nearly Men

The intricacies of Test cricket allow a team to be utterly outplayed, yet still leave the field in a happier state than its opponent. Likewise, a batsman who is out for 99 may feel more peeved than one who bags a duck. Glorious failure is an all too common occurrence.

Hanif Mohammad

No matter the depth of runs, being out on 99 adds a degree of failure to the effort. Brian Lara's 400 not out in Tests and 501 not out in first-class cricket both left the spectator wondering how many more he could have added. The latter innings over-took the astonishing effort of 499 runs made by Pakistan's 'Little Master' Hanif Mohammad in 1959 for Karachi against Bahawalpur. Hanif had proved his strength of purpose during a marathon knock of 337 against the West Indies in Bridgetown the year before, finally dismissed after surviving over 16 hours (999 minutes) at the crease. But his legendary concentration wavered in Karachi, as he attempted to pinch the strike in the last over of the day. His short, tired legs could not carry him to the right end quick enough and the opportunity of scoring the 500th run was lost.

Mushtaq Mohammad

The third Test between Pakistan and England in Karachi in 1973 fizzled out into a tame draw, leaving both sides stymied in the series. Batsmen flourished on a friendly pitch, although none of the seven players who reached fifty in the match continued to a hundred. Three of them, however, were undone on 99. Pakistanis Majid Khan and Mushtaq Mohammad (one of Hanif's three brothers to play for Pakistan) set the example for Dennis Amiss, who would have notched his third century of the series. The first and last of this hapless trio were dismissed by the opposition, both of them caught. Mushtaq, on the other hand, brought about his own demise. He had sweated on 99 for several overs. As the pressure built, he pushed the ball for a quick single, took off, but then saw to his horror that fielder Norman Gifford had swooped in from the covers. His batting partner, Intikhab Alam, offered to sacrifice himself, but Mushtaq panicked and bolted back to his crease, only for Alan Knott to collect a wild throw and complete the run out. 'I was the bloody dumbest of them all,' Mushtaq told the BBC. 'At least they got out properly.'

Australia

In 1982 at the MCG, Allan Border and Jeff Thomson almost completed a nail-biting last-wicket smash-and-grab against England in the fourth Ashes Test, as they whittled down the target from 74 runs to just four. Border, who had struggled for runs in the series, was invited to take singles by opposition captain Bob Willis, so playing himself back into form. Thomson, at the other end, played a cool hand, adding his own singles where available to contribute a valuable 21 runs. The other Aussie players superstitiously remained in the same seats until stumps on the fourth day, returning to the exact positions the next morning, with 37 runs still needed. Neither batsman truly believed the victory was possible, until they came within just one hit of winning back the urn. Ian Botham was bowling and he served up a wide-ish long-hop outside the off-stump, which Thomson ought to have smashed to the boundary. Instead, he tried to guide the ball for one, succeeding only in edging the ball to Chris Tavaré at first slip. Tavaré parried the ball, nearly becoming the latest Englishman to have dropped the Ashes. But second slip Geoff Miller came to his rescue, diving full-length to snaffle the rebound. For the Aussie onlookers, the sequence was horror, followed by joy, ending with renewed agony. Yet, Australia had the last laugh, as Kim Hughes hit a century and a reinvigorated Border knocked two eighties in the final Test in Sydney to secure the draw that regained the Ashes.

Don Topley

Lord's groundstaff teenager Don Topley so nearly wrote himself into the annals of cricketing history by clutching a brilliant one-handed catch on the boundary during the Lord's Test against the all-conquering West Indies in 1984. The batsman was Malcolm Marshall and the bowler Bob Willis, who watched his bouncer fly off the Barbadian's bat to the square leg boundary. The young substitute fielder made good ground and pulled off a memorable catch, only to place one foot over the rope. The umpire raised both hands to the sky to signal that Topley's valiant effort had been in vain.

Graeme Hick

Zimbabwean Graeme Hick may not have reaped the international rewards of his considerable talent, but he remains one of the best batsmen to have graced the county circuit, scoring a record 64,000-plus runs in all cricket, with 136 first-class centuries during his 25-year career. Would a lighter touch from the England management have brought more runs from Hick? After all, he was thrown in at the deep end against a full-throttle West Indian attack with the weight of his adopted nation's expectation on his shoulders. Under the current set-up of closed-shop contracts and sports psychologists, perhaps both he and fellow international underachiever Mark Ramprakash would have fulfilled their potential. Hick did manage six Test centuries. But he could feel aggrieved that it was not seven, after Michael Atherton declared with his man stranded on 98 not out during the third Test of the 1994-95 Ashes in Sydney. Hick, who had scored his runs at a much faster rate than Atherton's 67 in the same innings, believed there would be another over before the declaration, so blocked out three deliveries. Atherton was nervous about having enough time to bowl the Australians out, which was necessary to retain the hope of winning back the Ashes. Personal milestones were irrelevant. As it happened, England did come close to winning the match, so the extra over could have been crucial. But for a batsman straining to find his feet at Test level, a ton against Australia at the SCG is a precious achievement. How many other skippers would have denied Hick that hundred?

Alex Tudor

New Zealand let slip a gilt-edged opportunity to win the first Test of the 1999 summer series in England, when they failed to capitalise on a hefty first innings lead. Opener Roger Twose was out for a diamond duck in the second innings (completing a four-ball pair), before his team-mates capitulated to 107. The total would have been much smaller had number ten batsman Simon Doull not slapped 46 in a 54-run ninth wicket partnership. Having struggled themselves in the first innings, the target of 208 to win was by no means a formality for England, especially when Alec Stewart fell for a duck just before stumps on the second day. Tall fast bowler Alex Tudor entered the fray as nightwatchman and not only survived the opening exchanges the next morning, but soon became the home side's most potent batsman. He dominated a 73-run partnership with Mark Butcher and then a 98-run stand with Nasser Hussain, to knock off the runs with ease. With his maiden hundred in sight and two-and-a-half days to get it, he was powerless to intervene when Graham Thorpe, his Surrey team-mate, came in and ruthlessly smashed the winning runs, leaving Tudor high and dry on 99 not out. He never came close to a Test hundred again.

Sachin Tendulkar

There is very little calamitous about Sachin Tendulkar's ODI batting record, scoring as he has 46 hundreds to date (2010) – 17 more than his nearest rival Ricky Ponting – except when one considers that the Little Master has reached 90 runs on 18 occasions without making a hundred. That figure is twice that of his nearest rival. Only once in those 18 innings was he not out, stranded on 96 as India won the match. Six of his nineties were made in one year, 2007, without a century in between, and included three scores of 99. That's hardly a failure – after all, he scored 1,425 runs in the year at an average of 47.5 – but then everything is relative.

Shane Warne

Australia's finest bowler never did make a hundred in Tests, although he came within a few yards of achieving the feat at the WACA in Perth in 2001. Australia had been totally outplayed by New Zealand up until Warne came to the crease on the third day, with the score at 192 for 6. Four New Zealand batsmen made hundreds in the opening innings (although none of the others had reached double figures) and the hosts were looking nervously at the follow-on target of 334. Warne ought to have been caught on 10 by Nathan Astle in the slips, but the reprieve allowed the right-hander to open his shoulders, hitting ten boundaries as he carried the score past the follow-on. Riding his luck, Warne hit his way to 99 just before the umpires pulled stumps. The crowd urged him to reach his maiden hundred that evening and the showman went for broke, hammering a ball from opposition spinner Daniel Vettori down towards deep square leg. Had it gone along the carpet, there was an easy single. A little higher and the ball would have cleared the fielder Mark Richardson. Instead, the wind slowed the ball's progress, allowing Richardson to settle underneath and pouch a simple catch. Despite knocking a couple of first-class hundreds, Warne could not pass the milestone in Tests. He remains the highest scorer of runs in Test cricket without a hundred to his name.

Asim Kamal

Pakistan's left-handed batsman Asim Kamal is the only man in Test history to be dismissed on 99 on debut, who did not then go on to score a hundred. He has grounds for complaint that he has not played more than twelve matches for his country, reaching his fifty on eight occasions and playing exactly the organised and gritty middle-order innings that the Pakistan Test team has so often lacked. His debut against South Africa in 2003 in Lahore promised much, as he dug in to establish useful partnerships in his first knock, at a critical point of the match. Taking 246 balls was no crime and he may well have reached a deserved century had he not lost the strike for several overs on 99. Nerves caused him to play the only rushed shot of his innings to seamer Andre Nel, and the ball ricocheted off the inside edge to clip his off stump. On another day, it might have beaten the keeper for four or bounced down off the pad for a scrambled single. Instead, Kamal had to trudge off. Scores of 87 in Australia and 91 in India further proved his ability, but he was then dropped, rueing that one extra run. Fellow Pakistani Zahid Fazal suffered the frustration of being carted off with cramp just two shy of a hundred in Sharjah against India in 1991. His knock of 98 not out would remain his highest score for his country.

Zimbabwe

It is uncanny how the same names seem to appear time and again in backs-to-the-

Nervous nineties

wall accomplishments. Premier West Indian fast bowler Fidel Edwards would ordinarily have passed unnoticed in batting circles, but for a series of rearguard efforts that saved no less than four Tests. The first came as a novice in 2003 against lowly Zimbabwe, a team which had come into the match on a sequence of twelve straight defeats. But the African side dominated from start to finish, racking up over 500 runs and then holding the visitors to 335. Time was freakishly lost from the game after a ball became stuck under the heavy roller, causing an indentation on a length, which had to be patched up. Whether it cost the hosts the match can only be guessed, but they eventually found themselves just one ball from victory. As the light deteriorated, forcing the Zimbabwean captain Heath Streak to bowl his slow bowlers, keeper Ridley Jacobs and number eleven Edwards saw off the remaining 71 deliveries for a draw that was ill-deserved.

India

The Antigua Recreation Ground provided the stage for so many thrilling West Indies performances throughout the 1990s and 2000s, but usually in an attacking sense due to its flat wicket. Brian Lara's record-breaking knocks against England and the highest ever run-chase against Australia in 2003 were all triumphs for the flashing blade. When the home team played India at the ARG in the first Test of 2006, scheduled as the old ground's swansong, the match was decided by a straight bat and a stout heart. But it was no less exciting for that. India were 130 runs behind after the first innings, but piled on a massive 521 for 6, as Wasim Jaffer scored a double hundred. Fidel Edwards had broken down, bowling just five overs before hobbling off to the pavilion with a pulled hamstring. But he would have to return to the line of fire, as the Indian bowlers prized out the top order on the last day, including Lara for a duck. Batting with a runner, Edwards survived 36 balls, while his childhood friend from Barbados, Corey Collymore, negotiated eight deliveries, including the last over from Sri Sreesanth as the stands rocked. It was a fitting finale for a venue that had provided so many wonderful memories.

England

In fact, though, that match wasn't quite the finale. Edwards and the ARG had one more unlikely triumph during the Caribbean tour by England in 2009. The scheduled match at the new Sir Vivian Richards Stadium was farcically abandoned after just ten balls for being an unsafe playing surface, so becoming the shortest Test in history. (It was a fortnight after the inimitable Test Match Special scorer, Bill Frindall, had passed away, who was coincidentally born during the longest ever Test in 1938.) The original St John's ground was quickly dusted off by curator Andy Roberts and the old girl laid on another nail-biting draw, although England should really have cantered home. Declaring on 566, after centuries from captain Andrew Strauss and Paul Collingwood, the West Indies were only ever playing catch-up. All out for 285, including a first baller for keeper Denesh Ramdin, England decided to rest their bowlers, rather than enforce the follow-on. In hindsight, whether a target as big as 503 runs was necessary is a matter for debate, but with the home team already three down at the end of the fourth day, the decision promised to be academic. Then Guyanan team-mates Ramnaresh Sarwan and Shivnarine Chanderpaul dug in all the next morning, setting the example for those below to follow. Every batsman did his bit, but it still came down to Edwards and fellow quick Daren Powell to keep the English out. Andrew Flintoff, who had bagged a pair in the match, ran through the pain barrier to deliver a hostile spell, while Graeme Swann spun the ball with fielders crowding the bat. But, as the locals flooded in to see the spectacle, and the Barmy Army booed every delay, the light failed. Edwards had done it again!

England (2)

Come the climax of the Port-of-Spain Test at the end of that series, Fidel Edwards must have been suffering from a queasy feeling of déjà vu. Again England's batsmen had filled their boots with runs, as the West Indies seemed determined to play for a draw from the outset, in order to defend their 1-0 series lead. It was a risky strategy from the captain, Chris Gayle, who would have been panned if it had failed, but he gave the appearance of a man with everything under control. Indeed, he scored a hundred of his own in response, before Chanderpaul and Brendan Nash combined with a 200-run partnership to seemingly make the game safe. After England charged to a 240-run lead by lunch on the fifth day, propelled by a Kevin Pietersen century (the seventh of the match), the West Indies needed only to bat out two sessions on a docile pitch for a famous series win. Edwards must have been tempted to crack open the Caribs. But the resolve of the last six weeks evaporated, as England's spinners and seamer Jimmy Anderson found life on the dead surface, aided by the odd dodgy umpiring decision. Eight wickets down, Edwards entered the fray, this time promoted to number ten, as Lionel Baker sweated in the pavilion. But this was old hat to Edwards, who calmly defended eight balls alongside Denesh Ramdin to send the fans into ecstasy. Gayle's strategy had worked, but only just.

England (3)

These disappointments were not the first witnessed by England skipper Andrew Strauss. In the epic 2005 series, when just a foot soldier, he had scored a hundred in the second innings at Old Trafford as the home team batted Australia out of the game (despite Kevin Pietersen's first primary), setting 423 runs to win. In truth, England should have been in a more dominant position, but a couple of dropped catches and a missed stumping had allowed Shane Warne to smash 90 in the first innings and so avoid the follow-on. Yet hope was high on the fifth day, as 23,000 spectators crammed into the ground, leaving another 20,000 outside. But such a stage befits the truly great batsmen and Ricky Ponting revelled in it, scoring a fluent and determined 156 to give his team an unlikely sniff of victory, before reining back to secure a draw. But he did not finish the job, leaving the door open for the English bowlers. Flintoff, who had been a titan all day, and Steve Harmison tore into the last batsmen, Brett Lee and Glenn McGrath, striving for that elusive coup de grâce. But the tailenders survived four overs of intense pressure to leave the field in triumph. For Lee, who had suffered the agony of falling short at Edgbaston in the second Test (*see* Chapter Nine **Umpiring Howlers**), this was just reward for his tenacity. For England, there was the disappointment of an opportunity missed, but the consolation that for the first time since 1989 Australia were celebrating a draw.

Australia (2)

Four years later, the shoe was on the other foot in Cardiff's inaugural Test, as England were battling to save the first Test of the 2009 Ashes summer. With the urn meekly surrendered down under (*see* Chapter Thirteen **One-Sided Affairs**), Andrew Strauss's troops were desperate to prove themselves a match for Ricky Ponting's tourists, who arrived without many of their leading lights from the last decade. Any team missing the talents of McGrath, Warne, Gilchrist, Langer and Hayden was bound to be considerably weaker, despite claims to the contrary, so the British public looked forward to a close contest. The controversy that surrounded the decision to play at Sophia Gardens, instead of Old Trafford or Trent Bridge, was soon forgotten as England's batsmen got in and then got out, but still accrued 435 in the first innings.

Any supposed weakness in the Aussie line-up was quickly dismissed, as they rattled off four hundreds in a rapid 674 for 6 declared, leaving plenty of time to force the win. Rain helped England enter the fifth day just two wickets down, but they were soon 70 for 5 and in need of a miracle. Plucky redhead Paul Collingwood was the saviour, digging in for a monumental 245-ball stay, scoring just 74 runs. The lower order all contributed with both time and runs, but eventually Collingwood offered a chance, clearing the stage for ten and jack, Jimmy Anderson and Monty Panesar. With at least ten overs left to survive, the draw still seemed unlikely. Even when Anderson cracked two boundaries, meaning that Australia would need to bat again and forfeit two overs, the feverish crowd feared the worst.

Delays for new gloves, drinks and the physio's attentions brought cheers from the stands and scowls from the Australians, but the clock eventually ticked past 6.40pm. Anderson and Panesar had faced 53 and 35 balls respectively. England had been thoroughly outplayed, but still left the field as victors, by achieving the draw.

South Africa

Paul Collingwood, since nicknamed Brigadier Block by the media, was again frustrating bowling attacks in the first Test against South Africa at Centurion towards the end of 2009. The home team had taken a healthy first innings lead, despite failing to polish off the visitors' tail, allowing Graeme Swann to carve 85 valuable runs. England had again been tasked with surviving the whole of the last day and a fine partnership between one-time locals Jonathan Trott and Kevin Pietersen appeared to snuff out hopes of a victory for South African skipper Graeme Smith. But after KP called for a non-existent single, running himself out, and Trott was dismissed by a brilliant diving catch by AB de Villiers at gully, South Africa smelled blood.

Debutant bowler Friedel de Wet made the new ball dance and the English batsmen followed each other back to the pavilion. Only Collingwood stayed resolute, facing 99 balls for just 26 runs, as he accepted that runs were irrelevant. But with Jimmy Anderson already dismissed as nightwatchman and Monty Panesar back in England, Andrew Strauss needed a new hero. Graham 'Bunny' Onions accepted the challenge. With eight balls left, Collingwood clipped one into the leg-side and called Onions through for a single, which would give him the strike for the last over. He grimaced as the ball ran away to the boundary. Unable to pinch a single on the last ball of the penultimate over, fellow Durham man Onions was charged with seeing off the final six balls. Smith, perhaps through a sentimental sense of occasion or a gut feeling, turned to his old warhorse Makhaya Ntini, playing in his hundredth Test, to bowl the last over, instead of de Wet, who had already done so much damage. Onions did enough, in particular smothering a shooter with just two balls remaining, to spoil the fairytale.

South Africa (2)

Two Tests later, in Cape Town, the Brigadier was at it again, battening down the hatches for his country. England had cruised to victory at Durban, leaving the South Africans frustrated to be 1-0 down in the series. The first innings scores were nearly level, as Jimmy Anderson and JP Duminy scooped primaries. But Captain Fantastic Graeme Smith took the game by the scruff of the neck, hammering 183 runs in a total of 447 for 7, leaving the opposition with more than five sessions to survive. England had lost three top order wickets by the end of play. Surely Paul Collingwood could not go to the well once more? Of course he could! After 188 deliveries and four-and-a-half hours of dead batting, he had reached 40 runs, ably assisted by fellow redhead Ian Bell, who scored 78 runs in 213 balls. Yet their demise in quick succession again allowed the tension to build. Again, Graham Onions was called upon to stonewall the final overs, this time alongside Graeme Swann. And again, Onions prevailed. It was the sixth nine-wicket draw that Strauss had endured in his career, but further evidence that Test blocking can generate tension every bit as titillating as the free hitting of ODIs or T20s.

South Africa (3)

The World Cup has engendered more heartache in South Africa than any other nation, although their first dismal dismissal in their first tournament post-apartheid was not entirely their fault. Having been readmitted into the international fold, the Rainbow Nation set about making up for lost time in the 1992 shindig in Australia. With the pace of Allan Donald, an inspired Peter Kirsten and the enthusiastic brilliance of Jonty Rhodes raising the bar for fielding, South Africa hit the ground running. In the semi-finals, an emotional journey to lift the cup was on the cards, although England had made a creditable 252 in their reduced 45 overs, thanks largely to a fine 83 by Graeme Hick. The match was poised for an exciting finish, as South Africa needed 22 runs off the last 13 balls, with 4 wickets in hand. Big-hitting all-rounder Brian McMillan had his eye in, as did keeper Dave Richardson. One of the overs would have to have been bowled by Chris Lewis, who had already been dispatched for nearly eight runs an over. In short, both sides fancied their chances. But then the rain fell. Without the complications of Duckworth/Lewis to call on, the target was revised to 22 runs off just one ball. Game over. The World Cup heartache for South Africa had begun. (D/L would have had it at four runs to tie, five to win.)

South Africa (4)

Any hangover from 1992 had been cleared by the next World Cup in India four years later. Led by Hansie Cronje, South Africa were the form team, romping through the group stages with five emphatic wins from five, including a cathartic dismantling of England in Rawalpindi. All of the batsmen had scored runs and the bowlers were hunting as a pack. Their opponents in the quarter-finals were the West Indies, recently humiliated by Kenya and fortunate to qualify for the knockout stages. The bookies did not give the Caribbean men a prayer. But when you have batsmen of the genius of Brian Lara and a bowler as restrictive as Curtly Ambrose, why worry about the team's form? Lara, accused of complacency against Kenya, was stung into action. His 111 runs from 94 balls in Karachi were sumptuous, guiding his team to 264 from 50 overs. Ambrose then suffocated the South Africans with his pace, length and line, bowling his ten-over allocation for just 29 runs. Cronje's men never came close and they were dumped from the competition, thanks to one reverse. Again, the format changed to make sure this would not happen again, introducing a carry-over points and run-rate system into the latter stages. But it was too late to help South Africa.

South Africa (5)

By 1999, Duckworth/Lewis and a new points system surely meant that the best two teams would reach the final. South Africa again bossed their pool group in England and then seemed to be cruising through the Super Sixes stages. When he wasn't smashing boundaries, Lance 'Zulu' Klusener was taking important wickets, eclipsing all other candidates for man of the tournament. Against Pakistan, he had bludgeoned his team to victory with an assault of flat sixes and blistering fours. And then Australia had felt his wrath in the last of the Super Six matches in Leeds, as he boosted the total to 271 with several late swishes of his heavy Duncan Fearnley bat. The Aussies lost three quick wickets to bring their indomitable captain Steve Waugh to the crease. He counter-attacked, galvanising Ricky Ponting at the other end, and the pair each notched up half centuries in quick time. Then came the pivotal moment of the match. Waugh flicked a ball from Klusener off his legs to midwicket, where Herschelle Gibbs was waiting.

It had been a nigglesome build-up to the match and Gibbs had been one of the taunters-in-chief, especially as Australia needed to win to stay in the tournament. But Gibbs had just scored a sumptuous hundred in the match and was one of the best fielders in the world. Surely he would not drop a dolly? In truth, he didn't, but such was his enthusiasm to celebrate the match-winning catch, he fumbled the ball as he threw it up in the air. Bizarrely, Shane Warne had all but predicted this in the team meeting the night before.

Waugh, usually so understated, confronted the red-faced South African with the cutting put-down: 'I hope you realise that you've just lost the game for your team.'

Perhaps the cricket gods were chiding Gibbs for his over-confidence, who knows, but Waugh was true to his word, leading his team past the total with an unbeaten 120 runs, in possibly the finest World Cup innings of all time. Australia marched on to the semi-finals to meet…South Africa.

South Africa (6)

When you three-putt at golf, it is not the nerve-jangling four-footer to blame, but the preceding weak putt that you left four feet short. The same could be said for South Africa's next blooper in Birmingham, just four days after the last. Had they seen off Australia, as they ought to have done, then the ignominy of their eventual demise would have been avoided. Again, without the magnificence of Klusener, they would not have come close to winning. Allan Donald, choosing to bowl second change, had helped restrict the Australians to 213 all out, with four of the batsmen making no contribution. He ought to have been the hero of the hour, but his top order succumbed to some everyday brilliance by Shane Warne. Klusener was asked to pull another rabbit from the hat. He obliged, bringing the total down to nine needed off the last over. Tellingly, however, Donald was at the other end, the last man in. As Australia had won the Super Six match, a tie would put them in the final and send South Africa home. Damien Fleming watched helplessly as his first two deliveries were hammered to the extra cover boundary. As the crowd went potty, one run from the last four balls would suffice. Hearts nearly stopped after the next delivery, as Donald was almost run out backing up. 'What on earth was he playing at?' asked the commentators. Once bitten, twice shy, Donald rushed back to his crease when Klusener bunted the next ball past the bowler. By the time he had realised that Klusener was coming, it was too late. Eventually, the fast bowler turned and ran, his bat left behind, only to see Adam Gilchrist breaking the stumps at the other end. Klusener was already half way to the pavilion. Neither player deserved such an ending to the match, but since when was cricket always fair?

South Africa (7)

By the time of the 2003 World Cup, given all that had happened, South Africa were due a little good fortune, especially as they were hosting the ruddy thing. But this time, there was nobody to blame but themselves for their premature exit. Another dazzling knock by Brian Lara in the curtain-raiser, when the world was wondering if he was past it, allowed the West Indies to win by three runs. (South Africa had been docked an over for a slow over-rate.) Then the rain and a career-best hundred by Stephen Fleming conspired to make the Proteas lose to the Blackcaps, meaning that the hosts needed to beat Sri Lanka to proceed. Marvan Atapattu provided a hundred for the Sri Lankans, but South Africa rallied behind Kallis, who took three wickets to rein the total back to 268. With rain about, all eyes turned to the D/L projections, which looked set to save South Africa, in what seemed divine retribution for the 1992 farce. Experienced campaigners Mark Boucher and skipper Shaun Pollock were in the middle, both armed with a paper graph that showed where they needed to be with the run-rate, should the match be called off. Even when Pollock was run out, bringing the hapless Klusener to the crease, Boucher seemed to have it all under control. An easy single was turned down, in accordance with the magic sheet of paper. But what Boucher did not know was that the projected score was to secure the tie and not the win that South Africa required. Nobody had thought to tell him that. The scores were level as the umpires pulled stumps and Boucher punched the air. Then it all started to sink in. They were going home. Well, you know what I mean.

Index

Retired, not out